# THE LAST DAYS OF
# DIETRICH BONHOEFFER

✝ ✝ ✝

# DONALD GODDARD

✛ ✛ ✛

HARPER & ROW, PUBLISHERS

New York   Hagerstown   San Francisco   London

# THE LAST DAYS OF
# DIETRICH
# BONHOEFFER

✠ ✠ ✠

Grateful acknowledgment is made for permission to reprint the following:

Excerpts on pages 14–15, 47–48, 51–55, 70–73, 84–85, 100–101, 116–117, 120–121, 126–127, 132–140, 143–146, 148–152, 154–162, 165–177, 184–187, 190–191, 194–195, 197–201, 209, 226–227, and 233 from *Letters and Papers from Prison*, The Enlarged Edition, by Dietrich Bonhoeffer. Copyright © 1953, 1967, 1971 by SCM Press Ltd. Reprinted by permission of SCM Press Ltd., London, England, and Macmillan Publishing Co., Inc., New York, N.Y.

Excerpts on pages 122–124 from *True Patriotism: Letters, Lectures and Notes 1939–45* from the *Collected Works of Dietrich Bonhoeffer*, Volume III, edited by Edwin H. Robertson and translated by Edwin H. Robertson and John Bowden. Copyright © 1973 in the English translation by William Collins Sons & Co., Ltd., and Harper & Row, Publishers, Inc. Reprinted by permission of the publishers.

FIRST EDITION

*Designed by Dorothy Schmiderer*

**Library of Congress Cataloging in Publication Data**

Goddard, Donald.
 The last days of Dietrich Bonhoeffer.

 1. Bonhoeffer, Dietrich, 1906–1945. I. Title.
BX4827.B57G58 1976      230′.092′4  [B]      75–25106
ISBN 0–06–011564–5

76 77 78 79 10 9 8 7 6 5 4 3 2 1

*To Natalie*

## ACKNOWLEDGMENTS

No one can write about Dietrich Bonhoeffer without incurring a heavy debt to his friend, biographer, and literary executor, Eberhard Bethge.

In attempting to reconstruct the last two years of Bonhoeffer's life, I have, of necessity, taken many liberties in fleshing out the bare bones of what is known, inventing the substance (though not the fact) of his interrogations, as well as conversation, incident, and even some minor characters in the story—all of which would have been unthinkable in a formal biography of the sort that Dr. Bethge has already published. To him and his monumental study of Bonhoeffer's life and work I therefore owe my thanks for establishing the limits within which imagination was free to work. If I should succeed in my main purpose of directing the reader to Bonhoeffer's own writings—and in particular to his *Letters and Papers from Prison*—I trust Dr. Bethge will forgive my temerity in venturing onto ground he has made uniquely his own.

D.G.

# THE LAST DAYS OF
# DIETRICH BONHOEFFER

✠ ✠ ✠

# 1

✳ ✳ ✳

HE HAD TELEPHONED CHRISTINE, and a stranger had answered.

"I would like to speak to"—he had almost said, "my sister"—"to Frau von Dohnanyi."

"Who is this speaking?"

And that was enough. The Gestapo were there. Hans had been taken, and he would be next.

He watched the lace curtains belly and ebb at the drawing-room window, allowing the calm of his parents' house to resettle about him. He had endured his own arrest so often in imagination that he felt no surprise, no emotion at all. And now the moment had come, there was still no ethical objection to killing himself that he could see.

He went to the piano, his usual place in this room. Not a week before, the whole family, children and grandchildren, had gathered around him here to perform the cantata they had rehearsed in secret for his father's seventy-fifth birthday—Walcha's *Praise the Lord*. Their joy in one another that day had revived his sense of purpose. This was the Germany they had to redeem, a civilized Germany of honor and high tradition. Even the Führer had played a fitting part. Among the birthday messages and telegrams piled neatly on the writing table was one from the Chancellery: "In the name of the German people, I bestow on Professor Emeritus Dr. Karl Bonhoeffer the Goethe Medal for Art and Science instituted by the late Reich President Hindenburg. Adolf Hitler."

The room was full of echoes. The portraits of the Bonhoeffers and the von Hases, his mother's family, looked down with the comfortable assurance of four centuries' prominence in public life. The idea of anything reaching in from outside to threaten him here was difficult to grasp; the past was so solidly present. He sat half-mesmerized by the slow tick of the ormolu clock on the chimney piece, breathing a familiar incense of polished wood and flowers.

He closed the piano lid over the keys. The objection to suicide was practical, not ethical. Like running away, his death might be taken as a sign of guilt and hurt Hans more than it helped him. He knew exactly what to do. They had gone over it a dozen times. In imagination, the Gestapo had always come without warning, allowing no time to think, but now he was ready. It was not time to think—it was time to have lunch.

He listened in the hall for a moment, but there was no one about. The last of the servants had long since been called up for war work, and his parents were still in their room. Deciding not to disturb them, he went through the garden to the house they had built next door for the Schleichers. The most levelheaded of his brothers and sisters, Ursula Schleicher was better prepared for this than the rest of the family, for her husband, Rüdiger, was also in the resistance.

Dear Ursel. Not much was said while she cooked him a meal. As always with the Bonhoeffers, the more serious things were, the less they discussed them—not for want of feeling, but rather the reverse: for fear of burdening one another additionally. They had acquired this reserve from their father, whose patrician distaste for emotional display belied his sensitivity to others, but they also shared their mother's warmth of sympathy and, in Ursula's case particularly, her practical grasp of detail.

She promised to break the news to Maria—what a terrible blow for *her*, poor girl, so soon after their engagement. And she agreed that the best place for the Dohnanyi children, at least until Christine was freed, was the family's country house at Friedrichsbrunn, well away from Berlin. She thought she might send her own girls there, too, although Renate couldn't stay long, of course. There was so much to do before the wedding. Or should she postpone it now?

No, not on any account, he said, listening to a car pass by on the Marienburger Allee.

As soon as he finished his coffee, he excused himself and went back to the house for a last unnecessary shuffle through his papers. Hans had warned him they were being watched, and since the last attempts on Hitler's life in March, he had been doubly careful. The Gestapo would find nothing they were not supposed to see.

On the desk was his unfinished "Ethics"—three years' work and, since he had never wished to concern himself with anything other than theology, a substantial sacrifice. And yet theology had brought him to it. Faith had obliged him to live in the world as it was and to take sides. Hidden in the rafters was an essay he had written at Christmas for Hans and their fellow conspirators. "Who stands firm?" he had asked. "Only the one for whom the final standard is not his reason, his principles, his conscience, his freedom, or his virtue, but who is ready to sacrifice all these when, in faith and sole allegiance to God, he is called to obedient and responsible action."

He straightened his tie in the closet mirror, trying to see through Gestapo eyes. He was too big, built too much like a prizefighter, to play the shrinking scholar, but he would try to look unworldly. High-minded and politically naïve. No great friend of the party, of course, but loyally serving the Fatherland in its hour of destiny. "I believe that in every trial, God will give us as much strength as we need to resist," he had said in his Christmas essay. "But in order that we shall rely on Him alone and not on ourselves, He does not give it in advance." Well, unworldly or not, he could hardly look more Nordic. Among the other attributes he owed the Hases were his thinning blond hair and short-sighted blue eyes. Satisfied that, outwardly at least, he offered his enemies nothing to seize on, he went downstairs again.

There was still no sign of his parents. Unwilling to wait by himself, he returned to the Schleichers' house, where, to his real delight, he found Ursula had been joined by Renate and her fiancé, Eberhard Bethge, his closest friend. Their constraint soon faded in his obvious pleasure at seeing them, and by midafternoon, they had gone over every particular of the plans he had made with Hans for their joint defense.

They then talked about the wedding, and what they would do together when this was behind them, breaking off each time they heard a car outside.

At about four o'clock, his father came through the garden to say that two men were waiting for him in his room, and he saw from his father's face there was nothing he had to explain. They walked back together in silence, neither finding it necessary to put the other through the usual banalities of leavetaking. Pausing at the foot of the stairs to gather himself, he shook his father's hand, smiled, and went up alone.

They were searching his desk. One was a Luftwaffe colonel, sharp-faced, with pale eyes. The other was in Gestapo uniform; thick-set, black-booted, withdrawn to the point of somnolence.

"Pastor Dietrich Bonhoeffer?" The colonel seemed surprised, as though he had pictured him differently.

"What are you doing?"

"Roeder. Judge Advocate. Luftwaffe."

He obviously expected Bonhoeffer to have heard of him, and so he had, though he gave no sign. Manfred Roeder was a friend of Hermann Göring's. Some months before, in the fall of 1942, he had prosecuted a Communist resistance group in the Luftwaffe, the Röte Kapelle, and seventy-five of its members had been executed. Bonhoeffer turned to the Gestapo officer, who had already resumed the search through his papers.

"Criminal Commissar Franz Sonderegger," said Roeder.

"Are you interested in ethics, Herr Commissar?" asked Bonhoeffer distantly.

Sonderegger ignored him, and Roeder laughed. "The ethics of dissent are a particular study of ours," he said. "You're involved with military intelligence, I believe."

"I am a confidential agent of the Abwehr. But I keep nothing here."

"Do you know a Dr. Schmidhuber?"

"Consul Schmidhuber was a colleague of mine in Munich."

"Was?"

"I heard he'd been arrested."

"Were you surprised?"

Bonhoeffer hesitated. "Not very."

4

"Would it surprise you to learn that he's told us all about your activities?"

"It would. He knew next to nothing about them."

Roeder shrugged. "Enough, I think, to warrant your arrest for treason. Have you finished, Herr Commissar?"

"For the moment."

Neither of them had even bothered to watch Bonhoeffer's reaction. "Treason?" Schmidhuber had been arrested for currency offenses. "What madness is this?"

"Shall we go?" said Roeder. "I have a car waiting."

Bonhoeffer blocked his path, filling the doorway. "This is preposterous. I am responsible to Admiral Canaris. On whose authority are you acting?"

Roeder looked back at Sonderegger, who casually unbuttoned his holster. "As chief of the Abwehr, the admiral is under orders from Field Marshal Keitel to cooperate. You would be well advised to do the same."

Bonhoeffer stood his ground, eying each in turn. "I'm required to keep the center informed of my whereabouts. I must ask you to wait while I telephone for instructions."

"That will not be necessary."

"On the contrary. My orders are very explicit."

"If you want to talk to your brother-in-law," said Sonderegger unexpectedly, "he's under arrest."

Bonhoeffer stared. "In that case, I'll speak to General Oster. He'll soon get to the bottom of this."

"Oster has also been relieved of his duties."

That ended the charade. It was one thing for the Gestapo to try to discredit the Abwehr through its vulnerable civilians—Reichsführer Himmler had always resented the existence of an army intelligence group outside his control—but quite another for them to bring down the admiral's chief of staff. They would need more than suspicion for that—much more than Hans had allowed for.

"I'll put a few things together," said Bonhoeffer.

"I'm sorry." Roeder stepped between him and the desk.

"Not even my Bible?"

As Roeder hesitated, Sonderegger picked it up and gave it to him. "Here. You want the hymn book as well?"

"Thank you."

"They may not let you keep them," he said indifferently.

There was no one downstairs to see him go, but Bonhoeffer fancied he saw the curtains move at the window of his parents' room as he looked back from the car. Then he climbed in between Roeder and Sonderegger, blackly oppressed by his helplessness. If they had arrested Oster, the Gestapo had aborted the army plot against Hitler without even suspecting its existence. With Hans gone as well, the mainspring was broken. Without them, Canaris would be hard pressed even to hide their tracks, although fortunately most of the documentary cover had already been planted in the Abwehr's files. The resistance would now have to regroup around some other nucleus in the army command and begin again. Five years' work had gone for nothing.

When he raised his head, he saw they were not, as he had supposed, making for Gestapo headquarters on Prinz-Albrecht-Strasse, but threading their way north toward Tegel. He drew some comfort from that. There was a park in Tegel he remembered from childhood. His governess had sometimes taken him there with his two younger sisters. On its southern edge, next to the Borsig locomotive works, was a gaunt old military prison. If that was where they were headed, then the army still had jurisdiction, which ruled out the use of torture.

Even so, when the car slowed in the shadow of the prison wall and turned in through the iron-bound gates, his teeth began to chatter uncontrollably. As they handed him over, it was all he could do to stop shaking. He meant nothing to anyone here. Roeder produced a receipt, the duty sergeant signed it, and they drove away and left him. No word of how long he might be there, or what was to happen next. Nothing.

The guards pushed and jostled him, unresisting, through the formalities of admission. Their shouting, their abuse, their impersonal hostility confused him still further—he had never dreamed he would be treated as a criminal. They flipped through the pages of his Bible and hymn book and tossed them on the guardroom table. They made him empty his pockets, and took away his watch and signet ring as well as his tie, belt, and shoelaces. When they gave him a list of his possessions to sign, he was tempted to ask for the Bible back, but he saw how much pleasure it would give them to refuse, and kept silent. Nothing mattered for the moment except to hold on.

Then they marched him across the yard to the cell block, a bleak three-story building pitted with rows of barred windows. Inside, it was dank as a cellar, the air stagnant with sweat and urine, but the noise dismayed him most. Behind the clump of boots on stone and the ringing crash of steel doors was a cavernous murmur, like surf, interrupted now and then by outbursts of shouting, too distant or muddled with echoes to make any sense.

He followed the leading guard along a gallery to where a cell door stood open and went inside, not waiting to be told. It was small and dark, about nine feet by six, with a narrow window high in the wall. Below it was a camp bed with some greasy-looking blankets, and in the corner, a toilet bucket blackened with filth.

He waited for the guards to lock him in, then stretched out quietly on the bed. But as his head touched the blankets, he recoiled, retching with disgust at the stench of sour vomit, and flung them aside. Furious, he worked the semaphore signal that was supposed to attract the guards' attention for almost half an hour, but no one came.

It grew bitterly cold as night came on, and the practical objection to suicide had lost its force. Now it could be attributed as easily to the shock of arrest as to a guilty conscience. It was not uncommon, or why would they strip a prisoner of the means to hang himself?

He had leaned toward death before, dogged from childhood by a recurrent melancholy that had something to do with self-knowledge. Alert to the least intrusion of vanity, he would always question his motives at precisely those times when others most admired him, so that the very qualities that commanded their respect were made to seem hollow and distasteful to him. More than once he had considered ending his life when he could no longer distinguish between God's will and his own.

He could not now. He was far from sure that vanity had played no part in bringing him here, that he took no inner pride in the totality of his sacrifice of church, vocation, family, fiancée—everything. And the uncertainty eroded him with guilt for the burden he had laid upon his parents, who felt deeply for their children, and upon Maria, so young, and still grieving for her father and a brother killed in Russia.

Overwhelmed with hatred for the imperfection of his life, he paced up and down to keep warm, listening to the restless sleepers along the gallery.

Suicide was an attempt to give a final human meaning to a life that was humanly meaningless. If the bomb planted on Hitler's aircraft three weeks before had not failed to explode, and if a second attempt a week later had not also miscarried, he would now be helping to dismantle the Third Reich. By choosing to share its experience of war and revolt, he would have earned the right to share in restoring Germany to sense and decency. But a faulty detonator on the first occasion and the Führer's unexpected change of plan on the second had denied him his justification, and now, without knowing it, the Gestapo had taken a prisoner who, while he lived, endangered every one of those still free to try again. He owed the resistance his death. Only then would his life have meaning.

And yet only a lack of faith could lead a man to seek his own justification, for God alone knew the end to which it was His will to lead him. It meant refusing to believe that God could give meaning to a failed life, or that a life might be fulfilled in failure. No man obedient to God's will was free to abuse the freedom to live or die. God maintained the right to life even against those for whom it had become a torment, for in dying, they would again fall into His hand, which they had found too exacting in life.

But might not a man take his own life and thereby meet the end that God prepared for him? It was beyond the reach of human judgment. If he killed himself for fear he might betray his friends and, through them, his country, then surely the act was so close in spirit to self-sacrifice that God would not condemn him for it?

The prison awoke with an ugly stir at first light. When the key rattled in his lock, he was composed and ready, but the door opened just wide enough for a hand to set down a tin mug and toss in a chunk of bread and then slammed shut again. The coffee was ersatz, a tepid black sludge, but he got some of it down, thawing his fingers around the mug. Then he brushed the dirt off the bread and ate the middle part.

An hour or so later, the guards opened all the cells along the gallery and ordered everyone out. Most of his fellow prisoners were very young,

Bonhoeffer discovered, and sullenly bewildered. Some of them looked at him twice, as he was the only one not in uniform, and he tried to smile back reassuringly. They were then marched across the yard to the administration block and lined up in front of a sergeant major seated at a wooden table. He was fat, disgruntled, and apparently absorbed in the papers before him.

When he at last condescended to look up, he called them forward one by one to account for themselves, commenting sarcastically on their answers as he wrote them down. But not all the NCOs who stood around listening seemed to find this amusing. When Bonhoeffer's turn came, two of the older men, both corporals, shook their heads and turned away.

"Been after the choirboys, have you, Pastor?"

A few of the guards sniggered, and Bonhoeffer looked at them until they stopped.

"No?" said the sergeant major. "What then? Too much organ practice?" His smile faded.

"I've not been charged," said Bonhoeffer evenly. "I've no idea why I'm here."

"Well, you'll find out soon enough." He consulted his list. "Prisoner Bonhoeffer. Solitary confinement. No privileges. No access without special permission. Step back into line."

"Am I allowed to buy tobacco and writing materials?"

"No privileges. Next?"

"Does that include newspapers?"

"It does."

"Then may I at least have my Bible?"

The sergeant major looked up at the guard beside him, who nodded, came around the table, and pushed Bonhoeffer roughly back into line.

When all the new arrivals had been checked against the sergeant major's list, they were moved forward from table to table to have their dossiers completed by the waiting clerks. Several NCOs tried to have a word with Bonhoeffer, but each time they were ordered away. As he was taking his compulsory bath, however, one of the two corporals he had noticed earlier appeared in the doorway, and asked:

"Do you know Pastor Niemöller?"

"I was with him the day he was arrested."

The corporal nodded. "He's a good friend of mine," he said, and walked on.

After a perfunctory medical examination, Bonhoeffer was taken back across the yard and up to the third floor. He was pleasant with his escort, a dour young man who limped heavily, but all he could get out of him was that he had been assigned to a condemned cell. While waiting for the door to be opened, he could hear the clink of his new neighbors' chains, and their plight put his own in better perspective. The sympathy he sensed in some of the NCOs had already relieved his sense of isolation, and he was now in no mood to oblige either man or the devil by giving way. He spent the rest of the day taking stock of his situation and devising a program to keep himself fit and alert.

He would eat all the food he was given, palatable or not, and though his new cell offered little enough scope for exercise—it was about ten feet by seven and furnished with a plank bed, bench, stool, and toilet bucket—he determined to walk at least ten kilometers a day. To keep his mind occupied, he would devote more time than usual to meditation, recall everything he knew by heart from the Bible and literature generally and practice translating it into English, French, Italian, Spanish, Latin, Greek, and Hebrew.

But the night undid him. A prisoner in a nearby cell sobbed until dawn, and the will of God remained hidden. The promptings of his heart were not to be confused with it. The will of God could be known only by renouncing attempts to know it out of his own resources and trusting in the belief that he was already sustained and guided by it. It could be known only to the man of faith—and faith had never come easily.

He had chosen theology as a career to distinguish himself from his brilliant older brothers, who inclined, like his father, to the natural sciences. Though not a churchgoing family, they respected his decision, for his mother presided over a Christian household and there were a number of eminent churchmen among their Hase ancestors—his grandfather Karl Alfred, for instance, had been court chaplain to the Kaiser at Potsdam, and professor of theology at Breslau. But Bonhoeffer had been required to defend his choice against his brothers' skepticism, and in his eagerness to excel, he had become a theologian first and a Christian later. He was twenty-six and lecturing at Berlin University before he knew that faith had at last overtaken ambition. Since then, the struggle had been to preserve his calling in true humility. He lived in constant dread of secretly priding himself on being a chosen instrument of God, and thus deluding himself that he followed His commandment when, in reality, he was merely asserting his own self-righteousness.

He thought again of suicide. Life was not a compulsion he could not throw off. By freely choosing death, he would raise the act high above petty moralizing; he would be exercising the counterpart of his right to life. Without the freedom to sacrifice life for a higher good, there could be no freedom toward God. If a man killed himself to protect a higher cause than self, just as the victim of an incurable disease might choose to spare his family from ruin, where was the sin? If people could remain alive for base motives, equally they could surrender life for noble ones.

He tried hard to pray. The sin was lack of faith. Over men there was God, who alone could justify a life or cast it aside. Toward morning, he saved himself from utter hopelessness by wrenching his thoughts back to the family and Maria—to the saving pain of a loss he could measure.

As though to signal a better day, a bird began to sing in the yard. By standing his stool on the bed and climbing up, he found he had a magnificent view through the grimy window of a sunlit forest of pines to the south, which set him to thinking of Friedrichsbrunn. Around noon, he was in the middle of his walk—three paces, turn, two paces, turn, three long ones across the diagonal—when the limping guard brought his midday ration of soup. He was accompanied by the corporal who had spoken to him in the bathhouse.

"I thought you'd want to have these," he said, jerking his thumb at the guard to leave them. He laid the Bible and hymn book down on the bench, and Bonhoeffer touched them wonderingly. "You'd be surprised what people hide in books. Knives. Saws. Razor blades. We have to be careful."

"I understand," said Bonhoeffer. "And I'm very grateful."

They both glanced at the door. Bonhoeffer would have liked to ask him how he knew Niemöller, but it hardly seemed wise with the guard in earshot.

"Does this mean my privileges have been restored?"

"Not yet, sir. But you're entitled to a Bible. I looked up the regulations."

"That was very considerate of you, Corporal. What do they say about writing materials?"

"I didn't notice. I'll have to see. But if you've any complaints"—he raised his voice so the guard would hear—"ask for me. Corporal Linke."

"I will—and thank you. My only real complaint, apart from being here at all, is that I've nothing to smoke."

"Well, there I can't help you." With another look over his shoulder, he shielded his left hand against his body and opened it to show three cigarettes and some matches. "Tobacco *does* count as a privilege, I'm afraid," he said, as Bonhoeffer hid them in his jacket pocket. "But I'll see what I can do." He smiled, nodded, and closed the door quietly behind him.

In penance for his doubts, Bonhoeffer decided to finish the soup and complete his walk before allowing himself to read or smoke. But the tobacco was burning a hole in his pocket, and as soon as the guard collected the empty mess tin, he climbed up to the window and forced it open. Then he lit a cigarette, his hands trembling with anticipation, and drew on it in an agony of pleasure, holding the smoke in until his head spun, and blowing it out hard between the bars. He did this with intense concentration, ignoring every frugal impulse, and eventually scorched his fingers. Reserving the last unsmokable scrap to go with future stubs, he then settled down on the bed to read the Bible through from Genesis.

There was still better to come. At four o'clock, when the guard brought bread and sausage for the last meal of the day, he was followed by the other corporal who had caught Bonhoeffer's eye the previous morning. He carried a cardboard box, which he set down carefully on the bed.

"What's that?" asked Bonhoeffer.

"Your sister left it," he said.

Bonhoeffer looked at him stupidly.

"Frau Dress? She said to tell you the family's all well and thinking of you."

Oh, Suse. He turned his head away.

"Sergeant Holzendorf took it in," the corporal went on awkwardly. "We're not supposed to accept food parcels—not for ordinary prisoners, that is—but the regulations are different for officers. In fact, I don't know what you're doing here at all. We don't have the facilities. They should have taken you to the officers' prison on Lehrter Strasse."

Bonhoeffer polished his rimless glasses severely. "You're very kind. Corporal . . . ?"

"Knobloch, sir."

"I'm much obliged. And thank Sergeant Holzendorf for me. But I'm not an officer, and I wouldn't want you to get into trouble on my account."

"We checked with the Judge Advocate's office. Chaplains count as officers. Always have done." Embarrassed, he went to look through the box. "I'm sorry we had to open everything, but it's all there. Bread. Cheese. Sausage. Butter. Coffee. Soap. Underwear. And a blanket."

"No tobacco, I suppose. Or writing paper?"

"No." He straightened up. "Linke said you'd been asking. Perhaps next time. We told Frau Dress you're entitled to a parcel a week."

"But how will they know what I need?"

"I inquired about that, too. You can send a letter out every ten days. Your family can write back as much as they like, but everything has to go through the Judge Advocate's office."

"You've gone to a lot of trouble, you and Corporal Linke." He touched Knobloch's arm, directing his attention to the parcel. "Is there anything you would like?"

"No," said Knobloch sharply. Then he saw he was not being patronized, and softened his tone. "No, thank you. I like to do what I can. We both know who should *really* be in this rathole."

He left the guard to close the door, and Bonhoeffer stared after him thoughtfully. At the bottom of the box, underneath the blanket, he found five hand-rolled cigarettes that had certainly not come from the family. That night he included Corporals Linke and Knobloch in his prayers and slept without stirring till 6 A.M.

After that, he saw or heard nothing more of them for a week, although three long nineteenth-century novels arrived one day with the soup. The despair of the first two nights had lifted, and despite the dirt, the bad food, and the endless clamor beyond his door, he found himself settling almost too readily into a daily round of contemplation, reading, and prayer. If God had put him aside for a while to learn modesty and patience, to make him a man for whom He would have use later on, he could only be thankful. The hardest time was when the light went out at eight. Then he knew his life was all in the past, and receding faster each day.

On April 14, nine days after his arrest, Knobloch reappeared with another parcel, his fountain pen, and a few sheets of prison notepaper. He had obviously been arguing with the guard who let him in, for they were both bristling with hostility, and after cautioning Bonhoeffer to write no more than a single page, he pushed the other man out the door. Bonhoeffer was sorry to see them go, for no one had spoken to him since Knobloch's last visit—the men who brought the food around and emptied his toilet bucket had ignored every overture—but disappointment soon gave way to the pleasure of holding a pen again. Knowing that Roeder would read every word as closely as his parents would for signs of strain, he had been planning what to say all week.

> A violent mental upheaval such as is produced by a sudden arrest brings with it the need to take one's mental bearings and come to terms with an entirely new situation—all this means that physical things take a back seat and lose their importance, and it is something that I find to be a real enrichment of my experience. I am not so unused to being alone as other people are, and it is certainly a good spiritual Turkish bath. The only thing that bothers me, or would bother me, is the thought that you are being tormented by anxiety about me, and are not sleeping or eating properly. Forgive me for causing you so much worry, but I think a hostile fate is more to blame than I am. . . .

That seemed just right. By reassuring his parents in this way, he was also disabusing Roeder of any idea he might have that a prolonged period of isolation would soften him up. Once he saw the futility of it, there would be no further reason for delaying his appearance before the

14

War Court. But Bonhoeffer was also worried about Maria. Though their engagement had not been publicly announced, Roeder was sure to find out and might think it odd if he failed to mention it. The problem was how to do so without arousing the Gestapo's interest in her as a possible source of information about him.

> You can imagine that I'm most particularly anxious about my fiancée at the moment. It's a great deal for her to bear, especially when she has only recently lost her father and brother in the East. As the daughter of an officer, she will perhaps find my imprisonment especially hard to take. If only I could have a few words with her! Now you will have to do it. Perhaps she will come to you in Berlin. . . .

He wanted her close at hand in any case—quite apart from the suggestion that he had nothing to fear from bringing her into the city. It would be a comfort to know the family was keeping an eye on her, and later she might also be allowed to visit him. But he would have to be careful. She was only eighteen. He would need to take care not to burden her unreasonably.

> Spring is really coming now. You will have plenty to do in the garden. I hope that Renate's wedding preparations are going well. Here in the prison yard there is a thrush which sings beautifully in the morning, and now in the evening, too. One is grateful for little things, and that is surely a gain. Goodbye for now. I'm thinking of you and the rest of the family and my friends with gratitude and love.
>
> Your Dietrich

He then checked the contents of his second parcel and added a postscript:

> When you have a chance, could you leave here for me slippers, bootlaces (black, long), shoe polish, writing paper and envelopes, ink, smoker's card, shaving cream, sewing things, and a suit I can change into? Many thanks for everything.

The following morning, two military policemen came to his cell, shackled his hands and feet, and drove him in a prison van to the Reich War Court on Witzlebenstrasse.

# 2

✠ ✠ ✠

THE GUARDS PUT HIM up in the well of the court and left him to stand in chains before the bench. Roeder was busy making notes from a folder at his elbow, and appeared not to notice. Above him hung a huge Nazi eagle, the swastika in its talons, and a framed photograph of the Führer, looking stern, wise, and confident. Below, at the head of a U-shaped table curving around three sides of the room, Roeder's assistants sorted through their papers. To the right, Sonderegger joked with three other black-uniformed Gestapo men, and on the opposite side of the court, four army officers, one of whom Bonhoeffer knew by sight from the Abwehr center, sat quietly reading their files. And except for one or two brief, uninterested glances, everyone ignored him.

Their indifference was not feigned, he could see that. They were not trying to unnerve him, although he could well imagine the effect it might have on the sort of prisoner he had seen at Tegel. What was momentous for the accused was commonplace for his accusers. He was caught in the machinery of state. It was not brilliance or heroism that would save him, but caution and self-effacement.

"You are Pastor Dietrich Bonhoeffer?" asked Roeder, without looking up. The murmur of talk died away.

"I am."

"You were arrested at the home of your father, Dr. Karl Bonhoeffer, Marienburger Allee 43, Berlin-Charlottenburg, on April 5, 1943?"

"I was."

"And since then you have been lodged in the Wehrmacht Interrogation Prison, Berlin-Tegel?"

"Yes."

Roeder checked his notes. "I see your registered address is in Munich."

"My aunt, Countess Kalckreuth, took me in when I was assigned to the Munich office of the Abwehr at the end of 1940."

"Indeed? Then we shall be interested to hear in due course how it is you seem to have spent more time under your parents' roof than hers—particularly in view of a Gestapo order banning you from Berlin."

"That's easily explained, Your Honor."

"It is?" He looked at Sonderegger. "You mean the order was rescinded?"

"It was modified on appeal," said Bonhoeffer. "I was allowed to come to Berlin and stay with my parents on condition that I took no part in church business here."

"Yes, yes. All in good time. We'll listen to your explanations later, when we've established the basic facts in the case."

"As you wish. I just thought it might be helpful to answer each allegation as it was made."

Roeder considered him for a moment. "I realize how tiresome this must be for a man of your exalted intellect, Pastor Bonhoeffer, but you will kindly allow me to conduct this inquiry in my own way."

"I'm at your disposal," Bonhoeffer said, jingling his handcuffs.

"Quite so. You will therefore confine yourself to answering my questions."

"Very well. But may I ask if I'm to remain shackled? Escape is the last thing I have in mind—you have my word."

This amused Sonderegger, and Roeder glanced at him. "I see no reason to vary the normal practice of this court," he said. "It may serve to remind you of your position here."

"Your Honor, I am painfully aware of my position, but so far no one has explained the reason for it. I've seen no warrant for my arrest."

"No warrant has been issued. You are held under emergency powers for examination on matters affecting the security of the Reich and, in particular, your part in various irregularities that have come to light in the conduct of military intelligence. At the end of this inquiry, I've no doubt we shall be able to gratify your passion for due process by laying formal charges against you, but until then, you will—as I have said—refrain from interrupting."

Bonhoeffer bowed his head. It had been worth provoking the rebuke. They still had no wind of the army conspiracy. Roeder returned to his notes.

"You were born February 4, 1906, in Breslau. Your father was professor of psychiatry and neurology at the university there. You are the youngest son in his family of eight children."

"Now seven. My oldest brother, Walter, was killed at the front in 1918."

Roeder amended the file. "Your reluctance to serve the Fatherland was not, then, shared by all the members of your family."

"Your Honor," said Bonhoeffer, stiffening, "the contribution my family has made to our national life is well known. It needs no defense from me. For my own part, I would simply draw your attention to the fact that I came home from America in 1939 as soon as I saw that war was inevitable, and in November, 1940, offered my services to the Abwehr."

"An offer which may not have been entirely unconnected with the fact that you had just been ordered to report for military service of a more hazardous nature."

"It was not for me to decide where I could be most useful," he said carefully.

"No. I'm sure you were quite content to leave that decision to your brother-in-law Hans von Dohnanyi. His conniving at your evasion of army service is typical of the way he abused his position of trust with the Abwehr."

"I believe my orders came from Admiral Canaris himself."

Roeder looked down at his papers with a tolerant smile. "You were educated at the Friedrichs-Werder and Grunewald gymnasia here in Berlin, and at the universities of Tübingen and Berlin."

"Yes." Then, as more seemed expected of him: "We moved to Berlin in 1912 when my father was appointed to the chair of psychiatry and neurology here. At seventeen, I went to Tübingen for a year—by family tradition—to begin my theological studies. After that, I returned to Berlin and took my doctorate three years later, in December, 1927."

"By which time, no doubt, you were already identified with those subversive elements who would later try to use the Evangelical Church as a propaganda instrument against the Reich?"

"Your Honor, I'm a theologian," he protested. "I opposed the Reich Church for its heresy, not for political reasons."

"But you'll not deny you joined with other self-important bourgeois intellectuals to divide the church and the German people at a critical moment in their national destiny?"

"I do most emphatically deny it. To suggest that our motives in proclaiming the Confessing Church were political is absurd. One might as well say that the motives for convening this inquiry are theological." He knew he had gone too far. "The truth is that the strongest influence in my student days was that of my professors, men like Adolf von Harnack and Reinhold Seeberg. Scholars of world renown."

There was a baleful silence. "So while the flower of German youth girded itself to cleanse the nation of dishonor," said Roeder, "you and your world-renowned friends were trying to decide how many angels could stand on the point of a pin."

The Gestapo men tittered, and Bonhoeffer studied his hands. "I would remind the Judge Advocate that the Führer himself has said that he found in Christianity the unshakable foundations of our people's ethical and moral life. To prepare oneself to preach the word of God would therefore seem to render a service of some importance to the state."

"The state alone will be the judge of that. The Führer himself is the foundation of our national life. As Reich Bishop Müller once said: 'The voice of the Führer is the voice of the people, and the voice of the people is the voice of God.' "

"Your Honor, as I said, I opposed the Reich Church for its heresy. The Confessing Church—"

"The Confessing Church," Roeder broke in, "is an illegal organization that stands condemned in the eyes of all true Germans for its treasonable attempt to seduce the credulous from their allegiance to the Führer, and for aiding the international Jewish-Bolshevik conspiracy."

"Your Honor—"

"Be silent!" he shouted, and Bonhoeffer blinked in surprise. "Must I again remind you of your position? You are not here to engage the court in debate. Nor have I invited you to comment on my observations."

"I'm sorry, Your Honor." The army observers were engrossed in their files. "I find it difficult sometimes to distinguish between question and statement. The one is often put in the form of the other."

Roeder hesitated, then busied himself with his notes. "So you disrupted the Reich Church for its heresy. Are you, then, the final authority on such matters? Do you enjoy some special access to the Almighty?"

He sighed.

"I don't hear you."

"Your Honor, to disrupt the church would indeed be godless if our faith were not as strong as Martin Luther's. We are concerned to protect the true church of Christ."

"Martin *Luther?*" Roeder looked around the court in amazement. "You oppose the will of the German people. You defy the Führer. You reject the authority of the Reich Church. And now you dare compare yourself with Martin Luther? We are used to the self-importance of your class, Herr Bonhoeffer, but this—why, it's sublime."

Bonhoeffer considered him in silence. "The church is the presence of God in the world," he said at last. "I believe that the confession of the Confessing Church is that of the true church. I believe that the question of the true church cannot be separated from the question of the soul's salvation. But these are not matters to be settled in a word, and with respect, Your Honor, I don't see how they are relevant."

They both glanced at Sonderegger, who yawned.

"Your attitude toward the Führer and the Reich could hardly be more relevant," said Roeder thinly. "By sowing doubt among the German people about their historic mission, you consciously aided their enemies."

20

"Your Honor, I have always tried to serve the best interests of my country. I am a loyal German."

"Indeed? How could a *loyal* German refuse to swear allegiance to the Führer?"

Bonhoeffer hesitated. "Every pastor takes an oath of allegiance at the time of his ordination. I did so in November, 1931."

Roeder waved this aside. "I refer to the service oath introduced in 1934." He cleared his throat. " 'I swear before God that I will be true and obedient to the Führer of the German people and state, Adolf Hitler, and I pledge myself to every sacrifice and service on behalf of the German people such as befit an evangelical German.' Now tell me —as a *loyal* German, what did you find to object to in that?"

"I was already bound by oath to serve God and the nation. I saw no useful purpose in swearing to do so again. In any case, it was not a requirement."

"But it *became* a requirement, did it not? I have here a copy of an order issued in April, 1938. 'Whereas only those may be office-bearers in the church who are unswervingly loyal to the Führer, the people, and the Reich, it is hereby decreed, Anyone who is called to a spiritual office is to affirm his loyal duty with the following oath: I swear that I will be faithful and obedient to Adolf Hitler, the Führer of the German Reich and people, that I will conscientiously observe the laws and carry out the duties of my office, so help me God.' And so on. 'Anyone who was called before this decree came into force' "— Roeder glanced at him meaningfully—" 'is to take the oath of allegiance retrospectively.' Now then. Did you—as a *loyal* German— thereupon swear allegiance in those terms?"

"No, Your Honor."

"Why not?"

"I again felt it would call in question the sincerity of my ordination vows. But more than that, I was not *asked* to take the oath. I was not then an office-bearer in the church, and my name did not appear on the list."

Roeder shook his head, as though saddened by the world's duplicity. "Is it not a fact, Pastor Bonhoeffer, that your stubborn refusal to swear an oath of loyalty to the Führer is because you were, as you have always been, an active opponent of National Socialism?"

"Your Honor, I am, as I have always been, an active defender of the Evangelical Church and of the truths revealed in the Christian gospel."

"Are you, then, saying that the government of the Third Reich is an enemy of the church and an enemy of the truth?"

"I believe that government serves God through its very existence, whether it is conscious of doing so or not."

"Then surely it's your Christian duty to obey its laws?"

"Every Christian is bound by faith to obey the law, except when it compels him to offend against the divine commandment."

"I see." Roeder glanced down at his papers. "Was it by divine commandment, then, that you publicly attacked the Führer within two days of his election as Chancellor? I have here the text of a broadcast you made over Berlin radio on February 1, 1933."

Bonhoeffer frowned. It was so futile. The outcome could hardly be different if he kept silent and saved his dignity.

"I did *not* attack the Führer, Your Honor. My purpose was to discuss the leadership principle as it applied to the church as well as the state."

Roeder waved the script at him. "I have marked certain passages. 'It is virtually impossible to find a rational basis for the nature of the Führer. . . . If he allows himself to succumb to the wishes of his followers, who will always seek to make him their idol, then the image of the leader will fade into the image of the *mis*leader, and he will be acting in a criminal way toward those he leads. . . . This is the Führer who makes an idol of himself and his office, and who thus mocks God.' If this treasonable rubbish is not an attack, then what is it?"

"Your Honor, I was simply trying to point out certain dangers inherent in the leadership principle. As you say, the Führer had been Chancellor for two days. My remarks could hardly have been directed at him personally."

"I think we might find that more persuasive, Pastor Bonhoeffer, if you had not subsequently confirmed your hostility by refusing to swear an oath of allegiance."

"Your Honor, if I were really the traitor you take me for, surely I would have sworn the oath so as not to arouse suspicion? If it would serve a useful purpose, I would willingly do so now, but I'm afraid you might doubt my sincerity."

"Yes, I'm afraid we would." Seeing no immediate way past this, Roeder turned to another folder. "Where do you stand on the Jewish question?"

Bonhoeffer did not reply at once. "I think Your Honor must know that, like many others, I opposed the so-called Aryan Clause because it excluded Jewish Christians from the church."

"That's not what I meant, but we'll start from there. Did you oppose it on personal or political grounds?"

"I opposed it for theological reasons, as I made clear at the time."

"The fact that your twin sister Sabine was married to a Jew had nothing to do with it?"

"My sister married Gerhard Liebholz in 1926." He looked at his feet.

"He's a Jew?"

"He's a distinguished constitutional lawyer. He was dismissed from the faculty of Berlin University in 1935, and left Germany with my sister and their children in 1938."

"It must have been a shock for your family—when she married a Jew."

"They were certainly very concerned about him," he said, not proud of the ambiguity.

"And where is he now, this Jew?"

"My brother-in-law is in England."

"Have you kept in touch with him?"

"Not since the war."

"Not even in the course of your journeys abroad for the Abwehr?"

Bonhoeffer hesitated. "Not directly. I've had word of him from time to time through mutual friends in Switzerland."

"I see." He made a note in his folder. "How many other Jews have you helped escape from justice?"

"I've helped no one escape from justice."

"What about Franz Hildebrandt?"

"Your Honor, Pastor Hildebrandt left Germany well before the war to minister to a German congregation in London. He can hardly be said to have escaped."

"He's a Jew?"

"I believe his mother was of Jewish origin, but he's an ordained pastor of the Evangelical Church."

"How long have you known this Jew?"

"Hildebrandt and I were students together."

"Would it be fair to say you were inseparable?"

"We were close friends," said Bonhoeffer. "We thought of a joint pastorate at one time. But then the struggle within the church took us in different directions."

"In July, 1937, he was detained by the Gestapo."

"He was Pastor Niemöller's assistant at Dahlem. He had the temerity to conduct Sunday services there after Niemöller's arrest." His tone was tarter than intended, and Roeder looked up sharply.

"He was arrested for preaching sedition. And your family procured his release."

"There was a national outcry. We did what we could."

"Did that include smuggling him out of Germany to join your friends in London?"

"Your Honor, I knew of a vacancy there for an assistant preacher."

"So." Roeder slapped the desk with the flat of his hand. "And you *still* deny you helped this Jew escape?"

"Pastor Hildebrandt traveled quite openly," said Bonhoeffer wearily. "I imagine the Gestapo could have stopped him if they'd wished to do so." There was simply no fending off this kind of attack.

"Do you keep in touch with him also? Through your mutual friends in Switzerland?"

"Your Honor overstates it. I've occasionally had word of him, as I have of my brother-in-law—at second or third hand."

"You mean you didn't even *write* to them while you were traveling abroad? I find that hard to believe."

"I—yes. I wrote to them. Surely that's understandable."

"Of course." Roeder smiled. "What more natural? You help these agents of international Jewry escape to England. They repay enemy hospitality by assisting the British government in its conduct of the war." He shrugged. "Of course, we understand. Naturally you would want to keep in touch with them through neutral channels."

"Your Honor is surely mistaken," said Bonhoeffer, unwilling to credit what Roeder seemed to be saying. "One a lawyer, the other a pastor—what could they possibly tell the enemy that would be of any value?"

"Whatever you told them from Switzerland?" He smiled encouragingly. "What with your Abwehr and family connections, you must have learned a good deal about the war effort."

"Your Honor, this is monstrous." Bonhoeffer was truly taken aback. In preparing his defense with Hans and Oster, they had never once considered even the possibility of such a charge. "I am quite appalled by the construction you are placing on this. I was sent abroad on official business. I took advantage of the opportunity to write to my twin sister and my friend, neither of whom had heard a word from me or my family since 1939. I assured them we were well and often thought of them—and if that constitutes treason, then yes—I'm guilty."

"You deny conspiring with these Jews against the Third Reich?"

"Of course."

"And you deny supplying them with information calculated to aid the enemy or blacken the reputation of the Third Reich?"

"I do."

"Very well." Roeder wrote in his folder. "I asked just now where you stood on the Jewish question—as an index of your attitude toward the Führer and National Socialism. Do you still subscribe to the views you expressed on that subject in *Vormarsch?*"

"That must be ten years ago, Your Honor. I hardly remember."

"Then I'll refresh your memory." He found the place and smoothed the page flat. "Now—you say there are three ways in which the church should act toward the state. This is in connection with the race laws, but they presumably apply generally. The first is to question the state as to whether its actions are legitimate."

"To question a law is not to break it."

"It's an essential preliminary, but no matter. You go on to say that the church also has an unconditional obligation toward the victims of any social order, even where those victims do not belong to the Christian community. By that you mean the Jews, of course."

"Yes." He sighed.

"Well, now. Tell me about this unconditional obligation you felt you owed the Jews. What form did it take? Was it an obligation to help them escape from justice? To assist their conspiracy against the Reich?"

"All I had in mind, Your Honor," said Bonhoeffer, realizing there was worse to come, "was the Christian injunction to do good to all men. If you wish to distort my meaning by choosing a sentence here and a sentence there, I cannot prevent you, but if so, there's little point in going on with this. You have only to convict and sentence me."

Roeder refused to be drawn. "If this *were* a trial," he said calmly, "you'd stand convicted out of your own mouth. For you say here that the third course open to the church—and correct me if I quote you out of context—the third course is 'not only to bind up the victims under the wheel, but to put a spoke in the wheel itself.' Now, what did you mean by *that?* Am I wrong, or were you advocating direct political action against the lawful government of the Reich?"

"The context *is* important," said Bonhoeffer. He glanced at Sonderegger, who was playing fixedly with a pencil. "You'll find I went on to say that this course would only be open to the church if the state deprived any group of citizens of its rights or tried to interfere with the character of the church itself or its Christian proclamation."

"But isn't that what you've been telling us? That the state *has* unlawfully deprived these Jew traitors of their rights? That it *has* interfered with the church?"

He took a moment to think. "I opposed the Aryan Clause on theological grounds. You have the arguments before you as I expressed them at the time. I am bound to resist any intrusion on the ministry of the church, because its authority to exercise spiritual dominion proceeds directly from God. But one must be careful to distinguish the church in this sense from the church in the sense of its congregation. Government has a full claim to obedience from the Christian congregation—just as the congregation has a full claim on government to protect the Christian ministry."

Roeder kept him waiting while he made another note. "Then, presumably, you and your fellow conspirators in the so-called Confessing Church should also be counted as 'victims' of the new order?"

"Only to the extent that the state encroached on our mandate to proclaim the word of God."

"And finding the state guilty of that offense, did you not in consequence resolve to put a spoke in its wheel?"

"Your Honor, my one aim in all this has been to arouse the church to its responsibilities, and that's all."

Roeder smiled indulgently. "And having resolved to put a spoke in the government's wheel, did you not conclude that the best way of doing so was to encourage foreign intervention in Germany's internal affairs?"

Bonhoeffer looked about him with real dismay. "If Your Honor is referring to my work with the ecumenical movement, I can only say that to put such a construction on it is grotesque."

"Can you deny that the Third Reich has been vilified throughout its glorious work of national regeneration by the propaganda agencies of international Jewry?"

"I'm afraid I don't see the connection."

"It's clear enough to me. By spreading lies and distortions calculated to inflame world opinion against us, you deliberately flouted the Treachery Law of March 21, 1933. And before you trouble to deny it, let me read you the relevant provision. It applies to anyone who—and I quote—'with malice aforethought spreads or puts out an untrue or grossly distorted assertion of a factual nature calculated seriously to impair the welfare of the Reich or of a province, or the reputation of the Reich government or of a regional government, or of the parties or associations behind those governments.' " He paused briefly for effect, pressing his fingertips together. "Is it so grotesque, then, to suggest that your so-called ecumenical work was little more than a cloak for high treason?"

Bonhoeffer puffed out his cheeks. Grotesque or not, Roeder would have no great difficulty in building a case along those lines. He was essentially right; in the early days, no opportunity had been lost of bringing the pressure of world opinion to bear on the government in its dealings with the church. "Your Honor, I have always been mindful of Germany's best interests."

"Indeed? Then I think we had better examine your connections abroad in a little more detail. It may help us understand why the Abwehr thought them so vital to the war effort."

Rewarded by another titter from the Gestapo men, he picked up a new folder. Bonhoeffer shifted from foot to foot. The dampness of his cell had given him rheumatism in his lower back.

"You spent a year in Spain." It was an accusation.

"Yes. In Barcelona. I had just passed the first theological examination, and the next step toward ordination was a year's parochial work."

"Germany wasn't good enough for you?"

"I was twenty-two. I wanted to see something of the world. It was not until I went to America in 1930 that I began to take an interest in the ecumenical movement."

"And discovered how much you had in common with Germany's enemies?"

"Your Honor, I went with a notebook full of arguments against the Versailles Treaty. I was ready to do battle with anybody on the question of German war guilt. I preached on the subject more than once."

"Are you saying that was the purpose of your visit?" Roeder smiled contemptuously.

"I went as an exchange student to the Union Theological Seminary in New York. I'd finished my thesis to qualify as a university lecturer and taken the second examination for the ministry, but I still had a year to wait before I could be ordained."

"So you decided to spend it with the Jew architects of Germany's humiliation."

"So I decided to broaden my experience. There was little enough theology taught at the seminary—at least, as I understood it—and so I studied American life and thought. I saw a lot of the country. I visited Cuba and Mexico, made several lifelong friends, and returned home in the summer of 1931 convinced that the Christian Church had to heal its divisions before it could properly serve the will of God."

"Or properly serve the purposes of a global conspiracy to keep Germany in chains."

"Your Honor, a few weeks after I returned home, my dean of studies sent me to England for the annual conference of the World Alliance of Churches. In a debate on disarmament, the American,

British, and French delegates all agreed on the need to restore Germany's equal rights."

"Equal rights?" Roeder laughed. "After we'd been robbed of our living space and bled white by so-called reparation payments?"

"Just so. The conference recognized the justice of our complaints."

"Well, I suppose we might call that youthful naïveté if you had not been warned against these crude attempts to distract the German people from their destiny in Europe."

"Warned, Your Honor?"

Roeder raked through his papers. "You don't remember two eminent colleagues of yours, Professors Althaus and Hirsch, denouncing the ecumenical movement as a threat to national unity?"

"I remember."

"Yes. 'It should be unreservedly recognized that Christian and churchly understanding and cooperation on questions of rapprochement between the nations is impossible so long as the others conduct a policy lethal to our nation.' "

"I didn't agree. I thought they were mistaken."

"I see. Their statement was endorsed by every responsible political party in the country, by most of its newspapers, by the German Evangelical Alliance, by a majority of the faculty and students at your own university—but you thought they were mistaken."

Bonhoeffer eased his back. "The world was on the brink of moral chaos. I thought it right for the churches to unite in taking a stand."

"Against Germany?"

"Against war as a means of settling international disputes."

Roeder sat back. "Well, that's an interesting admission." They both looked at Sonderegger, who continued to make his presence felt without a word or even much change of expression. "You're a pacifist?"

"As a Christian," said Bonhoeffer, "I felt it my duty to work for peace. In no sense could war be regarded as God's commandment. On the other hand, as a German now faced with the *fact* of war, I am also bound by Christian duty to share the burdens of my countrymen. It was in this spirit that I joined the Abwehr."

"We'll get to that later. I want to know why working for peace, as you call it, always seems to mean siding with the enemy. When did you first meet the English Bishop George Bell?"

"Toward the end of 1931. He had just been elected chairman of the Ecumenical Council of Life and Work. And far from being an enemy, Germany has no better friend in England than Bishop Bell."

"You traveled a good deal after your return from America," said Roeder, consulting his notes.

"It was not then considered a crime, Your Honor. I'd been elected one of three youth secretaries to the World Alliance. But I was also very busy at home. Besides lecturing at the university, I was chaplain at Charlottenburg Technical College, and I had a confirmation class in Wedding."

"Did you attend a so-called peace conference at Bad Schwarzenberg?"

"Yes. In July, I think."

"And with your customary eloquence, did you again denounce the German people's legitimate aspirations in Europe?"

Bonhoeffer blinked. "Not even by quoting me out of context could Your Honor support such a view. The German people did not aspire to war, and war was all I denounced. Otherwise I consistently defended our national aims on every platform the ecumenical movement could provide."

Roeder threw himself back. "Your presumption is intolerable. The will of the people was expressed in the Führer's implacable resolve to restore German greatness. Did you suppose a true German would shrink from war if the struggle required it?"

"Your Honor, it was 1932. Germany was helpless. I tried in every way I knew—at home *and* abroad—to show that the justification for struggle could not be used as a justification for war, but there seemed to be a conspiracy against peace. It was argued that because there were different orders in creation, the nations should preserve and develop their differences out of obedience to God's will. Everything was sanctioned by this argument—war, national rivalry, class struggle, exploitation. Nothing was easier than to insist that because these things existed they were God-willed and God-created, and that we should therefore glory in conflict. But it was bad politics and worse theology, and that was why I supported the ecumenical movement—in spite of its shortcomings. Those who argued in this fashion had forgotten that the world

30

is fallen. They had forgotten, or never realized, that creation and sin are so wound together that no human eye can separate them. They could not, or would not, see that each human order is an order of the fallen world, not an order of creation, and that the will of God could no longer be perceived directly in what they saw about them. In a world fallen from God, nothing can happen without struggle, but war destroys His creation. War can no more be justified by the necessity for struggle than—than torture can be justified by the need for law. It obscures the light of His revelation."

He had not intended to say so much, but when no attempt was made to stop him, he had thought that if Roeder could somehow be made to see some part of the truth, that it was theology, not politics or ambition that had brought him into opposition, then the inquiry might afterward proceed on less punishing lines. Roeder might then concentrate on building a legal case against him—a game for which he was better prepared.

"If that's a sample of the sermons you preached," Roeder said, "I'm not surprised you had to move to England to find a congregation." There was a dutiful laugh, but it was hardly a vote of confidence. He reapplied himself, frowning. "But why would a man in whom God had such confidence exchange the international arena for the obscurity of a small parish in London?"

"I didn't. I continued as youth secretary of the Alliance, but I was anxious for pastoral work."

"Come, now. You needed this post abroad in order to exploit the dissension your confederates were stirring up at home."

"No, Your Honor." He was getting tired. "It's true the church had become heavily embroiled in questions of heresy and reorganization, but I think I was trying to escape them. I found it hard to see my way clearly."

"You saw it clearly enough to resist the patriotic reforms of the German Christians in 1933. You joined the so-called Young Reformers and engineered such an upheaval that the Führer himself had to intervene."

Bonhoeffer shook his head. "Your Honor, that summer the Minister of Church Affairs replaced the general superintendents of the Old Prussian Union with state commissars. It was a blatant attempt to

31

capture the church for political purposes, and the outcry was so great that President Hindenburg himself interceded with the Führer. The state commissars were then withdrawn and a general church election took place in July."

"An election that proved what? That the people stood behind you? That you were right and the Minister wrong?"

"No, Your Honor."

"No. You were crushed. In a free vote, the German people installed Bishop Müller at the head of the Prussian Church, and a little later as national bishop of a unified Reich Church."

"The election had decided who would hold office in the church, Your Honor. It did not decide who was in possession of the truth. Besides, the vote was not entirely free."

"Not *free?*" Roeder shouted. "It was a secret ballot supervised by the Ministry of the Interior."

"I mean that candidates opposing the German Christians were systematically intimidated. Their meetings were broken up, they were threatened with violence and the loss of their jobs."

"Well, you can hardly hold the party responsible for spontaneous outbursts of public feeling."

"No," said Bonhoeffer cautiously. "But by identifying itself so closely with the German Christians, the party inevitably turned the election into a vote of confidence for National Socialism, so that the significance of the event as a *church* election was rather lost."

"Is that what you told your contacts abroad?"

"I think the position was as clear to churchmen abroad as it was to us, Your Honor. But we didn't contest the result. The Young Reformers turned at once to the theological issues. I was myself sent into retreat to help draft a new confession of faith to which we hoped all the clergy of the Evangelical Church might subscribe. We were not entirely successful, but it showed a constructive response."

"Would you also describe your part in the so-called Pastors' Emergency League as constructive?"

Again Bonhoeffer hesitated. Roeder was damnably well informed, but there was a constant danger of telling him more than he knew. "That was in September, Your Honor. By then, I had more or less made up my mind to go to London—I'd already applied for leave of

32

absence from the university. My part in the Emergency League was not prompted, therefore, by any thought of intervening directly in the church struggle, but by theological reasons that seemed to me *entirely* constructive."

Roeder looked down in silence for a moment. "You were a co-founder with Martin Niemöller of a dissident group that aimed to split the Reich Church even before its constitution could be ratified by a national synod," he said. "You were out to sabotage the contribution that a united church could make to the spiritual regeneration of Germany under the Führer's inspiring leadership. Having stirred up dissension among the clergy, you then retreated to London by prearranged plan to exploit the situation that you yourself had helped create. While Niemöller stayed behind to fan the flames, you used the dispute to promote foreign interference in Germany's internal affairs. And in this way, you hoped to succeed in your stated aim of putting a spoke in the government's wheel."

Bonhoeffer rubbed his eyes, much hampered by the handcuffs.

"I'll try to answer that in order, Your Honor." He replaced his glasses. "After the election, the Prussian Church Synod passed a law applying the Aryan Clause to the Christian ministry. The next day, some of us met at Pastor Niemöller's house to consider our position. My own first thought was to resign from the church and urge others to do the same, but there was little support for that. Instead, Pastor Niemöller and I put our names to a declaration which said simply that the Aryan Clause violated the confession of our church, and that anyone who assented to such a breach excluded himself from the communion of the church. In two weeks, the declaration attracted two thousand signatures, and by the end of the year the Emergency League had six thousand members. So it's quite wrong to suggest it was merely an instrument for creating discord in an otherwise united church. It was a spontaneous expression of disquiet on the part of the German clergy—quite beyond the ability of anyone to engineer for disloyal purposes."

"But it wasn't beyond your ability to *exploit* for disloyal purposes," said Roeder angrily. "What happened in Sofia that September?"

"In Sofia? The World Alliance held a conference there."

"And were you the only German delegate?"

"There was one other, I think."

"Do you remember the conference resolution on the Jewish problem? 'We especially deplore the fact that the state measures against the Jews in Germany have had such an effect on public opinion that in some circles the Jewish race is considered a race of inferior status. . . . We protest against the resolutions of the Prussian general synod and other synods which apply the Aryan Clause of the state to the church,' etc., etc. Doesn't that have a familiar ring?"

"Your Honor, a resolution in very similar terms had been passed a few days earlier at a Life and Work conference in Novi Sad, at which I was *not* present. The German delegation there was led by Bishop Heckel, whose loyalty to the government has never, to my knowledge, been questioned. The situation of the church in Germany was causing great concern abroad. I remember going to the German embassy in Sofia to warn them. I made it clear I was powerless to prevent the resolution's being passed, but that it should not be taken as an attack on the German government."

"It could be construed in no other way," said Roeder, his irritation now very evident. "Your visit to the embassy was no more than a lame attempt to cover your tracks. You'll be telling me next it was just a coincidence that Bishop Bell's impudent interference in our affairs began the moment you moved to London."

"Your Honor, as chairman of Life and Work, Bishop Bell wrote to Bishop Müller in accordance with the resolution passed at Novi Sad." He was on easier ground here, although the Treachery Law had sowed it with mines. "For my part, I was at pains to have everything clear before I left for London. I insisted on seeing the Reich Bishop to explain in person that I could not represent the German Christian view abroad, nor could I avoid expressing my opinion of recent events in the German church if asked—and given my connections with Bishop Bell and other English churchmen, I certainly *would* be asked. I put all this in a letter to Bishop Heckel, asking that it be placed on record."

Roeder was writing in his folder.

"I also pledged my loyalty to Germany, and offered to give up going to London altogether sooner than leave any uncertainty behind."

Roeder again slammed his hand on the desk. "Did you seriously imagine that by doing this you could defeat the provisions of the Treachery Law?" he demanded. "Didn't Bishop Müller himself warn you of the need for discretion? Didn't he tell you that in the eyes of the church and the German people, our enemies abroad had forfeited the moral right to pass judgment on our affairs?"

"He did—but I needed no instruction from him in either the law *or* my duty to Germany." His own temper was fraying now, and he pulled himself together.

"Was it out of respect for law that you chose to defy the Reich Bishop's decree of January 4, 1934, forbidding all further public discussion of church policies?" The Judge Advocate's tone was dangerously restrained. "Is *that* how you saw your duty to Germany?"

"Your Honor, by then the authority of the Reich Bishop was seriously in question. He owed his position to the German Christians, but the Führer himself had publicly disowned them for their scandalous blasphemies. Consequently, for many of us, the Reich Bishop's decrees no longer had the force of law."

Sonderegger shifted in his seat with an audible sigh, and Roeder glared at him. "In conspiring with Bishop Bell and your Jewish friends to use this dispute as the pretext for a vicious propaganda campaign against the Reich, you knowingly broke the laws of both church *and* state."

"There was no such conspiracy." Bonhoeffer raised his hands, and let them fall. "Does the court seriously suppose that Dr. Bell of Chichester, a bishop of the Anglican Church with a seat in the House of Lords, would allow himself to be used for political propaganda by the pastor of an obscure German congregation in south London?"

"Be careful. The court *does* seriously suppose that you allowed *yourself* to be used for political purposes—and that this was the sole reason for your move to London."

"Your Honor, I was recommended for the post by Bishop Heckel. And I was bitterly reproached by some of my colleagues in the Emergency League for accepting it."

"Not, surely, when you made your intentions clear?" He glanced again at Sonderegger. "Isn't it a fact that in February, 1934, only four months after your departure from Berlin, Bishop Heckel found it necessary to visit London in order to curb your activities?"

"Your Honor, Bishop Heckel visited London to warn *all* the German pastors in England against criticizing the government of the Reich Church." His lower back hurt so much now he could hardly stand upright.

"Isn't it also true that he saw Bishop Bell and asked him to refrain from further comment on Germany's internal affairs? A simple yes or no will be sufficient."

"Then I must say no, Your Honor."

*"No?"* Roeder jabbed at the file in front of him. "It's a matter of record."

"Bishop Bell was asked to consider remaining silent on the issues of the church struggle for a period of six months," said Bonhoeffer patiently. "As chairman of Life and Work and a council member of the World Alliance, he considered them to be matters of general Christian concern, and declined."

Roeder stared in frustration. "Just as *you* declined to sign the declaration of allegiance that Heckel asked for."

"It was a declaration of allegiance to a church government he knew I opposed. My allegiance to Germany was not in question."

"The church government had another opinion. You were recalled to Berlin a month later. Why?"

"Why? Because the Archbishop of Canterbury had asked to see me—and no such invitation had been extended to Bishop Heckel during his visit." Before he had finished, he regretted saying it. It was gratuitous, and gave Roeder an opening he was not slow to see.

"Indeed? Then perhaps you'll tell us what it was that the archbishop preferred to discuss with the pastor of an obscure German congregation rather than with the bishop in charge of the External Affairs Office of the Reich Church?"

"Like Bishop Bell, he was concerned to hear from *both* sides of the church dispute," he said. It had been a stupid lapse.

"But didn't Bishop Heckel tell you in Berlin that discussions of this kind would be regarded as intervention in our affairs? Yes or no, please."

"Yes."

"Yes. And did he not remind you that Reich Bishop Müller had denounced as high treason the betrayal of church information to foreigners?"

"Yes."

"And did he not again ask you to sign a declaration renouncing this so-called ecumenical work as a pledge of your loyalty to church and state?"

"He did."

"And yet you *still* went ahead with this meeting?"

"Yes."

"In spite of these warnings, you actually discussed the internal affairs of the German church with the archbishop?"

"Your Honor, to have refused a summons to Lambeth Palace would have caused the gravest offense to the archbishop at a time when Germany was making every effort to improve its relations with England."

There was a silence. Then Roeder laughed, and the court joined in.

"The same applied to Bishop Bell," Bonhoeffer went on evenly. "To have refused to see him was unthinkable. We were colleagues in the two great ecumenical movements, and often had to discuss things that had nothing to do with the German church. And far from seeking to defame Germany, he was then, like the archbishop, a strong supporter of Anglo-German friendship. I would remind the court that Herr von Ribbentrop not only went to see him in Chichester at about this time, but also invited him to Berlin in 1935 to meet the Deputy Führer and the Minister of Church Affairs."

Roeder found this less amusing. "Your actions could have had no bearing on the matter. They neither explain nor excuse your defiance. Reich Bishop Müller derived his authority from the Führer. To defy one was to defy the other."

"Your Honor, by the end of 1934 that was no longer true." They were both watching Sonderegger, who had just finished scribbling a note and given it to one of the Gestapo men to take up to Roeder. "The opposition clergy had met in free synod at Barmen in May to condemn the German Christian heresy and assert themselves as the true church, the Confessing Church."

No one was listening. Roeder read the note, looked at his wrist watch, and scratched his chin thoughtfully. Then he whispered something to the Gestapo man, who nodded and made his way out of the court.

"In retaliation, Müller called in the police and tried to centralize the church by force," Bonhoeffer went on, rather than meekly await their pleasure. "This led to demonstrations in the streets, and another synod was convened at Dahlem in October to declare the Confessing Church the only legal church in Germany. At this point the Führer stepped in."

"Yes?" said Roeder absently, looking over his head to the courtroom door.

"Yes. He announced, in effect, that membership in the Confessing Church was not inconsistent with loyalty to the Reich or to himself —a point which I have tried repeatedly to bring to Your Honor's attention."

Roeder woke up to what he was saying. "So then you came back. You thought you'd won a great victory, was that it? You'd put a spoke in the wheel?"

"I was called home to take charge of a preachers' seminary." He heard the clink of chains in a stir of movement behind him, and a pulse began to thump in his head. "I was under no illusions about the future."

Roeder was again looking past him. "The only future for a traitor is the gallows."

He dared not turn around, suddenly terrified that they might have taken his parents. Sweat ran down inside his clothes. He could hear Roeder speaking, at a great distance, but not what he said. Nor could he see him as the darkness closed in. He was afraid he would fall. Then the weakness began to pass and his vision slowly cleared. He looked to his left, moving his shoulders uneasily to free them from his sodden shirt, and saw Hans and Christine, both handcuffed, not ten feet away.

"A most convincing picture of guilt," said Roeder.

The guards were alert to keep them apart, but they stayed where they were, studying one another's faces for signs that only they would recognize. His sister was tense and worried, but not on her own account. She could hardly take her eyes off Hans, who looked ill, although his gaze was direct and untroubled.

"We've heard a most interesting account of your activities," said Roeder. "We managed to persuade Pastor Bonhoeffer to tell us the whole story."

Hans smiled politely. "Knowing his faith in God and German justice, Your Honor, I'm sure he needed little persuasion."

There was nothing they could say to one another in front of these people. There was nothing they *had* to say. The longer they stood there, the more strongly Bonhoeffer felt the bond between them. They were another breed.

Roeder looked at Sonderegger, who shrugged.

"Remove the prisoner Bonhoeffer," he said.

# 3

Bonhoeffer slept so heavily that he heard nothing of the usual uproar next morning, and woke to find a guard standing over him. It was a moment or two before he remembered where he was. Then he groped for his glasses on the stool, and swung his legs over the side of the bed with a muttered apology.

The guard held out a mess tin with an uncommonly generous ration of bread and sausage, and a mug of what looked and smelled like real coffee. "Compliments of Corporal Knobloch," he said. "When you've finished that, you're moving to another cell."

"Another cell? Why?"

The guard shrugged. Bonhoeffer had not seen him before, but he recognized his manner. The long-service staff shared a common indifference. Not responsible for anything, they were capable of anything, but he took the coffee gratefully and set the mess tin down on the bench.

Then the guard went outside and came back propelling a prisoner in front of him. Lanky and pale, he was dressed in greasy scraps of uniform and carried a bucket and mop.

"This man will clean up," said the guard. "Get on with it. And no talking."

He watched for a few moments, then walked off down the gallery, leaving the cell door open. As soon as he had gone, the prisoner straightened up, spat on the spot he had just cleaned, and sat down on the bench.

"What happened to your face?" asked Bonhoeffer.

The other touched his left eye, which was swollen and purple. "Him," he said, jerking his head at the door. "Bastard." But he was more concerned with Bonhoeffer's breakfast.

"I thought guards weren't allowed to strike prisoners."

He shook his head tolerantly. "You going to eat that?"

"You can have some if you like," said Bonhoeffer, but the other already had his mouth full of bread. He then took a huge bite of sausage, looked from the bread in one hand to the sausage in the other, stuffed them into his side pockets, and rubbed his hands down the front of his jacket.

"What are you in for?" he asked, not much interested.

"I don't know," said Bonhoeffer. "What about you?"

"Theft." He wiped his mouth on his sleeve. "You belong to the party? *We* don't get rations like this."

Bonhoeffer shook his head. "What part of Berlin do you come from?"

"Wedding."

"I thought so."

"How would *you* know?" The belligerence was as automatic as Bonhoeffer's hint of patronage.

"I know Wedding very well. I took a confirmation class there years ago. Fifty boys. You might know some of them."

"You're a minister?"

"Pastor Bonhoeffer. Who are you?"

"Otto Meiser." He raised himself an inch or so above the bench, farted, and sat down again. "That's what I think of religion."

Bonhoeffer scratched his chin. "Well, I don't think much of it either. But hadn't you better do something? Before the guard comes back?"

"You don't think much of religion?" Meiser laughed and levered himself up with the mop.

"Faith is what counts." He lifted his feet out of harm's way as the other slopped water around with abandon. "Religion is man reaching for God on Sunday. It makes him feel virtuous. Faith is God reaching for man."

"Yeah? Well, he never did anything for me."

"He just gave you my breakfast," said Bonhoeffer mildly.

As Meiser leaned on the mop to consider this, the guard reappeared at the door, and without a word, kicked the mop out from under him. Meiser pitched forward, boots skittering for purchase on the wet floor, and fell heavily on his hip, his face contorted with pain and alarm.

"I told you no talking," the guard said.

Bonhoeffer pushed him aside and helped Meiser to his feet. "Are you all right?"

He tested his leg cautiously, and nodded, wincing. Then Bonhoeffer straightened to his full height and turned to look down on the guard.

"Army regulations specifically forbid the striking of prisoners," he said, and was distantly amused to hear in his voice the authentic note of the officer class.

The guard heard it, too. "He slipped."

"I saw what happened. And it's not the first time you've mistreated this man." Meiser pulled at his sleeve.

"He slipped," the guard repeated sullenly.

"That's right," said Meiser. "I slipped. Lost my balance."

Bonhoeffer ignored him. "If I see or hear of any further incident of this kind, involving you or anyone else, I shall report it immediately to the commandant and insist on the strongest possible disciplinary action. Is that clear?"

The guard lowered his eyes and shuffled uneasily. Then he noticed the empty mess tin on the bench. "Your cell's ready," he said. "Meiser will bring your stuff."

Puzzled by this unexpected deference, Bonhoeffer followed him along the gallery. He had earned no reward for his performance in court, but his new quarters were bigger and cleaner. Smelling spring on the air, he stood beneath the bars of the open window and waited for them to leave. Then he rearranged his belongings—he had a table now—and picked up the thread of his daily routine. After fifteen minutes' strenuous exercise, he washed himself down as thoroughly as a shallow bowl of cold water and a sliver of soap allowed, changed into clean underwear, dressed, and began his morning walk, looking forward to the modest challenge of recomputing the number of times he would have to crisscross this larger cell to cover ten kilometers.

At about nine o'clock, he was repeating to himself as he walked the Bible passages he had learned by heart the previous day, when Knobloch came to fetch him.

"Prisoner Bonhoeffer for exercise," he yelled, with a broad wink. "Step outside and follow me."

"Are you *sure?*" Bonhoeffer looked past him, at the guard.

"Captain's orders. He's waiting in the yard."

Bonhoeffer buttoned his jacket and strolled downstairs with Knobloch as though on a tour of inspection, nodding affably at everyone they passed and sometimes securing a respectful smile or half salute in return. Whatever had happened to raise his stock, he intended to make the most of it. As he stepped blinking into the sunlight, a slightly built officer in cap and greatcoat changed direction to meet him, the fat sergeant major waddling a pace or two behind.

"Captain Maetz." He clicked his heels. "Good morning. I regret this pleasure has been long delayed, but there are many calls on my time. Seven hundred prisoners, you understand . . ." He waved the sergeant major and corporal away, acknowledging their salutes with a flick of his cane. "Would you care for a turn around the yard?"

"Thank you," said Bonhoeffer. "I've been looking forward to it."

"Yes." They set off together in step, Maetz with his gloved hands clasped behind his back. "Sergeant Major Weber tends to be overzealous, I'm afraid," he said suddenly. "He has a literal mind. No bad thing in a field NCO, of course, but it sometimes makes for difficulties in more sensitive situations."

"I can well imagine."

"Yes." He scuffed at the gravel with his mirror-bright boots. "He was told to keep you apart from the other prisoners. And there was to be no inessential contact with the prison staff—Colonel Roeder was most insistent on that. But I'm afraid Weber took this to mean solitary confinement. Without privileges."

"I'm afraid he did."

"Well, I see no reason for it. From now on, you will be brought down for half an hour a day to exercise here in the yard. Weather permitting, of course."

"Thank you."

"Does this time suit you?"

"Perfectly."

"Good. Then that's settled. And if there is anything else I can do to make your stay more comfortable, then let me know. Subject to regulations, of course."

"Of course."

Bonhoeffer turned his face to the sun. Maetz was a bureaucrat—well enough disposed, no doubt, but unlikely to have gone to this trouble without being prompted. The thrush was singing in one of the lime trees. They were misted gray-green with new growth. "Such a beautiful day."

Maetz looked up briefly. "Yes. Beautiful. Of course, the real problem is that the men aren't used to dealing with prisoners of your type. We get the scum of the army here. Deserters, looters, murderers, thieves—animals, most of them. The best I can do, I'm afraid, is keep you out of their way."

"In a condemned cell?"

"Well, it *is* the quietest part of the prison." He laughed. "And the cells are better than most."

"They *are?*"

"Oh, yes. At least you can breathe up there. Didn't you notice the stench as you came down? No ventilation. I wouldn't keep dogs in a kennel like that."

"Just these unfortunate young men."

Maetz broke stride, then recovered. "Your sympathy does you credit, Pastor, but it's entirely wasted."

"Is it necessary to keep them chained?"

"Only those awaiting execution."

"But why? No one can escape from here, surely?"

"You miss the point." He mastered his annoyance. "They are chained to protect my men. We deal with degenerates here, Pastor—vicious, subhuman degenerates. If we left them free in their cells, what's to prevent them attacking the guards? They can only hang once. My men would never go near them."

44

"And if they want to make their peace with God?"

"The prison chaplain has a free hand. So long as the regulations are observed, I never interfere."

"Then will you allow *me* to visit them? It must be hard enough to number the days in a place like this, without being chained like a beast."

"I'm sorry. You don't understand what we're up against here. And with respect, Pastor, I think the gallows will make better Christians of them than you can."

Bonhoeffer bit down on his temper.

"I'll take leave to debate that someday," he said. "Meanwhile, I'd like to meet the chaplain, if you'll be good enough to arrange it."

Maetz looked doubtful. "I think, for the moment, that may not be possible. But I'll ask Colonel Roeder at the first opportunity."

Halting under a lime tree, Maetz produced a silver cigarette case from the inside pocket of his greatcoat, hesitated, and offered it to Bonhoeffer, who took one and thanked him politely.

"Did Colonel Roeder give you any idea of how long I might be here?" he asked.

"None. Until his investigation is complete, I presume."

"And you've no impression of when that might be?"

"I know nothing of your case. He didn't confide in me."

Maetz's tone had turned hostile. Bonhoeffer saw he was looking at the cigarette in his hand, and guessed that prisoners were probably not allowed to smoke in the yard. Maetz was embarrassed at having offered it, and even more at not being able to ask for it back.

"Then I must learn to be patient," said Bonhoeffer, renouncing his pleasure in Maetz's predicament. There was more to be gained from sparing his feelings. "And if you will allow me, I'll save this till later. I sometimes think it might be easier to give up my hope of salvation than a cigarette after lunch."

"Well, of course," said Maetz cordially. "By all means. Why don't you ask your family to send you some? I'd have no objection to that."

"Thank you. I will. And if my parents were to bring them, is there a chance I might see them, perhaps?"

"Ah. Now, there again, I regret that Colonel Roeder has forbidden all visitors for the time being. They can always apply for permission to the War Court, of course, but without it I'm afraid there's nothing I can do." He had been watching Knobloch double across the yard to head them off. "What is it, Corporal?"

"Berlin Command on the telephone, sir."

"Very well." Maetz turned to Bonhoeffer with the rueful air of a man in constant demand. "You'll excuse me, Pastor? The corporal will see you back to your cell." He checked his watch. "At 0940."

"Thank you, Captain."

"Until tomorrow, then." He sketched a salute, again clicked his heels, and strutted away toward the administration building. Knobloch spat reflectively into the gravel.

Bonhoeffer walked on. "As you see," he said over his shoulder, "there's been a great change."

"Yes, sir," said the corporal, falling in behind. "If he had any sense, he'd have done this last week."

"Why? What happened?"

"A telephone call from General von Hase. The Berlin commandant."

"Ah, yes. Well, that would explain it."

"Is he a friend of yours, sir?"

"He's my uncle."

"Your *uncle.*"

"Well, the captain couldn't have known that, and the Gestapo are interested. We all have to be careful these days."

Bonhoeffer was hoping to draw Knobloch out, but he only grunted. When Bonhoeffer turned to pursue the point, he noticed that Sergeant Major Weber was watching them, and changed his mind. Knobloch had seen him, too, and fallen back several paces. They completed the half hour in silence.

At midday, he was served with a generous helping of stew, and had to cut short the guard's almost servile excuses for the incident with Meiser. In the afternoon, Corporal Linke stopped by, ostensibly to discuss the books in the prison library, but in fact to gossip generally for almost an hour, and by evening, when a new guard came on who already knew all about him, Bonhoeffer realized that his walk with Captain Maetz was the talk of the prison. The prospect was suddenly brighter.

But the moment the lights went out at eight, he was again beset with such longings for the life he had lost that he wandered about his cell for hours, trying to master his incredulity at being there.

Easter Day, 25 April 1943

Dear Parents,

At last the tenth day has come round, and I'm allowed to write to you again! I'm so glad to let you know that even here I'm having a happy Easter. Good Friday and Easter free us to think about other things far beyond our own personal fate, about the ultimate meaning of all life, suffering, and events; and we lay hold of a great hope. Since yesterday, it has been marvellously quiet in the house.

Good Friday was Maria's birthday. If I didn't know how bravely she bore the death last year of her father, her brother, and two cousins of whom she was particularly fond, I would be really alarmed about her. . . . Give her my love, tell her that I long for her very much, but that she is not to grieve, but to be as brave as she has always been. She is still so very young—that is the hard thing.

First of all, I must thank you very much for all the things that you brought me and for father's and Ursel's greetings. You can't imagine what it means to be suddenly told, "Your mother and sister and brother have just been here, and they've left something for you." The mere fact that you have been near me, the tangible evidence that you are still thinking and caring about me (which of course I really know anyway!), is enough to keep me happy for the rest of the day. Thank you very much indeed for everything.

Things are still all right, and I am well. I'm allowed out of doors for half an hour every day, and now that I can smoke again, I even forget sometimes, for a little while, where I am! I'm being treated well, and I read a good deal—newspapers, novels, and above all the Bible. I can't concentrate enough yet for serious work but during Holy Week I at last managed to work solidly through a part of the passion story that has occupied me a great deal for a long time—the high priestly prayer. I've even been able to expound to myself a few chapters of Pauline ethical material; I felt that to be very important. So I really have a great deal to be very thankful for.

How are things with you? . . . I want to make it clear that it is my express wish that Ursel should not postpone the date by a single day, but should let Renate get married as soon and as happily as possible; don't let her worry. Anything else would only distress me. Renate knows all the good wishes for her in my thoughts, and how much I share her joy. In recent years we have really learnt how much joy and sorrow can and must fill the human heart at one and the same time. So, the sooner the better. Do give her my love. . . .

Now a couple of requests: I would very much like the brown, or better still, the black boots with laces. My heels are going. My suit is very much in need of cleaning; I would also like to give it to you and to have the other brown one instead. I also need a hairbrush, lots of matches, a pipe with tobacco, pouch and cleaners, and cigarettes. Books: Schilling, *Morals,* Vol. II, and a volume of Stifter. Excuse me for troubling you. Many thanks.

It is surprising how quickly the days pass here. I can hardly believe that I have been here three weeks. I like going to bed at eight o'clock (supper is at four), and I look forward to my dreams. I never knew before what a source of pleasure that can be; I dream every day and always about something pleasant. Before I go to sleep, I repeat to myself the verses that I have learnt during the day, and at 6 A.M. I like to read psalms and hymns, think of you all, and know that you are thinking of me.

The day is over now, and I hope you are feeling as peaceful as I am. I've read a lot of good things, and my thoughts and hopes have been pleasant, too. But it would put my mind very much at rest if one day Maria were quietly with you. . . .

Goodbye for now, and excuse all the worry that I'm causing you. Greetings to all the rest of the family. Love and thanks with all my heart.

Your Dietrich

In fact, he was not sleeping well, and his dreams were not always pleasant. He was learning to support life by changing particular griefs into general abstractions. It was his only defense against a loss that was still ungraspable. While whole, he had imagined what it might be like, and thought he could endure it. What he had never stopped to consider was what it would be like to think of his loss without *being* whole, when the mind was crippled with longing and self-reproach. All he could do was force his thoughts outward, to think about separation and time passing as intellectual problems, and arrange his ideas as though preparing a paper on the subject. And when that failed, he would consider the relativity of suffering, pitting his own against that of the men around him. All night long, even while dozing fitfully, he sensed them moving about, opposing the hours to their death like cattle scenting the slaughter.

There was also the resistance to think about. It now seemed in retrospect too weak and irresolute ever to have had much chance of achieving its purpose. Hans, Oster, and the others had kept it going by force of will, but they were too few. The Germany they served, if not dead, was blind and besotted. They had not realized that obedience, a sense of duty, the capacity for self-sacrifice—all the great strengths of the nation—could be exploited as readily for evil purposes as for good ones. Faced with the success of National Socialism, it was now hard to say which was the more responsible course: to battle on quixotically against the reality of a new age, or to admit defeat and serve it. After all, the ruler of history had repeatedly brought good out of evil over the heads of the history-makers, and the idea of going down fighting like heroes in the face of certain annihilation was not really heroic at all, but merely a refusal to face the future.

Nevertheless, there were lives to be protected. The emergency code he had agreed on with Hans in anticipation of their arrest was now working smoothly. If his name was underlined on the flyleaf of a book sent in with his weekly parcel, there was a message inside. On every tenth page, starting from the back, there would be the faintest of pencil marks under a letter or number. By stringing these together, he had learned that his friend Josef Müller, an Abwehr colleague in the Munich office and a key figure in the conspiracy, had also been arrested. This was serious, for he and Müller had been due to go to Rome on April 9 to explain to the British through the Vatican the failure of the attempts on Hitler's life in March. Worse still, the message had gone on to say that while searching Hans's office, Roeder had seized a slip of paper referring to this assignment which bore the code letter "O" of General Ludwig Beck, signifying his assent, as resistance leader, to the mission. Sonderegger had spotted Oster trying to hide it, and assumed the initial was his, but Oster had then denied all knowledge of what was on the paper—an assertion so unlikely in view of his attempt to keep it from them that Roeder had at once suspected treason.

Bonhoeffer could well imagine how much harder Hans's interrogation was going in consequence. Forewarned, he would now take care not to make matters worse, but the only solution was to get Oster to acknowledge the initial as his own, and for Canaris to insist that the slip of paper was a normal Abwehr document relating to a normal Abwehr assignment. As soon as it was light enough, he encoded a message to this effect in a book to be returned with the next batch of laundry, adding that if the issue cropped up before he received a reply, he would assume it was being dealt with along those lines.

But he was in a bleak mood when the guard brought breakfast. He looked suspiciously at an even more generous portion of sausage than usual and insisted on comparing it with the other prisoners' breakfasts. When his turned out to be considerably larger, he exchanged it for the smallest he could find, sharply reminding the bewildered guard that he looked for no favors, least of all at the expense of men condemned to death.

That evening, Corporal Linke came to see him. Setting aside the notes he had been making for Renate's wedding sermon, Bonhoeffer sat him down, and they chatted and smoked like old friends. Linke had stayed over Easter with his niece and her children in Dahlem, Martin Niemöller's old parish. Her husband had been reported missing at Stalingrad.

"He may be a prisoner," said Bonhoeffer.

"I don't know that it makes much difference, Pastor. Not with the Russians."

"I could make inquiries. Through my family."

He shook his head. "Best leave it. I wouldn't want to raise her hopes."

It was another lesson in the difference between suffering and inconvenience. To change the subject, Bonhoeffer went on to tell Linke about *his* niece, Renate, and how she was soon to marry his closest friend.

"I was going to start them off with one of my better sermons," he said, making light of it. "Now they'll just have to get along as best they can."

There was no answering smile from Linke. "Have you written it yet? The sermon?"

"The wedding was six weeks off when they came for me. I've been making a few notes, but that's all."

"Well, you write it out," said Linke, "and I'll see she gets it."

Bonhoeffer frowned.

"It's not the same as being there," the corporal went on, misunderstanding his silence, "but if you'd like me to take it, I will."

"Herr Linke, I don't know what to say. I couldn't allow you to run any risk on my account."

"Well, I wouldn't want to make a habit of it," he said, "but once won't hurt. Do you have enough paper?"

"I think so."

"Good. I'll bring more from the guardroom next time." He pinched out the end of his cigarette and replaced the butt in his tin.

"You're quite sure about this?" asked Bonhoeffer. It was the first time he could remember accepting a favor he knew he could never repay.

"It'll give me pleasure. What day is the wedding?"

"May 15."

"Good. But don't leave it too late. Otherwise you can be sure I'll get extra duty that day."

"I'll start tonight," said Bonhoeffer, shaking him warmly by the hand. "God bless you, Herr Linke."

The moment he left, Bonhoeffer sat down at the table, took a fresh sheet of paper, and began to write, hesitantly at first but then with growing confidence.

> It is right and proper for a bride and bridegroom to welcome and celebrate their wedding day with a unique sense of triumph. When all the difficulties, obstacles, hindrances, doubts and misgivings have been, not made light of, but honestly faced and overcome —and it is certainly better not to take everything for granted—then both parties have indeed achieved the most important triumph of

their lives. With the "Yes" they have said to each other, they have by their free choice given a new direction to their lives; they have cheerfully and confidently defied all the uncertainties and hesitations with which, as they know, a lifelong partnership between two people is faced; and by their own free and responsible action they have conquered a new land to live in.

He and Maria had conquered one, too, although God alone knew when they might be free to live in it.

Was that envy? He wrote on of the pride they should feel in helping to shape their own destinies. They should not be too quick to speak of God's will in these matters; the course they were taking was one they had chosen themselves. Unless they were secure in their resolve and their love, they would be hiding behind a false piety. At the same time, they had special cause to look back in thankfulness for their lives so far, for the blessings and joys that had been showered on them, and the love and friendship that had smoothed their way. No one could make such a life from his own strength. What was given to one was withheld from another—that was what was meant by God's guidance. So in adding His "Yes" to their "Yes," in confirming their will with His, God had created out of their love for each other something quite new.

> Marriage is more than your love for each other. It has a higher dignity and power, for it is God's holy ordinance, through which He wills to perpetuate the human race till the end of time. In your love you see only your two selves in the world, but in marriage you are a link in the chain of generations, which God causes to come and to pass away to His glory, and calls into His kingdom. In your love you see only the heaven of your own happiness, but in marriage you are placed at a post of responsibility towards the world and mankind. Your love is your own private possession, but marriage is more than something personal—it is a status, an office. Just as it is the crown, and not merely the will to rule, that makes the king, so it is marriage, and not merely your love for each other, that joins you together in the sight of God and man. As you first gave the ring to one another and have now received it a second time from the hand of the pastor, so love comes from you, but marriage from

above, from God. As high as God is above man, so high are the sanctity, the rights, and the promise of marriage above the sanctity, the rights, and the promise of love. It is not your love that sustains the marriage, but from now on, the marriage that sustains your love.

As he was reading it over, knowing Maria would read it, too, and speaking as much to her as to them, the light went out. It was a few minutes before eight. He paced about the cell, as restless as an adolescent on a summer night, and went to bed at last thinking out the rest of his wedding present for Renate and Eberhard.

But the morning brought other distractions. Meiser was sullen, and it was some time before he could be talked around. He then taxed Bonhoeffer's patience with some rather impudent cross-questioning about the relevance of his faith, adopting an air of superior worldliness that Bonhoeffer found most irritating. Soon after, Captain Maetz tested his temper still further by treating him to another annoying lecture on original sin and the unregenerate nature of the prisoners in his care. But on returning to his cell, Bonhoeffer found that two letters had been left on the table in his absence, and the day was at once transformed. One was from his oldest brother, Karl-Friedrich, and the other—almost beyond belief—from Hans von Dohnanyi.

Karl-Friedrich's was short, controlled, and entirely in character, allowing only the barest hint of his feelings to show through; it could as easily have been written by their father.

> I've been in Berlin often during the last two weeks. You need not worry about the parents; of course, they are very shaken, but full of confidence and trust that the matter will soon come out all right. . . . I'm brooding on a manuscript which I really wanted to get ready for publication in the Easter holidays, but my thoughts often go astray and end up with you. Keep your spirits up. All the best.
>
> Ever your Karl-Friedrich

Bonhoeffer read it twice, smiling. He had always been a little in awe of Karl-Friedrich, a brilliant physicist who had abandoned his researches sooner than run the risk of becoming involved in the development of nuclear weapons. When Hitler seized absolute power in 1934, he had turned instead to physical chemistry, of which he was now professor at Leipzig. An agnostic like their father, Karl-Friedrich had sometimes teased him as a boy for choosing theology as a career, and to be told now that his brother's concern for him was interfering with his work meant far more than any ordinary protestation of affection might have done.

But Hans's letter was even more affecting, not least because in sending it, he had forfeited his chance of writing to Christine in Easter Week. It was dated Good Friday, April 23.

My dear Dietrich,

I don't know whether I shall be allowed to send you this greeting, but I want to try. The bells outside are ringing for worship, and memories flood back of the marvelous, profound hours that we spent together in the garrison church, and those many joyful, happy, untroubled Easters with children, parents, brothers, and sisters. You will feel the same, and one needs a great deal of strength to master these memories. You cannot know how much it oppresses me that I am the cause of this suffering that you, Christel, the children, our parents now undergo; that because of me, my dear wife and you have been deprived of freedom. . . .

If I knew that all of you, and you in particular, were not thinking of me reproachfully, a weight would be lifted from my spirit. What wouldn't I give to know that the two of you were free again; I would take everything upon myself if you could be spared this testing. It was marvelous that I could see you; I have also been allowed to speak to Christel, but what can one say in the presence of other people? How immeasurably difficult, impossible it is to open one's heart. . . .

You know me well. We are, I feel, more than "just" relatives by marriage, and you know what my wife is to me. I simply *cannot* be without her, when she has shared everything with me hitherto. That I am not allowed now to endure with her what has been laid upon us—who can fathom what that means? It certainly does not further the *case;* I am completely taken aback. . . .

I hear from Ursel that the children are in Friedrichsbrunn. Our idea of a perfect holiday is there.

I want you to know that I'm grateful to you for everything that you have been and are to my wife, my children, and myself. So goodbye.

Your Hans

The "goodbye" dismayed him. Knowing Roeder would see the letter, Hans had again taken all the responsibility upon himself, and relied on Bonhoeffer to read what he could between the lines. Some of it was plain enough, and he was relieved to know the Dohnanyi children were safe with Ursula at the summer house. But the last sentence, and that final "goodbye," were chilling.

He was still reading the letter, trying to wring some other meaning from it, when Sergeant Major Weber came to say he had a visitor.

# 4

IT WAS SONDEREGGER. He sat at the end of a plain wooden table in a small, windowless room with green-painted walls. He was going through his papers under one of two bare light bulbs hanging from the ceiling. It was the first time Bonhoeffer had seen him out of uniform. But for the party badge in the lapel of his neat blue suit, he might have been a shopkeeper dressed for church.

"Come in," he said affably, waving Weber away. "Sit down." He leaned over the arm of his chair, rummaged in his briefcase, and threw a sheaf of typescript on the table. "I want you to sign these."

"What are they, Herr Commissar?"

"They're the minutes of your interrogation. Here—use my pen. Just sign at the foot of each page."

Bonhoeffer looked at him suspiciously. "May I read them first?"

"If you like. But you've nothing to worry about. It's not a confession. Do you smoke?" He pointed to the open pack of cigarettes in front of him. "If you find anything you don't agree with, make a note in the margin and initial it."

"Thank you." Bonhoeffer lit a cigarette and began to read, looking up frequently, expecting to catch him out. These were not the Gestapo methods he had anticipated. After a lengthy silence, Sonderegger exchanged one file for another.

"As you see, they don't get us very far," he said.

"The minutes? They seem accurate enough."

"Oh, it's all there. Except there's *nothing* there. You might as well sign the lot and not bother."

"I'd still like to read them first, if you don't mind." He finished another page, signed it, and turned to the next. "I'm sorry you found my answers unsatisfactory."

Sonderegger shrugged, without looking up. "They were as good as the questions."

Bonhoeffer eyed him curiously. "The Judge Advocate did sometimes confuse me with his vehemence," he said.

"Dr. Roeder is a lawyer. He wants a conviction. I'm just a policeman. I want the truth."

"It's not always easy." Bonhoeffer was reluctant to let him go back to his papers. "The truth is, I'm utterly bewildered by what's happened. All that ever concerned me was trying to follow the will of God."

Sonderegger threw down his pencil. "You really *mustn't* take me for a fool, you know," he said amiably.

"I don't understand."

"Yes, you do. You're more devious than poor Roeder ever learned how to be, you and Dohnanyi. You know exactly what to say. This bewilderment, this injured innocence . . ." He shook his head. "Read the minutes. There's not an unguarded word from start to finish."

Bonhoeffer polished his glasses. "If you find nothing there, Herr Commissar, it may be because there's nothing to find."

"You're too perfect. Too clever. You can't help it. An innocent man would have tripped over himself a dozen times. He'd have said the wrong thing, contradicted himself, walked into traps—but not you. Not once. Dohnanyi's the same. And so's Müller."

"You arrested *Müller?*" said Bonhoeffer, remembering just in time that they had never told him so. "*Josef* Müller? In heaven's name, what for?"

"For the same reason we arrested you. And there you go again. Covering up. Read the minutes. It's always the fish playing the angler."

Bonhoeffer replaced his glasses. This had to stop. "Forgive me, Herr Commissar, but you seem to be saying that by *not* incriminating myself, I have somehow incriminated myself. I am not familiar with this legal principle."

"Go on," he said encouragingly.

"Go on? I don't know what you want to hear. You and Dr. Roeder have obviously made up your minds that I'm guilty, and you're determined to find the proof of it in everything I say or don't say. Indeed, if I said nothing at all, you would probably regard *that* as conclusive."

"Undoubtedly."

"Well, then." He sat back with a shrug. "I *am* inexperienced in these matters, but I can't pretend to be stupid or unaware of what you are trying to do. I'll answer your questions as best I can, and you must draw what conclusions you will."

Sonderegger eyed him for a moment. "There's something going on, Pastor—I can smell it. I smell it on Dohnanyi, and I smell it on you. I don't know what it is yet—and I don't expect you to tell me," he added, raising his voice as Bonhoeffer tried to interrupt, "but I'll find out. One day you'll let something slip. And until then we'll get along better if you don't insult my intelligence." He picked up his pencil, glanced at his watch, and showed every sign of settling down to read again.

"This is intolerable," said Bonhoeffer, mastering his alarm. "My life and work are to be totally disrupted; my family, my fiancée, my friends are all to be worried and inconvenienced—and for no better reason than *that?*"

Sonderegger considered him impassively, lighting another cigarette. "Tell me what you know about Colonel General Ludwig Beck."

"General Beck?" It was all right. The hesitation had been momentary, and surprise was the proper reaction. He cleared his throat. "He was chief of the General Staff, wasn't he?"

"You know him?"

"We've met once or twice."

"At Dohnanyi's house?"

"I can't remember. Why do you ask?"

"But Dohnanyi does know him?"

"I imagine so. Through his work. I'm sure he knows every officer of general rank, active *and* retired. But why Beck?"

Sonderegger smiled. "What about Dr. Carl Goerdeler?"

Bonhoeffer was ready this time, but it was still a frightening blow. After the *Putsch*, Beck was to be president and Goerdeler chancellor of Germany. "He was mayor of Leipzig, and at one time a government minister, I believe."

"Is he a friend of yours?"

"I've met him."

"At Dohnanyi's house?"

"There, and in other places."

"With your brother Klaus, perhaps?"

Bonhoeffer had started to sweat. He was afraid Sonderegger would notice. "My family is very active in public life. We meet a great many people through the university, the law, the church, and so on."

"And politics?"

"Not as a rule. We never had much to do with politicians." If he wiped his face, Sonderegger might put it down to the stuffiness of the room.

"Diplomats, then. Do you know Ulrich von Hassell?"

"Yes." Sonderegger was playing with him. Germany's former ambassador to Italy had been a key figure in the resistance since 1938. "As I say, we know a great many prominent people. I don't see where this is leading."

"I think you do." He looked at him critically. "Why don't you take your coat off?"

"Thank you." Bonhoeffer wiped his forehead with the handkerchief already in his hand. "I prefer to keep it on. It's not a crime, is it, to have a wide circle of acquaintance?"

"Depends what they have in common." He might have said more, but the door opened and a short, stout man in Luftwaffe uniform stamped in and threw his briefcase down on the table.

"Heil Hitler," he said furiously. "This is most irregular, Herr Commissar. The hearing was called for ten-fifteen." Another man, in civilian clothes, followed him and closed the door quietly behind them.

"Oh, was it?" Sonderegger consulted his watch. "I thought you were late. I had it down for ten. Well, no matter. While we were waiting, the pastor's been signing the minutes. Where would you like him to sit?"

"I would prefer the prisoner to stand."

"Very well." He motioned Bonhoeffer to his feet. "This is Dr. Moeller," he said. "Dr. Roeder's assistant."

Bonhoeffer pulled himself together. It was the usual Gestapo game of cat and mouse. If they had anything positive on Beck, Goerdeler, and the rest, they would have crushed the resistance long since —certainly long before it threatened the Führer's life.

"You were questioning the prisoner as I came in, Herr Commissar," said Moeller, grabbing the files he wanted as his clerk arranged them on the table. "Was there anything of which we should take official note?"

"We'd just discovered some mutual acquaintances, that's all."

Moeller sniffed. "He's read the minutes? Then we'll start from there. And let me warn the prisoner—I'll tolerate none of the evasions we had from him last time, nor any long, involved statements. You'll answer the questions clearly and concisely, keeping to the point."

Bonhoeffer bowed slightly.

"You returned from England in April, 1935, to take charge of an illegal seminary at Finkenwalde."

"No."

"No?" Moeller reached for the minutes and began to search through the final pages. Sonderegger settled back in his chair with a sigh.

"Finkenwalde was one of five seminaries founded by the Old Prussian Council of Brethren to train ordinands for the Confessing Church," Bonhoeffer explained, "but it was not illegal. It was September, 1937, before the Gestapo closed it."

Moeller slammed down the typescript. "The closure was ordered under the Law for the Protection of the German Evangelical Church, promulgated in December, 1935. Do you wish me to continue, or would you prefer this investigation to be handed over to Reich Security Head Office?"

Bonhoeffer looked at his feet.

"Very well, then. Is it not a fact that under your direction this so-called seminary at Finkenwalde became a center for indoctrinating German youth with pacifist and subversive propaganda?"

"No."

"Do you *deny* you're a pacifist?"

"In the sense you mean it, yes. I was against war because we were then at peace. Now war is the present reality, and other considerations apply. At Finkenwalde, my one purpose was to show students the strength and liberation to be had from life in a Christian community, but we were an arm of the Confessing Church, and could not stand aside from its struggle to survive."

"Are you saying your pacifist ideas had no influence on the students?" he asked scornfully.

"They were not children, to be told what to think. I took as much from them as they from me—perhaps more. You'll find your answers in the casualty lists."

"An honor you've been careful to avoid."

"It would seem we were both called to serve Germany in other ways, Herr Doctor."

"Take care," said Moeller, struggling. "To serve Germany is to serve the Führer. That is the only test."

"Didn't we discuss this last time?" asked Sonderegger, bored.

Moeller slapped the table, sweating freely. "His answers were as unsatisfactory then as they are now. There's a consistent pattern of resistance and subversion here. It's essential that the prisoner's actions be seen in that light."

"As you wish. But can't we concentrate more on his actions and less on theology?"

"With respect, Herr Commissar, theology is a key to this case. The prisoner is always trying to hide behind it, to explain his actions in terms of some higher imperative than loyalty to the Führer. Finkenwalde was closed by the Reich Minister of Church Affairs to stamp out this very practice of cloaking sedition in the language of religion. The prisoner cannot again be allowed to escape behind that smokescreen."

Sonderegger subsided. "Well, so long as you think it's relevant."

But Moeller had lost some of his confidence. "The Minister himself said that National Socialism was the fulfillment of God's will. It was not the church that had shown the faith which moves mountains, he said—it was the Führer." He looked at Sonderegger almost anxiously. "I would have said the prisoner's attitude toward the Führer and National Socialism was therefore crucial to this case."

"What do you say to that?" asked Sonderegger.

Bonhoeffer shrugged. "I don't doubt that Reich Minister Kerrl was sincere," he said, "but he claimed far more for the Führer than the Führer ever claimed for himself."

"Do you or do you not regard National Socialism as the fulfillment of God's will?" Moeller shouted.

"Man and all his works are subject to His will—nothing can stand before God except under His sentence and grace."

"You see?" He turned to Sonderegger. "Another evasion. I demand a simple yes or no."

"I cannot give it to you. The will of God is not a given set of rules. It cannot be fulfilled in any final sense, once and for all. The will of the living God is new and different in every new and different situation, and our knowledge of it depends solely upon His grace."

"Very well." Moeller drummed his fingers. "Let's come at it another way. Do you acknowledge the Führer as the spiritual leader of the German people?"

Bonhoeffer blinked at them thoughtfully. "When the Führer condemned the injustice we labored under, he spoke with the voice of the people. He also spoke with their voice in appealing for a return to German greatness through the virtues of industry, courage, and love of country. In this, he embodied their spirit and gave expression to it in his leadership."

Sonderegger had been watching Moeller's color rise, and headed him off. "What exactly were your duties at Finkenwalde?" he asked.

"As director, I was responsible for the administration of the seminary, for its syllabus, and the quality of instruction."

"I thought you rejected the leadership principle."

"I don't believe the relationship between teacher and student falls quite in that category," he said. There was no dealing this side of madness with Roeder and Moeller, but Sonderegger at least lived in the same world.

"What did you teach?"

"Nothing more seditious than homiletics, Herr Commissar."

"You were also lecturing here in Berlin, at the university?"

"Yes."

"And you were still active in the so-called ecumenical movement?"

"I went to London once or twice in 1935 to advise Bishop Bell on the ecumenical implications of the church struggle, but that was all."

Sonderegger raised his eyebrows. "Didn't you also take your students to Denmark and Sweden?"

"Yes," said Moeller eagerly. "In defiance of the Foreign Ministry?"

"We were invited there as guests of the Swedish Church, and I advised the Foreign Ministry before we left."

"When it was already too late for them to act," said Sonderegger.

"It was a field trip. An educational visit to see how the Swedish church ordered its affairs. It never occurred to me that anyone might object."

"Bishop Heckel objected," said Moeller. "He wrote to your Provincial Church Committee denouncing you as a pacifist and an enemy of the state. He also recommended that you no longer be allowed to train German theologians."

"The bishop and I had not seen eye to eye for some time, but no law had been broken. No action was taken against me."

"Except by the Ministry of Education," said Sonderegger, now clearly bent on moving things along.

"Well, yes. My right to lecture at the university was revoked in 1936, but I think that had more to do with my work at Finkenwalde than anything else."

"You were breaking the law there, weren't you?"

Bonhoeffer pushed out his bottom lip. "Technically, perhaps. But when the so-called Law for the Protection of the German Evangelical Church was introduced, every student at the seminary chose to stay on, knowing full well that they might never find employment afterward. Could I, as their teacher, risk less?"

"You risked more." Sonderegger looked down at his file. "You announced that anyone who knowingly separated himself from the Confessing Church separated himself from salvation."

"Including the Führer," shouted Moeller, banging his fist on the table so unexpectedly that his clerk jumped and had to correct his shorthand note. "He dared insult the Führer."

"I did?" said Bonhoeffer.

Sonderegger looked at Moeller through a haze of tobacco smoke. "Didn't you work on a memorandum to the Führer at about this time?"

"No—but I saw the final draft," said Bonhoeffer warily.

"Then you knew what was in it," said Moeller. "You agreed with what it said."

"There were certain questions the Confessing Church felt it should bring to the Führer's attention. We wanted to know if it was government policy to lead the people away from Christianity, to secularize German society. We also felt that people were being forced into hating the Jews, and we were anxious about the erosion of civil liberties."

"In other words," said Moeller, looking to Sonderegger for support, "you wanted the Führer to sit back and let you sabotage the work of national reconstruction."

"Quite the opposite. We wanted the Führer to know that his promises to the German people were being dishonored by his officials."

"His officials?" Sonderegger smiled. "You mean the Secret State Police?"

"Since you mention it, Herr Commissar, we did feel that the powers of the Gestapo and the practice of detaining people in camps without trial should be subject to legal restraint, and said so in the memorandum."

Sonderegger grunted. "If it was meant for the Führer, how did the foreign press get hold of it?"

"That was a great shock, Herr Commissar—and it served our interests very badly," he added, as Moeller threw up his hands. "All hope of receiving a reply from the Führer vanished when the text was published abroad. It was so embarrassing that we asked the Gestapo in to get to the bottom of it."

"You asked the Secret State Police to investigate the theft of a document attacking the Secret State Police."

"It was still more ironical, Herr Commissar, that the culprits should have turned out to be not enemies of the Confessing Church trying to discredit its message, but two former students of mine who had allowed impatience to get the better of their judgment."

"What about the Jew traitor Weissler?" asked Moeller sarcastically. "More youthful high spirits?"

64

"Dr. Weissler was a valued employee of the church. He was certainly ill-advised in allowing these two to make a copy of the memorandum, but he was no traitor."

"He assisted the enemies of the Reich."

"His only crime, Dr. Moeller, was indiscretion. And for that, he was beaten to death by the guards in Sachsenhausen camp."

"Which is also ironic," said Sonderegger. "He conspired to publish a document criticizing the camps, only to die in one. But where were you while this was going on?"

"At Finkenwalde, I imagine." Bonhoeffer was in two minds about him. Though hostile in tone, Sonderegger's interventions invariably allowed him to get his answers and counterarguments on the record. "The whole seminary was on an evangelical mission in Further Pomerania at about that time. It must have been June. I know I was back in Berlin for the Olympic Games because I remember I preached here in August. And soon after that, I went to Chamby for the 1936 'Life and Work' conference."

Moeller aimed his pencil at him. "A moment ago, you said you were too busy for this so-called ecumenical work."

"I was instructed to go. Far from interfering in Germany's affairs, the ecumenical movement was now working closely with Bishop Heckel and the Reich Church. Chamby was the last conference I attended. In 1937, I resigned as youth secretary."

"The job no longer suited your purpose," said Sonderegger, yawning. The air was layered with smoke.

"My purpose had been to help bring the churches together so that a Christian people would never again make war on a Christian people. When the movement allowed itself to be distracted from this, the church struggle at home claimed all my attention."

"You turned instead to undermining the will of the German people from within," Moeller suggested.

Bonhoeffer looked at him, and then at Sonderegger. It was useless, but he had to go on. "I mean that in 1937, Reich Minister Kerrl set about suppressing the true church by every means short of direct proscription. Everyone involved in the Christian ministry outside the Reich Church was forced to choose between apostasy and prison. Hundreds were arrested, Pastor Niemöller among them, and the offices of the Confessing Church were sealed. It seemed to me then, as now, that to go on proclaiming the word of God in that gathering darkness was the best way to serve the German people."

"So you went on," said Sonderegger. "You continued at Finkenwalde until we closed the place down in September."

"Yes."

"But you'll agree there was a difference now. You could no longer pretend it was just a church dispute. You were deliberately breaking the law."

"No, the law was unclear," said Bonhoeffer firmly. "Preachers' seminaries were nowhere mentioned. We were not certain—not until Reichsführer Himmler published the closure order."

Sonderegger yawned again. "Well, let's not quibble. Once you knew that communities like Finkenwalde *were* illegal, and that it was forbidden to teach theology anywhere but in institutions approved by the state, what did you do?"

"The Confessing Church had not been formally proscribed, Herr Commissar. I continued to serve it in ways that did not bring me into conflict with the law."

"Yes, but what exactly did you *do?*"

"I became an assistant minister in the parish of Schlawe in Pomerania."

Moeller laughed, but Sonderegger raised his hand. "As a former university lecturer and seminary director, weren't you a little overqualified for that?"

"I could only be grateful for the opportunity to serve God wherever I was called."

"Yes, yes—humility is no doubt very commendable in a country pastor, but what *kind* of service were you called upon to perform?"

"My colleagues and I had noticed," said Bonhoeffer delicately, "that no objection had been raised to the traditional practice of assigning theological students to pastors with teaching ministries in order to train them in parish work. There were a number of these student ministers in the neighborhood of Schlawe, and others in the nearby town of Köslin. They lived together to save money and because their respective pastors were not always able to accommodate them."

"So you became a teaching minister."

"Yes."

"And you taught these student ministers."

"It was a collective pastorate."

Sonderegger inspected the end of his cigarette. "Then will you explain how these arrangements differed from those at Finkenwalde?"

"The only similarity was that each group lived together," said Bonhoeffer indignantly. "And to avoid suspicions of the sort you are evidently entertaining, Herr Commissar, I made a point of not staying with either one, although this would have been more convenient. Instead, I took lodgings with Superintendent Block in Schlawe, and registered with the police there."

Moeller stood up from the table so abruptly that the legs of his chair screeched backward on the floor and his clerk flinched with apprehension. "I've heard enough," he said. "I shall recommend to the Judge Advocate that he ask the Führer for special permission to deal summarily with this prisoner." He began to collect his papers together.

Sonderegger slumped lower in his chair.

"I warned him what would happen if he persisted in these evasions."

"So you did," agreed Sonderegger. "But if you're going to turn him over to us anyway, you won't mind if I carry on? There are still a few points I want to clarify."

"That's up to you, Herr Commissar." Moeller frowned and fiddled with his case. "I don't think you'll get very far."

The other shrugged.

"Unless, of course, you can persuade the prisoner to adopt a more cooperative attitude," he went on, uncertainly. "Does he ask us to believe that these so-called collective pastorates were anything other than a deliberate evasion of the order closing Finkenwalde?"

"Dr. Moeller, the interpretation of law is a matter for the courts," said Bonhoeffer. "As far as we knew, what we did was perfectly legal. The authorities took no action against us."

"No action? You were arrested at an illegal church meeting in January, 1938, and expelled from Berlin."

"That had nothing to do with the collective pastorates. Otherwise

I would have been expelled from Schlawe. We continued our work there for two more years—until the war began and all our ordinands were called for military service."

"Not quite all," said Sonderegger. "That's something we have to discuss."

Moeller had gone too far to back down. "I'm not satisfied," he said savagely. "This session of the War Court stands adjourned. I will consult the Judge Advocate and notify you of his decision. And let me warn the prisoner that his behavior today may lead to the most severe consequences for his family and anyone else in a position to throw light on his activities." Moeller's clerk moved around the table to join him, but was pushed roughly aside. "Shall I order the guards to return the prisoner to his cell?"

"Not yet," said Sonderegger, leaning over the side of the chair to look in his briefcase. As Moeller stumped out, the commissar placed on the table a package wrapped in a white linen napkin, and unfolded it carefully. "Sit down," he said.

Bonhoeffer lowered himself into the chair he had occupied before, and rubbed his thighs.

"Have a sandwich."

"No, thank you. But I would like a drink of water."

Sonderegger pushed the carafe and a glass toward him, and ate in silence for a few minutes. "Moeller doesn't like the look of this case," he said eventually. "He needs a confession."

"A confession? I'm expected to make good the lack of evidence against me?"

"Well, it's not a *total* lack, is it?" He sucked his teeth. "They've established reasonable grounds for questioning your loyalty to the Führer. There are some unsatisfactory aspects of your activities abroad. If the case *is* turned over to us, that in itself would be enough."

Bonhoeffer took another sip of water.

"You're in the same kind of position as your friend Niemöller was. He was acquitted, yes, but we couldn't very well leave him at large."

He sat dumb.

"Except in your case, of course, it might just be possible to eliminate our suspicions."

"How?" he asked mechanically.

Sonderegger took a thoughtful bite from his sandwich. "I'm concerned with what happened when you realized you were no longer opposing the government of the church but the government of the Reich. Now, don't misunderstand me," he went on, as Bonhoeffer started to protest. "I'm not suggesting you decided one day to join the Jews and Bolsheviks. All I'm saying is that while *your* position may have stayed the same, the government's position has changed. Do you follow me? Bit by bit, its definition of treason has altered. The line you took in the beginning, which was then just a nuisance, has come to be regarded, little by little, as entirely hostile to the national interest. You see what I'm driving at?"

Bonhoeffer saw very well. He had not credited the Gestapo with so much finesse.

"Now, my guess is you realized what was happening with the closure of Finkenwalde. Or perhaps with the prohibition order on your coming to Berlin. Because whatever you say about these collective pastorates, they were formed in clear defiance of the law's intent. Moeller was right about that. Whether you liked it or not, your opposition had become political."

"Because the state now said it was?"

"Exactly. No one can blame you for holding on to your convictions. It's a great German virtue. I even sympathize to some extent. But I don't see why, as a matter of conscience, you should feel it necessary to protect people who don't share your beliefs and whose motives are less honorable than yours. That's what interests me in all this—the circles you were drawn into when church politics began to merge with secular politics. That's how you could show us, perhaps, that no matter how strongly you felt you had to oppose the *church* policy of the Reich, underneath, your loyalty to the Führer and the German people remained as staunch as anyone's."

They eyed each other.

"Think about it," said Sonderegger, reaching for his cigarettes.

# 5

✚ ✚ ✚

5 May 1943

My dear Hans,

Your letter so surprised, delighted, and moved me that I could not refrain, at the very least, from attempting to reply to it. Whether this letter reaches you does not lie within my power; but I fervently hope so. For you must know that there is not even an atom of reproach or bitterness in me about what has befallen the two of us. Such things come from God, and from Him alone, and I know that I am one with you and Christel in believing that before Him there can only be subjection, perseverance, patience—and gratitude. So every question "Why?" falls silent because it has found its answer. . . .

He allowed himself an unscheduled cigarette; it was Wednesday, and another parcel was due. Writing for Roeder as well as for Hans was not easy. If "Why?" fell silent in submission, "How?" and "What?" were still clamorous. How could they endure? What was still to come?

No, you must not and need not worry about us at all; another has now taken this worry from you. What we cannot do we must now simply let go of and limit ourselves to what we can and should do, that is, be manly and strong in trust in God in the midst of our suffering. . . .

Keep well and in good spirits. I think with gratitude of the many good hours with you at home, making music, walking, enjoying the garden, playing and talking. The children are in good hands with their grandparents and they are old enough to know what sort of behavior they owe themselves and you.

God bless you. I think of you faithfully each day.

Your Dietrich

He folded the sheet of paper and set it aside to give to Linke or Knobloch when one of them came with his parcel. It was foolish, but the fewer the unsympathetic hands his letters passed through, the less invaded he felt. And this time there was a special reason for not simply giving it to the guard. He drew toward him the letters he had just received from his mother and Rüdiger. Having replied to Hans, as he was bound to do, he was not now entitled to write to anyone else for another ten days. But he had an idea that one or the other of the corporals might be able to do something unofficially if they knew the circumstances.

Dear Parents,

Many thanks for the letters from mother, K. Friedrich, and Rüdiger. I'm so glad that you are at ease and confident, and also that K. Friedrich can be with you frequently. I'm sure that it is good for me personally to undergo all this, and I believe that no more is laid upon any man than he can receive the strength to bear. The hardest thing for me is that you must bear the burden, too, but the way in which you do it is again infinitely cheering and a great strength to me. . . .

I've now had four weeks in prison; and whereas I was able from the outset to accept my lot consciously, I'm now getting used to it in a kind of natural and unconscious way. That is a relief, but it raises problems of its own, for one rightly does not want to get used to being in this position. . . .

There was no other vein in which he could write to them. The load was not to be spread. Part of it was maintaining this outer serenity, to the edge of unreason.

The wedding at the Schleichers will soon be here now, and I won't be able to write again before then. . . . I wish them a very happy day with all my heart and will be there with them with many happy thoughts and wishes. I would so like it if they in turn could think of me only with happy thoughts, memories, and hopes. . . . Here in the quietness I hope that one day we shall all be together to celebrate my and Maria's wedding day—when? At the moment, that seems fanciful, but it's a splendid hope and a great one. . . .

Now once again, thanks for everything you brought, for all your trouble, consideration, and love—Wednesday is always such a specially good day, and how I look forward to it!—and a few requests: a clothes brush, mirror, towel, face cloth, and if it keeps being so cold (it seems to be warmer today), a warm shirt and long socks; also Holl, *Church History,* the volume on the West, and something to smoke, whatever is going, and some matches. I don't understand either why you can't find my suit and jacket. . . .

I hope that every worry will soon be removed from you and all of us.

Your grateful Dietrich

In fact he had given up hope of the case being quickly resolved. The interrogation had so far gone both better and worse than expected; better in that he was now more confident of being able to protect his fellow conspirators from Roeder and Sonderegger, despite the Gestapo's suspicions, and worse because it had left him soiled and humiliated. Torn between resentment at being badgered by party hacks and submission to God's unrevealed purpose behind it, he found their incessant attack on his motives chiming in uncomfortably with his own self-questioning. Was it faith and obedience to God's commandment that had brought him here, or pride and self-will?

Corporal Linke brought him the parcel unopened late that afternoon, and they unpacked it together, as the regulations required—another sign that his rights as a prisoner were being restored. But it was clear from the contents that his parents had not yet received the letter he had sent ten days earlier, and he added a postscript about this to the one he had just written, hoping it would prompt Roeder's office to forward his mail more quickly in future. Then he gave it to Linke along with the note to Hans. The corporal shook his head dubiously, but when Bonhoeffer explained his dilemma, that his parents would fret if he missed writing to them but that Hans would inevitably construe his silence as a reproach, Linke sighed and put them both in his pocket, promising to see what he could do.

"Have you finished the sermon yet? I've got a two-day pass."

"I'll have it ready in the morning. Am I imposing on you, Herr Linke? You must say. I owe you too much to do that."

"I'll do what I feel like doing," he said crossly, and shook his head as though he would never forgive those who had overturned the social order he was used to.

Bonhoeffer finished the sermon a few minutes before the light went out.

> Most people have forgotten nowadays what a home can mean, though some of us have come to realize it as never before. It is a kingdom of its own in the midst of the world, a stronghold amid life's storms and stresses, a refuge, even a sanctuary. It is not founded on the shifting sands of outward or public life, but it has its peace in God, for it is God who gives it its special meaning and value, its own nature and privileges, its own destiny and dignity. It is an ordinance of God in the world, the place in which—whatever may happen in the world—peace, quietness, joy, love, purity, discipline, respect, obedience, tradition, and, with it all, happiness, may dwell. . . .
>
> "Welcome one another, therefore, as Christ has welcomed you, for the glory of God." In a word, live together in the forgiveness of your sins, for without it no human fellowship, least of all a marriage, can survive. Don't insist on your rights, don't blame each other, don't judge or condemn each other, don't find fault with each other, but accept each other as you are, and forgive each other every day from the bottom of your hearts.

At about six o'clock the next evening, Sergeant Holzendorf unlocked the door and stood staring at him critically. Bonhoeffer, who was stretched out on the bed reading, sat up by degrees as he took in the other's expression.

"Is something wrong?"

The sergeant clicked his tongue. "You don't look well, Pastor. You look pale. Very pale. You'd better come with me." He opened the door wider, inviting him through.

Bonhoeffer, who felt perfectly well, laid down his book and followed him onto the gallery. Still mystified, he raised his eyebrows as the guard bent to unlock the barred gate at the end, but the sergeant gave no sign. He marched him briskly downstairs and along a dingy corridor toward a pair of scuffed swing doors at the far end. As they got nearer, he heard talk and laughter on the other side and, very faintly, an orchestra playing Mozart.

Holzendorf grinned. "It's the sick bay," he said. "We thought you might like some treatment."

"You've a *radio?*" said Bonhoeffer, so starved for music that he had taken to playing the piano in his head for hours on end.

"For the air raid warnings. It's on all the time."

As they pushed through the doors, the talking stopped. Corporal Knobloch and three other men, two in uniform and one swaddled in a rough gray blanket, sat at a table in what was obviously the dispensary. Seeing who it was, they relaxed and produced from under the table the hands of bridge they were playing. Beyond, through a glass-paneled door, Bonhoeffer could see into the prison hospital ward, as bleak as any barracks, with a row of iron cots on each side, only two or three of which seemed to be occupied. After introducing the bridge players, who were clearly in no mood for idle conversation, Holzendorf seated him by the stove with a medicinal glass of schnapps and then left to complete his evening rounds.

The last two movements of the *Prague* Symphony combined with the cheap spirits to bring Bonhoeffer his first really pleasurable moments since the arrest. He stretched out in the warmth, smiling companionably at Knobloch and trying not to stare too obviously at the burn-disfigured face of one of the men playing with him, Corporal Bergmann. Only the eyes were alive. The rest, lividly seamed and creased, looked less like flesh than lumpy pink wax. It was a child's attempt to model a face, with a hole for a mouth and half-melted ears. Almost every time Bonhoeffer looked in his direction, the eyes were on him, clear blue and impersonal, and would hold his gaze for an instant before returning to the cards.

When the concert ended, he got up regretfully, finished his schnapps, and stood watching the game for a while. Then, establishing in pantomime with Knobloch that it was all right to look around, he went into the ward and found Meiser lying there, wanly staring at the ceiling. For the past three mornings, another young prisoner had been brought in to clean Bonhoeffer's cell, but he had put that down to the general arbitrariness of prison life, and had not thought to ask anyone why. He sat on the edge of the bed, meaning to twit Meiser for malingering, but changed his mind when he saw how pale and subdued he was. He had been urinating blood, and once his curiosity was satisfied, about Bonhoeffer's appearance in the ward, he answered his questions with growing reluctance until finally he turned on his side and closed his eyes.

Bonhoeffer let him be. He wished he had the power to charge a few simple words with the confidence of faith so that they would pierce like bullets, but that, too, was probably vain—the desire that God should speak through *his* mouth to reclaim the indifferent. He lingered for a moment by the two other occupied beds in the ward, but both men were sleeping soundly and, with a last glance at Meiser, he went back to the cardplayers.

They had just finished a rubber, and Knobloch, like his partner, Bergmann, was not disposed to start another. After trying unsuccessfully to find some more music for Bonhoeffer on the radio, the corporal gave him the *Deutsche Allgemeine Zeitung* instead, and rejoined his companions at the table. But Bonhoeffer sensed that his presence was a constraint they might soon resent, and at the first opportunity he asked if anyone knew what was wrong with Meiser. The others looked at Bergmann, who, Knobloch explained, was the senior medical orderly.

"Kidney damage," said Bergmann, straining like a stutterer to frame the words with his lipless mouth. "Says he fell, but he was more likely kicked."

"He thinks he's dying." Bonhoeffer was distracted by the eyes.

"He may be." Bergmann brought his chair over to the stove. "Do you mind? My voice." He raised his chin to show his flayed throat. "It's hard to shout."

"Please." Bonhoeffer made room for him. "What makes you think he was kicked?"

"Heavy bruising. Ribs broken. Couldn't do that slipping on the washhouse floor."

"Then who did it?" All at once he was furiously angry. "Whoever it was should be court-martialed."

Bergmann shrugged. "He won't say."

"Well, I simply won't tolerate this. I've already had to speak to the commandant about the way the prisoners are treated."

This amused the man in the gray blanket. "It may not have been a *guard,* you know," he said. "In fact, this time it probably wasn't."

"No?" Bonhoeffer frowned. "I'm sorry. Herr . . . ?"

"Engel. Max Engel. It was probably one of his clients. Meiser services several of the older men here, and there's always a lot of jealousy. It's not the first beating he's had, by a long way."

Bonhoeffer looked at their faces in turn.

"It's not uncommon," said Engel gently. "Coop men up with nothing else to think about, and . . ."

"Yes, I know." He met Bergmann's disconcerting gaze. "Shouldn't he be in hospital?"

"There are trainloads of wounded in need of a bed. He's lucky to be where he is."

There was no way of telling from the eyes alone if he was callous, vindictive, or neutral in feeling. The voice betrayed nothing but the effort of speaking.

"Well, he can't just be left there to die," said Bonhoeffer flatly. "My father is a doctor—perhaps he can do something. He still has some influence with the Charité Hospital."

Bergmann nodded. "He could throw out someone like me to make room."

"That'll do," said Knobloch.

"No, he's right." Engel brought his chair over to join them. "That's what it would mean. And I don't see it. If you're going to pull strings, do it for some poor devil parked on a railroad siding with his guts hanging out. Meiser's a thieving little pervert who stopped someone's boot in a faggots' quarrel. So what?"

"It's not for us to judge him," said Bonhoeffer mechanically.

"Okay. But we still have to use our judgment as to who's the more deserving. I mean no disrespect."

"Nor I, Herr Engel, when I suggest we do all we can for one another and leave the final decisions to God. I'll speak to Maetz in the morning. Perhaps something more can be done for him here."

Engel nodded, content to leave it at that.

"You could pray for him," said Bergmann.

"Yes."

"You're a pastor—God may listen to you."

Bonhoeffer felt in his pockets for a cigarette, but he had left them in his cell. "If miracles could be had to order," he said, "nothing would be asked of *us*. We'd acknowledge God's power and go on unchanged."

"Unchanged?" Bergmann took Bonhoeffer's hand and pressed it against his cheek. "He burned my face off."

They sat like that in silence, the others watching. "He took our flesh," said Bonhoeffer. "He made our suffering His." Bergmann released his hand. "He is our Father."

Engel stirred impatiently. "What kind of father nails his children to the cross?"

"A merciful father." Bonhoeffer was embarrassed. "The cross was not the last word. Christ was raised from the dead, to deny the world its victory. And because His flesh was our flesh, what happened to Him now happens to us. We suffer and die and are raised with Him."

He had not realized before how much was normally conveyed between people by their facial expressions. Talking to Bergmann was like talking to a masked man. With nothing to guide him, his habitual reluctance to speak about God with strangers deepened into a longing for silence; having approached the inexpressible, there was nothing to do but stand silent before it.

"I respect what you say, Pastor," Engel said, breaking a cigarette in two and handing half to Bonhoeffer, who accepted it gratefully, "but I'm afraid you'll find us more concerned with the realities of *this* world."

"Christ came to save this world, Herr Engel. *Our* reality is *His* reality—He made it so. The revelation of God in Christ is present and open to all of us."

"Not to me," said Bergmann, and Engel punched his arm affectionately.

"Well, perhaps He overlooked the Eastern front," Engel said.

"I'm sorry, Pastor, but the sort of reality we've had to face just recently hasn't inspired much trust in the Almighty."

"How much has it inspired in man?" It was easier to get angry with Engel than with Bergmann. "What you saw was the reality of man *without* God."

"Perhaps." He shrugged good-naturedly. "A little proof of His concern might help."

"A little magic to win His way into our good graces? God is not accountable to us, Herr Engel. We live under His judgment, subject to His will and dependent on His mercy."

"Which He expects us to take on trust."

"That is the nature of faith."

"It's a lot to ask."

"He demands everything, and gives back everything—forgiveness, life, fulfillment."

The fourth man, who had been listening at the table with Knobloch, stood up noisily, buckling his belt. "Well, while He's about it," he said, "see if He can find a blind girlfriend for Bergmann. I've got to go. Good night, all."

"Good night, Helmut." Engel held up his hand as though conferring a blessing, and wrung a reluctant smile from the other as he pushed through the swing door.

"I'm sorry, Pastor," said Knobloch. He joined them at the stove. "There was no call for that."

"Oh, you mustn't mind us," Engel said. "Helmut would like to believe in God, but it isn't easy to believe in one with less compassion than he has himself."

Bonhoeffer shook his head, puzzled. "The world is not what it should be, Herr Engel. We live in wickedness. He came, not to give us proof of His power, but to take our guilt and suffering upon Himself, and that is compassion beyond all understanding. A God who let us prove His existence would be just a reflection of ourselves."

"Well, we thank you for the words of comfort—even if they *did* fall on deaf ears." Engel pushed Bergmann's shoulder in mock reproof.

"I think Herr Bergmann shares my own unwillingness to talk about these things," said Bonhoeffer. "There are times when reality is too oppressive. Whatever we have to say sounds so flat and empty that we destroy the mystery of God behind it. All we can do is surrender our lives to Him, even when this seems against all sense."

Now Bergmann avoided his eye. "I have to go shit," he said. "Excuse me."

Engel watched him through the door. "You just told a cripple to get up and walk," he said, and when Bonhoeffer made no reply, grimaced at Knobloch. "Well, I suppose there's a precedent for that, too."

Knobloch wagged his finger. "You mind your manners."

"No offense. I just don't understand what a pastor is doing here anyway, buried in a hole like this."

"It's none of your business. You'd better get back to bed before Holzendorf comes."

"Oh, all right." He stood up reluctantly. "I'm sorry, Pastor. Any enemy of theirs is a friend of ours—right, Knobloch?"

The other turned to Bonhoeffer, shaking his head. "It's not hard to understand what *he's* doing here—not with a mouth like his."

"You're a prisoner, Herr Engel? I hadn't realized."

"You mean you took me for one of *them?*" He pretended to bridle. "It must be my naturally commanding manner."

"It's your naturally loose tongue," said Knobloch. "It got you here on a stretcher. It'll take you out in a box."

"Oh?" Bonhoeffer smiled politely.

"It was nothing," said Engel. "A misunderstanding."

Knobloch snorted. "He had a fight with the SS."

"Well, it wasn't really a fight. They were pacifying a bunch of prisoners by shooting them in the balls. So I sort of mentioned in passing that the Russians had caught a few of our people, too, and I hoped it wouldn't give them ideas. It was just a friendly word, but you know how they are. One turned nasty, and I had to be quite firm with him."

"He hit him in the groin," said Knobloch. "With his rifle."

"It was an accident. I was just trying to keep him off me, that's all."

"It's a wonder they didn't shoot you on the spot," said Bonhoeffer.

"Oh, they did." He rummaged in his blanket and pulled it aside to show a ragged blue scar under his right nipple. "Went through the lung and broke my arm."

"Lucky for him his mates were there," said Knobloch. "Otherwise they'd have finished him off."

"That's right. There were four of us and six of them, but the SS don't like odds like that—not unless you're on your knees with your hands tied. They're still after me, so I'm trying to heal slowly."

"Well, if I know anything about the army's legal department," said Bonhoeffer, "they'll be in no hurry—although they've got a good witness in the man you hit."

"Oh, no," Engel said cheerfully. "My rifle went off as I fell."

"Accidentally, of course," said Knobloch.

"Of course. Do I look the sort who'd shoot a party man on purpose?" Engel patted his knee. "But you can't always go by appearances. Just look at Herr Bonhoeffer. I wouldn't have said that a man of his stamp—a Christian pastor with his mind on higher things—I wouldn't have said he was the sort to know how the army's legal department feels about the SS, would you?"

"The pastor is very well connected," said Knobloch severely. "Even a Bolshevik like you should know that. His uncle is commandant of Berlin."

"So I hear." Engel bowed. "No wonder Maetz was pleased. It's improved the tone of his stinking jail no end. But with all that influence, you can't help wondering what the pastor is doing here at all."

Knobloch stared. "You think he's here for his health?"

"Maybe. Perhaps he's hiding, like me."

"Well, go hide in bed. I'm sorry, Pastor. As soon as someone comes, I'll take you back up."

"No, no," said Bonhoeffer. "I'm interested. And I'd be still more interested if I'd remembered to bring my cigarettes with me."

"Here." Engel held out his tobacco tin and sat down again. "Pay me back next time. And don't be such an old woman, Knobloch. The pastor doesn't look like he needs protecting. It's the other way about, most likely. You and me, we just bitch about our glorious leader. He must have *done* something."

Bonhoeffer smiled in spite of himself. "Are you really a Bolshevik?"

"I'm as much of a Bolshevik as you're a country pastor."

"Then you must be something of a Bolshevik, for I am at least a pastor."

"And I'm sure that *is* the least of it." He winked. "You won't ask me to believe the Gestapo were here the other day for a Bible class."

"You must believe what you like. I rarely confide in strangers."

"That may cost you friends, Pastor—without reducing the number of your enemies."

"There is that danger. Equally it may protect those I know to be friends against enemies I don't recognize."

"You're not strong enough alone. If strangers remain strangers, Germany is finished."

"That may be. But gossip won't save us. Those still free to act are best served by silence."

"Who? You mean the generals?" Engel clutched his head. "My God, they're the *architects* of ruin. You must look to the people for your friends."

"The people follow success, Herr Engel—we've seen that. I don't blame them for it, but how can you build on quicksand?"

"You should have set them a better example."

"I don't deny it. We're still learning that obedience is a virtue only when we're ready to accept the responsibility for what follows."

"Well, don't look at me. And don't look at Knobloch. He'd like to have the Kaiser back."

"Yes, I would," he said stoutly.

"You see? He doesn't care *whose* boots we lick. But you can't expect the German people to go on forever paying in blood for your education. Twice you've herded us over the cliff. So now *we're* learning, too. Like not to be grateful when you condescend toward us. And that bourgeois ideals of service and sacrifice, like bourgeois notions of art and refinement, are fig leaves for naked self-interest." He smiled disarmingly.

"That's a heavy charge," said Bonhoeffer. "I'm not sure it's deserved."

"Oh, Pastor, it's the failing of your class—to assume that a God-fearing people can aspire no higher than to place themselves in your hands and have you tinker with their welfare."

Bergmann, who had come back as Engel was speaking, went to stand behind his chair.

"I told you he was a Bolshevik," said Knobloch, edging closer to Bonhoeffer.

"Oh, I don't know. Ten years ago, a National Socialist might have said much the same. That's the trouble with populist movements. They all seem to end in worse tyrannies than the ones they were meant to replace."

Engel was a little slow with his answering smile. "And the trouble with the ruling class, Pastor, is that it learns from everyone's mistakes but its own. In the end, it retreats into narcissism and leaves the people defenseless. But we know you now. It won't happen again. Next time, we'll make sure your ideals of service and sacrifice really mean something."

"You see?" said Knobloch. "A Bolshevik."

"No. The pastor was right about that. Ten years ago, I voted for Hitler. I was a union man. Some of my fellow members had been out of a job for five years. You won't understand what that means, Pastor, and I'm too bored with misery to tell you about it, but our glorious leader promised to get everybody back to work and I thought he stood a better chance of doing it than the Reds. They're like you aristocrats. They worry about doctrinal purity the way you worry about traditional values. And anybody who doesn't share your concern is obviously unfit to govern himself."

Bonhoeffer feigned dismay. "The values I worry about, Herr Engel, are honesty, justice, brotherhood, dignity, trust, and service to others. And anybody who *doesn't* share my concern *is* obviously unfit to govern himself. Although if the past ten years are any guide, it doesn't seem to disbar him from governing others."

"Can't argue with that." Engel grinned back cheerfully. "The Führer put us to work, all right, but it turned out we had different ideas about the purpose of trade unions. I thought it was to serve the members. *He* thought it was to serve the party."

"We had the same experience in the church," said Bonhoeffer.

"Did you? Well, some of *my* flock were getting their faces kicked in to cure them of being Jews and Socialists. And when I asked the district leader about this, he thought I might be in line for some of the same unless I joined the party. So I took up teaching instead."

"We've more in common than you think."

"I'm flattered—but I doubt it. I traveled around talking to workingmen. And when that got too hot, I joined the army."

"And he's *still* talking," said Knobloch. "If words were bullets, he'd win the war single-handed."

Bonhoeffer laughed. "What did you talk to them about, Herr Engel? The iniquities of the ruling class?" And he heard it again in his voice, the same insufferable note of patronage. "I don't mean to make fun."

"I used to tell them about their rights," Engel said. He had lost interest.

"Their legal rights?"

"Yes. But mostly about the rights that you and your class have denied them. Equality. Freedom. Respect. That sort of thing."

"*Are* they rights? I don't know. Aren't they rather privileges to be earned?"

"From whom? Not everything is in your gift."

"From those who live by them and die for them. Can one be the equal of the wisest and bravest without being as wise and brave as they?"

"One can be as free, and as deserving of respect."

"One *can* be. But that's a matter of aspiration, isn't it? All have a right to law and order, but not everyone is ready for the responsibility of being free."

"They might like to have the choice."

"The choice is order or chaos. Do you respect the freedom of the SS?"

"I judge people by what they do, not what they are." He gathered his blanket about him and stood up. Holzendorf had just pushed through the swing doors.

"By what standards do you judge them?" asked Bonhoeffer.

"By ordinary standards of decency and humanity, such as are common among workingmen."

"Which is to say by standards of love, justice, and brotherhood, which are pleasing to God and common to all men of goodwill."

"And equality." Engel grimaced at Holzendorf, as though only politeness were detaining him.

"In other times, it may have been the business of Christianity to champion equality," said Bonhoeffer, "but now I think it's to defend human dignity and order."

"Which is to say, defend the rights and privileges of the ruling class against the working class."

"I find it hard to think in those terms."

"Then how about nobility versus the mob?" He again glanced apologetically at the sergeant.

"That's closer. Only a social order based on quality can save decency and order. Thank God, there's a new nobility binding men together that has nothing to do with birth or wealth or success."

Engel considered this, half smiling. "So once again the few will rule the many."

"Until the few *become* the many."

"And how will that come about?"

"Through sacrifice and courage and a clear sense of duty."

Engel laughed. "Not a chance. They'll sacrifice you instead. It's a lot less trouble."

15 May 1943

Dear Parents,

By the time you get this letter, all the final preparations and the wedding itself will be over, as will my own bit of longing to be there myself. . . .

Of course, people outside find it difficult to imagine what prison life is like. The situation in itself—that is, each single moment—is perhaps not so very different here from anywhere else; I read, meditate, write, pace up and down my cell—without rubbing myself sore against the walls like a polar bear. The great thing is to stick to what one still has and can do—there is still plenty left —and not to be dominated by the thought of what one cannot do, and by feelings of resentment and discontent. I'm sure I never realized as clearly as I do here what the Bible and Luther meant by "temptation." Quite suddenly, and for no apparent physical or psychological reason, the peace and composure that were supporting one are jarred, and the heart becomes, in Jeremiah's expressive phrase, "deceitful above all things and desperately corrupt; who can understand it?" It feels like an invasion from outside, as if by evil powers trying to rob one of what is most vital. But no doubt these experiences are good and necessary, as they teach one to understand human life better.

I'm now trying my hand at a little study on "the feeling of time," a thing that is specially relevant to anyone who is being held for examination. One of my predecessors here has scribbled over the cell door, "In 100 years it will all be over." That was his way of trying to counter the feeling that life spent here is a blank; but there is a great deal that might be said about that, and I should like to talk it over with Father. "My time is in your hands" is the Bible's answer. But in the Bible is also the question that threatens to dominate everything here: "How long, O Lord?" . . .

If only we could talk to each other about these things. For all my sympathy with the contemplative life, I am not a born Trappist. Nevertheless, a period of enforced silence may be a good thing, and the Roman Catholics say that the most effective expositions of Scripture come from the purely contemplative orders. I am reading the Bible straight through from cover to cover, and have just got as far as Job, which I am particularly fond of. I read the Psalms every day, as I have done for years; I know them and love them more than any other book. . . .

Many congratulations to Ursel on her birthday; I think of her a lot. Greetings to all the family and friends and especially to the young couple. I hope Maria will come to you soon. I feel myself so much a part of you all that I know that we live and bear everything in common, acting and thinking for one another, even though we have to be separated. Thank you for all your love and concern and loyalty day by day and hour by hour.

Your Dietrich

# 6

✠ ✠ ✠

"LET ME REMIND THE PRISONER that this is his last chance to convince the court of his readiness to cooperate. If there is any more obstructiveness of the sort that led to the summary adjournment of your last examination, I will refer the case at once to Reich Security Head Office. Is that clear?"

"Yes, Your Honor," said Bonhoeffer. Sonderegger had his head propped up in both hands and, as usual, seemed not to be listening. "I would ask the court to accept that the unfortunate impression I seem to have created is due solely to inexperience and certainly not to any desire to deceive."

"Only the most complete candor will persuade us of that." Roeder was at his most irritatingly condescending. "You have had several weeks to reflect on your position. I shall assume that your answers are final and complete. Dr. Moeller?"

His assistant rose from his place on the lower bench with an unmistakably vindictive air and surveyed Bonhoeffer in silence for a moment. Then he consulted his notes.

"You became liable for military service in 1938, and registered your address in the military subdistrict of Schlawe on November 3 of that year."

"Yes."

"Yes, *what?*" he shouted.

Bonhoeffer sighed. "Yes, Your Honor."

"Yes. You've made no secret of your contempt for this court." He looked again at his notes. "Having registered, you were then required to report any subsequent change of address or prolonged absence to the military authorities, and to apply for permission to travel abroad."

"That is correct, Your Honor."

"Did you remain in Schlawe to await the call-up of your age group?"

"No, Your Honor. I was already committed to visit England on church business, and in March, 1939, I was granted permission to do so."

*"Church* business?"

"Yes. I was anxious to see my sister, Sabine, but the main reason was to renew the ecumenical links of the Confessing Church."

"The visit had nothing to do with your impending military service?"

"Why, no, Your Honor. Nothing whatever. As I said, it was arranged before I registered."

"Who, then, did you meet in England, apart from your sister and the Jew traitors Liebholz and Hildebrandt?"

"Well, now. Besides my brother-in-law and my oldest friend, I saw Bishop Bell once or twice; Visser 't Hooft, general secretary of the new World Council of Churches; Reinhold Niebuhr, the American theologian, and various other people I knew from the days of my pastorate in London."

"And did you discuss with them ways and means of avoiding military service?"

Bonhoeffer looked bewildered. "The fact that I returned home in April is surely the best answer to that."

"You will allow the court to decide what are the best answers to its questions," said Moeller loudly. "Do you expect us to believe that your meeting with the American Niebuhr had nothing to do with the invitation you received to lecture in New York?"

"Well, it was discussed, certainly, but not as a means of avoiding the call-up. My subsequent actions show that quite clearly."

"Do they? You returned from London on April 18. Five days later, you applied to the recruiting station in Schlawe for permission to go to America for a *year*. Not for a few weeks, to lecture, but for an entire *year*—is that correct?"

"Yes, Your Honor. Quite correct."

Moeller seemed disappointed. "But you were notified instead to report for military service on May 22?"

"I was. Then, as you know, my application for leave was approved and the instructions to report were canceled."

"How fortunate. And how useful to have such influential connections. Your Junker friends in Pomerania seem really to have exerted themselves for once."

Some of the Gestapo men laughed, and Bonhoeffer stiffened. "As far as I know," he said, "my application was dealt with in the usual way. If I'd intended to evade conscription by leaving the country, I would hardly have drawn attention to myself by asking for a *year's* leave. A weekend pass would have been enough. In fact, if your suspicions were correct, I need not have returned from England."

"Oh, I think you had to come back," said Moeller. "You had your family to think of, your affairs to put in order. And no doubt there were last-minute instructions from your colleagues in the so-called Confessing Church?"

"Instructions? No. I merely had to ask the Council of Brethren for leave of absence."

"Well, they seem to have granted it willingly enough." He looked up at Roeder as though this were significant. "You left for America on June 2, stopping off again in London on the way."

"That is correct."

"Had you discussed the purpose of this journey with Dohnanyi?"

Bonhoeffer frowned. "I was going to lecture at Union Theological Seminary that summer, then at other colleges and universities across the country. My brother-in-law would have known this, like the rest of the family and most of my friends and colleagues. I don't remember discussing it with him specifically, although I may have."

"Did you discuss it with General Oster? Or Admiral Canaris?"

"I don't think so. In fact, I don't think I even knew them at that time—certainly not the admiral. If you're suggesting there was any ulterior motive in making the trip, Your Honor, or any hidden connection with military intelligence, that is not so. My brother-in-law was then a supreme court justice in Leipzig. He didn't join the Abwehr until a few days before we marched on Poland."

"By which time you had returned from New York."

"When I saw that war was inevitable, I cut short my visit and came home at once—which I think you'll agree was a strange way of trying to *avoid* military service. I arrived back in Berlin at the end of July."

"Now let's be clear about this." Moeller hitched up his trousers and looked around the court to make sure everyone was listening. "You saw the war coming, so you cut short this important American tour and rushed home to serve your country—is that it?"

"It was unthinkable that I should not be with my own people in time of war."

"A noble sentiment. Does you credit." He nodded emphatically, and Bonhoeffer began to see where he was heading. "So what did you do? Did you surrender your deferment and report for immediate induction into the army?"

"No, Your Honor."

"No? What then? You besieged the Reich ministries for a post better suited to your talents?"

"As soon as the war began," said Bonhoeffer patiently, "I applied for employment as an army chaplain."

"You were not, of course, aware that army chaplaincies were restricted to men with a record of active service. And none of your illustrious army connections saw fit to tell you."

"I was not aware of it—and my rejection was a great disappointment."

"But no great surprise, I think," said Moeller, hardening his tone. "Your application was turned down in February, 1940—more than six months after you'd come rushing home to serve your country in its hour of destiny. How did you manage to restrain your impatience?"

Bonhoeffer braced himself for the inevitable tirade. "While I was waiting to hear from the army authorities, I returned to the collective pastorates in Further Pomerania and continued my work there as a teaching minister."

"I see." Still holding back, Moeller put down his notes so as to have both hands free. "You mean you hurried home from America not to fight for your country, but to continue preaching pacifism and sedition."

"Your Honor, having placed myself at the disposal of the military authorities, I carried on with my work as best I could while awaiting their instructions."

Moeller invited everyone present to share his contempt. "Prisoner Bonhoeffer, you are straining the court's credulity. Is it not a fact that in March, 1940, the Gestapo stamped out your rats' nest of traitors at Schlawe?"

"The collective pastorates had already been dissolved, Your Honor," said Bonhoeffer. "My student ministers had all joined the army."

"And is it not a fact that in July the Gestapo broke up an illegal gathering you had called in Bloestau?"

"It was a Bible study group, Your Honor."

"And is it not a fact that in September you were forbidden to preach or speak in public because of your disruptive activities and ordered to report regularly to the police at Schlawe?"

"The order was not directed at me personally, Your Honor—that is to say, not exclusively. At least five other pastors were placed under a similar ban at the same time."

Moeller went on as though he had heard nothing. "And is it not a fact that no sooner had this order been issued by the Gestapo than your brother-in-law Dohnanyi decided to use the Abwehr as a cover for your illegal activities, thereby relieving you of the necessity to report your movements to the police and also of any further danger of your being called for military service?"

Bonhoeffer had long been prepared for this. He looked from Moeller to Roeder and back again, blankly at first, then with mounting indignation.

"Your Honor," he said. "What is Dr. Moeller suggesting? I *was* called for military service. With the Abwehr."

"I'll tell you what I'm suggesting," shouted Moeller, incensed that Bonhoeffer should appeal over his head. "I'm suggesting that you're a self-confessed Jew-loving pacifist and a tool of foreign interests. I'm suggesting you hurried back when you thought war was coming not, as you say, to share the historic mission of the German people, but to

90

divide and confuse them in their hour of trial. I'm suggesting you stand guilty of treason against the Führer and the German Reich."

"Your Honor," protested Bonhoeffer. "This is beyond belief. Am I here to answer questions, or simply to be abused?"

"You are here to help us inquire into certain irregularities in the conduct of military intelligence," said Roeder, with an unexpectedly dispassionate air. "And I'm inclined to agree that a more temperate approach might better assist the court in that purpose." Moeller's head settled between his shoulders as though struck from behind. He turned in furious dismay, but Roeder motioned him to sit down. "Nevertheless, it is clear that your association with the Abwehr followed very closely upon the restrictions imposed upon you by the Gestapo."

"That is so, Your Honor," said Bonhoeffer. He attributed this sudden impartiality to the much larger number of army observers in court. "I reported for duty in January, 1941, but the matter had been under discussion for months—long before the Gestapo order was issued. My brother-in-law had asked me to consider putting my church contacts abroad at the Abwehr's disposal, and I remember writing to him about it—although I can't recall exactly when."

Roeder examined his notes. "In November?"

"Possibly." They had found it. He and Hans had concocted the letter and planted it in the Abwehr's files only a short time before their arrest to cover this very point. "But we'd been talking about it since the summer of 1940 at least."

"I notice you wrote to him from Munich."

"Yes. After protesting the Gestapo's order, I thought I'd better leave Pomerania for a while to avoid any further complications. So I went south to Ettal in the Bavarian mountains to work on a new book."

"Are you sure it wasn't to avoid the complications of military service? All the men of your age group in Schlawe were called up that autumn."

"I was not aware of that, Your Honor. And may I say again that the exemption I received in January, 1941, was not to *avoid* military service, but expressly so that I could serve with the Abwehr. I found it a great relief to be employed by a military department after the damaging charges brought against me by the Gestapo."

"Weren't you afraid your Gestapo record would embarrass your brother-in-law—and through him, the Abwehr itself?"

"I often asked *them* that question."

"And how did they answer it?"

"I was always told that the Abwehr worked with anyone who could be useful, including Communists and Jews. All that mattered, they said, was the value of the information they obtained."

"Then how do you account for the attitude of your church colleagues? General Superintendent Dibelius, for example, and Superintendent Diestel are both under the impression that the purpose of the exemption was to enable you to continue with your church work."

"Your Honor, if all I had wanted was a dispensation for church work, then this could have been arranged in Schlawe at the request of Superintendent Block."

"Indeed? Could he also have relieved you of your obligation to report to the Gestapo?"

They were on dangerous ground. "I was anxious to be of some use, Your Honor. The fact that I came to do my war service with the Abwehr was not by my choice nor yet by my brother-in-law's—although I won't pretend it didn't suit me well. It was by direct order of Admiral Canaris."

"Yes, I imagine it suited you and Dohnanyi extremely well," said Roeder, and Bonhoeffer wondered suddenly just how secure Canaris still was as the sheet anchor of their defense. "But it doesn't explain why your colleagues thought this exemption was so that you could carry on with your church work."

"Your Honor, I was anxious to maintain the fiction that my work was still mainly with the Confessing Church because many pastors would regard the use of my ecumenical contacts for military purposes as highly improper. It could easily ruin my standing as a theologian, and to some extent, it may have done so already."

"Well, we must all expect to make sacrifices in wartime," said Roeder, elaborately unimpressed. "No matter what face you put on it, you'll not deny that your employment by the Abwehr meant doing nothing you would not have chosen to do in any case?"

"On the contrary. Had I been free to choose, I would have carried on preaching and lecturing."

"Nevertheless, while Germany was building a new order in

Europe, you were safe in Bavaria writing a book."

"After reporting for duty, I was sent almost immediately to Switzerland," said Bonhoeffer. "It was thought that my former associates there could provide a useful assessment of British and American reaction to the Führer's victories in the field."

It had been an even better way of alerting the British to the renewed preparations for a revolt against Hitler, and preparing the ground for a discussion of possible peace terms, but Roeder was impatient to return to what he obviously considered to be the essential point. "You say you left Schlawe in September. Did you go straight from there to Munich?"

"No." Bonhoeffer hesitated, loath to involve others unless he had to. "I spent most of September and October with friends, working on my new book."

Roeder leafed through his notes. "That was on the estate of the Kleist-Retzows? They're related to your fiancée's family?"

"That is so." It was another warning to lie only when it was strictly necessary. "And from there I went to Munich in November."

"To stay with your aunt Countess Kalckreuth?"

"Well, no. Or rather, I should say that while her house became my official residence, I decided to accept an invitation to work in the library of the Catholic monastery at Ettal. I stayed there until the arrangements for my journey to Switzerland were complete."

"Until February 24, in fact."

"If that was the date of my departure, yes."

"I see." Roeder sat back to survey the court. "So for six months after avoiding the military call-up in Schlawe, you worked on this book of yours."

"Yes, Your Honor."

"Did you consider that an adequate contribution to the war effort?"

Bonhoeffer caught Sonderegger's eyes. "The delay was not of my choosing, Your Honor. The formalities of joining the Abwehr took longer to complete than we'd anticipated, and then there were difficulties over my Swiss visa. While these were being attended to, I simply got on with my work. And if Dr. Moeller still believes I returned from America expressly to sabotage the war effort, perhaps he will explain how much damage he thinks I could have done in a remote Benedictine library."

"That will do," said Roeder, but he did not seem unduly displeased. "You say there were problems with your visa?"

"Yes, Your Honor. I was delayed for some weeks. Consul Schmidhuber had to go to Bern before it came through, and even then I was held at the frontier until a Swiss guarantor could be found to vouch for me."

The guarantor had been the eminent theologian Karl Barth, whom the Gestapo had forced into exile in 1935. Bonhoeffer was reluctant to mention him by name, as Roeder would inevitably see this as further evidence of conspiracy, but on the other hand, his failure to mention it might be equally damaging. The only answer he had so far found to the constant risk of saying too much or too little was to lead the questioning away from potentially dangerous lines of inquiry by opening up new ones, over ground prepared in advance.

"Ah, yes," said Roeder. "The talkative Schmidhuber. How closely did you work with him?"

"Not at all closely, Your Honor. He attended to the visa and one or two other matters, but that was all. There was some doubt about his discretion, so I told him as little as possible."

"That's not the impression he gave *us*. By his own account he was intimately involved in planning your missions abroad."

"By his own account, Your Honor, we can hardly win the war without him. But he knew no more about my work than anyone else in the Munich office."

"No more than Josef Müller?"

"With the *exception* of Dr. Müller," he said carefully, "whom I had known for some years. I valued his advice because he was well versed in church affairs. But he had no more to do with planning my missions than Schmidhuber. My instructions came through my brother-in-law from Admiral Canaris himself."

Roeder returned to his notes, and Bonhoeffer bent to ease the cramp in his right calf. The cover was obviously holding. So far, everybody's story had obviously tallied.

"Whom did you see in Switzerland?"

"I prepared a full report on the mission, Your Honor. No doubt it's still on file. The objective, as I've said, was to renew my contacts with the World Council of Churches in Geneva."

Sonderegger then surprised them both by lurching noisily to his feet. "With the court's permission, Herr Judge Advocate, I would like to ask the prisoner a question."

Roeder frowned. "I am in the middle of my interrogation, Herr Commissar."

"I realize that, but my question bears on the matter you've just raised."

"No doubt. I haven't finished with it myself."

"I think it's important, Your Honor," persisted Sonderegger, at his most bleakly impersonal.

"Oh, very well." Roeder fell back in his seat, and Sonderegger turned toward Bonhoeffer with the deliberation of an artillery piece locking on target.

"You say the purpose of your mission was to assess world reaction to our victories in Europe?"

"That was the general aim, yes."

"And in order to do this, it was necessary for you to enjoy the fullest confidence of your informants, which was why you disguised your connection with the Abwehr."

"Just so. They were hardly likely to discuss so sensitive a question with an official representative of German military intelligence."

"No." Sonderegger inspected his nails. "How, then, did you explain the fact that you had been permitted to travel abroad in wartime?"

His mind jammed for a moment. "You credit my friends with too little tact, Herr Commissar," he said, with a confidence he was far from feeling. He had thought they were over that hurdle. "I was not *asked* to explain it. No doubt they assumed I was on official business of some kind, but when I saw them, it was as a churchman long connected with the ecumenical movement. Most of them had known me, and I think trusted me, for many years."

Sonderegger shook his head slowly. "Most of them had known you for many years as an enemy of National Socialism. Why would they assume you were there on official business? Did they think you'd changed sides?"

"They knew me for a patriot," said Bonhoeffer, but there was no escape this time. "They knew I had returned to Germany in 1939 to stand or fall with the German people. But they did *not* know the nature of my war service. Nor did they have any suspicion that my conversations with them were the object of my visit—of that I am quite certain."

"You mean, none of them said, 'My God, what are *you* doing here? How did you manage to get out?' I find that hard to believe."

"They may have been curious, Herr Commissar, but my friends know me too well to press for information I choose not to volunteer."

"Well, I'm afraid we suffer from no such inhibition," he said. "Are you sure you didn't say to them in reply, 'The Gestapo thinks I'm here to pick your brains for information that may be useful to the High Command, but the real reason is so that I can bring you up to date about the resistance movement in Germany'—didn't you say something like that? Isn't *that* why they greeted you so warmly?"

Bonhoeffer clung to his vision of how an innocent man would behave. He turned to Roeder with all the dignity he could summon. "I have done my best to reply to these questions, but the Herr Commissar obviously prefers his own answers to mine. I don't think he understands that in *our* circles, Your Honor, friendship implies trust, confidence, and a general unwillingness to pry. It was enough that I should be there in Geneva. My friends would not risk embarrassing me with questions, not in such difficult times. Whatever they may have thought, they were content to take me on trust—as I'm sure your own friends would have done in similar circumstances."

Roeder nodded judiciously, and Sonderegger stopped smiling.

"The prisoner says he played a double game with *them*," he said, "so why not with us, too?"

"Why not indeed?" agreed Roeder. "Isn't that exactly what we're trying to determine? If that's your point, Herr Commissar, rest assured I have it in mind." He turned back to Bonhoeffer, but Sonderegger stayed on his feet.

"The point, Your *Honor*," he said heavily, "is that the prisoner traveled to Switzerland on papers provided by the German government. Now, I don't know whether he told his informants that or not, but they would have known it in any case. If he told them, I want to know what he said that induced them to confide in him. If he did *not* tell them, then perhaps he can explain what value there was in talking to enemies of the Third Reich who knew he was there in the service of the German government."

"I've already answered that," said Bonhoeffer. "I did *not* tell them, and they had no inkling of my purpose. Furthermore, they are *not* enemies of the Reich, but servants of the world's Christian churches."

Sonderegger shrugged. "Well, whoever they are and whatever was said, we could hardly rely on information gathered in those circumstances. The Abwehr must have known that before he went."

"I agree," said Roeder. "We've both read the report. It's of no particular value."

"Then why did they send him? Obviously, for some other purpose. And I want to know *what.*"

Roeder adjusted his papers impatiently. "The evidence so far suggests that Dohnanyi sent him abroad on what was little more than a social visit in order to justify the prisoner's exemption from military service. But I've no doubt he took the fullest advantage of the opportunity to renew his connections with the Jewish conspiracy and promote the interests of his illegal church."

Sonderegger washed his hands of it, and sat down. "I'll question him later."

"The prisoner is available to my Gestapo colleagues at any time," said Roeder. "But I think you'll find my reading of this is correct. After all, what followed this so-called mission? Nothing. What happened after you returned from Switzerland in March?"

"I reported to the Abwehr center in Berlin," said Bonhoeffer. "Where I was assured that Admiral Canaris was quite satisfied with the results of the mission. And I believe he must have been, for a second journey was then arranged for me."

Roeder referred to his notes. "Not for another six months. What happened in the interval?"

"After submitting my report, and while my next journey was being planned, I went back to my work."

"Your theological work? This book you were writing?"

"Yes, Your Honor. I was to have gone to Scandinavia in June, but the mission was canceled after several months of preparation."

"I see. And where did you spend this second six months, while you were waiting for Dohnanyi to find something for you to do? In Munich? At your official residence?"

"No," he said. "I spent some weeks at my parents' country home, and several more with friends. But I was in Berlin for most of that summer, preparing for the Scandinavian trip."

"And also keeping in touch with your former students at the front, isn't that right? By means of a monthly pastoral letter?"

"I corresponded with them, yes. I still held my teaching post with the Confessing Church."

"I see." Roeder looked smug, and Bonhoeffer resigned himself to another mauling. "Now, I just want to go over that again—so as to get everything clear in my mind. In the six months after your return from Switzerland, you worked mainly on your book—is that correct?"

"When I was not preparing for my next journey, yes."

"But wasn't there an order from the National Office for Literature prohibiting you from any further activity as a writer?"

"I took that to be a ban on *publishing* my work, Your Honor."

Roeder found a copy of the order in his file. "The exact words were: 'This has the effect of an official occupational prohibition of literary activity.' Are you saying that writing a book doesn't *count* as a literary activity?" He looked for, and received, a dutiful chuckle from the Gestapo bench.

"Your Honor, it seemed to me that 'occupational' was the key word—otherwise even the writing of letters would have infringed the order. I'm not a writer by profession, but a theologian."

"Well, you *did* say your principal occupation during those six months was as a writer, but never mind. Let's call it church work instead. As you say, you *did* still hold a teaching post. Where were you for most of that time?"

"Here in Berlin, Your Honor."

"In Berlin?" He looked puzzled. "I was under the impression you were still prohibited from conducting church business in the city and from practicing your profession as a theologian here."

"Yes, Your Honor."

"Yes, Your Honor," he repeated. And then, in a sudden shout: "Well, if writing a book is neither literary work nor church work, what is it?"

Bonhoeffer gestured helplessly. "It was a means of passing the time between assignments, Your Honor. No one else was concerned in it or affected by it in any way."

"Can you say the same of the pastoral letters you were writing to your former students? Weren't *they* literary? Weren't *they* theological? As the holder of a teaching post, wouldn't you call writing pastoral letters church business?"

"I don't think it was what the Gestapo had in mind when they made the order, Your Honor. I took it to mean that I was not allowed to come to the city for church meetings and conferences."

"Then perhaps you'll tell us what you thought Reich Minister Kerrl had in mind when he issued his order of July, 1940, expressly forbidding the dispatch of religious literature, including mimeographed pastoral letters, to members of the armed forces?"

"Mine were not mimeographed, Your Honor. I wrote to my students individually."

Roeder collapsed in his chair, well pleased with himself. "He wrote to them individually," he said in wonderment. "Now, here is a man who claims to be a loyal German. He tells us how anxious he is to serve his country. But what does he *do?* Does he joyfully answer the Führer's call to arms? No. He gets his brother-in-law in the Abwehr to have him exempted from military service. And why does he do that? So that he can perform some vital *civilian* service? No. So that he can spend the next six months in comfort writing a book. He is then sent abroad on a useless, but no doubt enjoyable, mission in case someone should question his exemption, and after *that* what does he do, this patriot? He settles down again happily for another six months, writing an illegal book, living illegally in Berlin, and illegally mailing religious literature to members of the armed forces."

Bonhoeffer returned his gaze stoically.

"And when taxed with this treasonable defiance," Roeder went on, "does the prisoner humbly admit his fault? Does he ask forgiveness and for a chance to make amends? No. He stands there as though insulted that anyone should dare question his actions."

Bonhoeffer looked along the line of army observers. "I cannot prevent the court from interpreting my actions in any way it chooses," he said, painfully conscious of the shake in his voice. "I can only assure the Judge Advocate that I was always unreservedly at the Abwehr's disposal. I should also like to say that the Abwehr found much more for me to do after my second mission to Switzerland in September."

"Did they indeed?" Now in great good humor, Roeder was writing busily in his folder. "How long after that was it before Dohnanyi sent you abroad again?"

Bonhoeffer rubbed his forehead. "I left for Norway in April, I think."

"In *April?*" Roeder looked up incredulously. "They found *more* for you to do? My God, it was *seven* months this time."

"But I was ill for most of that winter, Your Honor. With pneumonia."

"Where? In Berlin, I suppose."

Bonhoeffer sagged a little. "At my parents' house."

Roeder dropped his pen and leaned back in disgust. "Get him out of my sight," he said.

June 14, 1943

Dear Parents,

. . . When the bells rang this morning, I longed to go to church, but instead I did as John did on the island of Patmos, and had such a splendid service of my own that I did not feel lonely at all, for you were all with me, every one of you, and so were the congregations in whose company I have kept Whitsuntide. . . .

It will be ten weeks tomorrow; as mere laymen we did not imagine that "temporary" confinement would amount to this. But after all, it is a mistake to be as unsuspecting in legal matters as I am; it brings home to one what a different atmosphere the lawyer must live in from the theologian; but that is instructive too, and everything has its proper place. All we can do is wait as patiently as may be, without getting bitter, and to trust that everyone is doing his best to clear things up as quickly as possible. Fritz Reuter puts it very well: "No one's life flows on such an even course that it does not sometimes come against a dam and whirl round and round, or that people never throw stones into the clear water. Something happens to everyone, and he must take care that the water stays clear, and that heaven and earth are reflected in it"— when you've said that, you've really said everything. . . .

# 7

✝ ✝ ✝

THEN IT WAS SUMMER. When they took him down for his walk with Captain Maetz, he stepped out of the shadows into a white flare of warmth that burned a blessing through his clothes. Lifting his face, squinting, to the sun, he uncoiled like an animal leaving its burrow, but it had come too late to help his rheumatism. The stone chill of the prison block had eaten into his bones, and was not to be thawed by a half hour outdoors or the exercises he still practiced stiffly each morning.

But even this had its compensations. Maetz had ordered heat-ray treatment for him in the sick bay, and while it had done nothing as yet to ease his aches and pains, it had much improved his social life. He now passed an hour or more every afternoon talking to the patients and drinking vile coffee with the guards, his circle of acquaintance widening each day as word got around.

The evenings were even better. On learning that he knew something about first aid, Maetz had appointed him medical orderly for his section, which meant that whenever an air raid alert sounded, he had to report to the sick bay and stay there until the all-clear. Worried by the prison's proximity to the Borsig locomotive works, Maetz was making up for the comparative lull in Allied air attacks with frequent practice alerts, so that, what with these and the rheumatism treatments, the guards were now accustomed to finding Bonhoeffer in the sick bay at all hours. Almost every evening after supper, Linke or Knobloch or Holzendorf would take him down to chat over a drink, play chess with Engel, or listen to the radio—sometimes even to the BBC if no one else was about.

Bonhoeffer was particularly grateful for this new freedom of movement because he had met Schmidhuber in the yard one morning and was hoping to run into him again. With Maetz there, it had not been possible to exchange much more than a reassuring nod, and he badly needed a few minutes with him in private to find out exactly what he *had* told the War Court. But the days went by without another accidental meeting, and one evening Bonhoeffer decided to risk asking about him. As Knobloch watched him work out a chess problem with Engel, he casually let slip that he had run into a friend of his in the yard a while back.

"Schmidhuber?" said Engel. "He was here."

*"Here?"*

"This afternoon. They think he's got an ulcer. But he said you weren't to worry. Everything would turn out all right."

"He's gone?"

"Yes. And just as well. He's a talkative fellow, your friend."

Bonhoeffer went still. "I'm sorry to hear that."

"I didn't know how to tell you. We were talking about Stalingrad. He said the Führer was mad, throwing twenty-two divisions away like that. And then he said he would do the same to the Afrika Korps as well unless he was stopped, so I asked him who he had in mind to do it."

"And what did he say?"

"He said we shouldn't be surprised if we heard one day soon that Hitler was dead, and the British and Americans were fighting *with* us against the Bolsheviks."

Bonhoeffer looked from one to the other. "No names?"

"No names," said Knobloch. "But he hinted you knew all about it."

He nodded. There was nothing to suggest that Schmidhuber had turned state's evidence, but Hans would have to be warned.

"It's Schmidhuber you've got to worry about, not us," said Engel.

"I know that, Max."

"It's a dirty business for a pastor."

"Is that sympathy or criticism?" Bonhoeffer pushed his tobacco tin across the table. "I wasn't *looking* for wrongs to right. I used to think it was enough to live a Christian life—or try to."

"You should have stayed in America."

"No. I should never have gone. As Christians, we had to choose between willing our country's defeat so that civilization might survive, and willing a victory that would destroy it. I couldn't make that choice in comfort and security. I had to come back. God wills us to live responsibly."

"Responsibly?" Engel pretended to faint in his chair.

"I knew what Hitler intended."

"But you'll have to *kill* him."

"Shut up," said Knobloch. He glanced over his shoulder at Bergmann, who was checking his medical supplies.

"If you don't, every SS and Gestapo man, every party member in the country, will rally around him."

"I think that's right," said Bonhoeffer.

Engel whistled softly. "You know what they're going to say, don't you? When you start talking peace? They're going to say you only turned on him because we're losing. Our own people will think so, too."

"Is that an argument for doing nothing? Must Germany be destroyed, and Europe with it? I fear God's judgment more than theirs. The war can't end till we're rid of this man."

"You know, that shocks me?" Engel looked at Knobloch and shook his head. "It really *shocks* me to hear him talk like that."

"Thou shalt do no murder," said Bergmann unexpectedly.

Bonhoeffer started at his voice, and twisted around. "That *is* God's commandment," he agreed. "Only an unconditional necessity can justify taking a life. But where the necessity exists, the killing *must* be performed. And I see no reason why pastors should be spared the anguish of the act."

"But who's to *say* it's necessary?" Engel asked. "You've let the lawyers in."

"No. The taking of life can never be one possibility among others. Sparing life has much the higher claim. If another possibility exists, then it *is* murder."

Bergmann came around the table to face him. "The commandments are absolute."

"Yes. But absolute righteousness is not attainable. The world is fallen. All human action is poisoned. If we refuse to incur guilt for the sake of others, we reject the example of Christ."

The others waited as Bergmann struggled to reply. "But He also said that all who take the sword will perish by the sword."

"My brother-in-law Hans once asked me how those words were to be understood," said Bonhoeffer tiredly. He took off his glasses. "I told him they should be taken as they are. We stand under the power of that judgment, but we need men who are ready to bring it upon themselves."

"What can you tell the court about Operation 7?"

"Very little, Your Honor. I was not directly concerned with it."

"You were aware of its purpose, though. You discussed it with Dohnanyi?"

"Only once, I think. As I understood it, the aim was to disguise a group of Abwehr agents as Jewish refugees and settle them in Switzerland."

"Disguise?" Roeder scoffed. "They *were* Jews, weren't they?"

"I believe so."

"You *believe* so. You knew them personally."

"I knew one of them slightly, Your Honor. Fräulein Charlotte Friedenthal. She had worked for some years in the office of the Confessing Church."

"And so you asked your brother-in-law to include this Jewess in the escape group?"

Bonhoeffer frowned. "These people were going abroad to serve Germany. I had no idea that Fräulein Friedenthal was one of them until she looked me up one day to ask if I thought she could undertake the assignment in good conscience. I assured her she could, although I knew nothing of what she was supposed to do in Switzerland."

"When was this?"

"It must have been, oh, two summers ago—in 1941. I can't remember exactly."

Roeder returned to his notes. "There are reports of other Jews visiting your parents' house at about that time. Were they also members of this group?"

"Your Honor, I've no recollection of that." He was genuinely startled. "Could it have been later—in the autumn, perhaps? When the deportations began, several former patients and colleagues of my father's called to say goodbye. But none of them were connected with Operation 7."

"The deportations began on October 16, 1941," said Roeder, still looking at his notes. "Do you happen to remember when the Jewess Friedenthal crossed into Switzerland?"

"It was some time after that, I believe."

"Quite right. It was almost a year after. So which do you think is more likely—that they were Abwehr agents posing as fugitive Jews, or fugitive Jews posing as Abwehr agents?"

"Your Honor—" Bonhoeffer looked about him helplessly. "I really think you should put these questions to my brother-in-law. I'd no reason to doubt the truth of what I heard."

Roeder smiled. "I'm putting it to *you* that Dohnanyi deliberately organized the escape of fourteen renegade Jews—and that you were not only aware of it, but actively assisted him."

"The operation was authorized by Admiral Canaris."

"In fact, I'm suggesting that you and Dohnanyi set out deliberately to sabotage the Jewish policy of the Third Reich—among other reasons, for motives of personal gain."

Bonhoeffer appealed to the court. "Your Honor, that's not merely absurd, it's offensive."

"Indeed? Consul Schmidhuber has already confessed to various crimes in connection with this affair—and implicated both of you."

"I know little of Schmidhuber's activities, and he still less of mine. But I *do* know that Operation 7 was ordered and supervised by Admiral Canaris himself. I also know that because of its sensitive nature, the mission was cleared in advance with SS Group Leader Heinrich Müller of Reich Security Head Office, and I simply cannot believe that two officers of their caliber would lend themselves to a deception of the type you're suggesting."

"Be careful," said Roeder, with a hasty glance at Sonderegger, who seemed to be listening for once. "Group Leader Müller may have

106

endorsed the operation in principle, but it was carried out by the Abwehr under Dohnanyi's direction. And the evidence is that he used it to smuggle Jews out of the country on the pretext of military necessity. Can you recall when you first discussed it with him?"

"I'm bound to say I cannot, Your Honor," he said. He had no idea what Schmidhuber had told them, but it seemed sensible to place it as far back as possible, certainly before the deportations began. "I know the preparations were very drawn out. I remember my brother-in-law telling me they took a year to complete. There were problems on the Swiss side. He asked me if I knew anyone there who might help."

"When was that?"

"I can't honestly remember. In the spring of last year? Perhaps earlier? I wrote a letter for Schmidhuber to take to the Swiss Evangelical Church Alliance, so perhaps *he* can remember. In fact, now I think of it, I'm not sure if I wrote at my brother-in-law's request or Schmidhuber's. At any rate, the letter was my only contribution to Operation 7."

"Schmidhuber remembers it differently." The tone was still forbidding, but the tension had eased, as though Roeder knew he would not get far on this tack. "He says you spoke to him directly about the Jewess Friedenthal."

"I may well have done, but I've no recollection of it. Schmidhuber was in charge of the Swiss arrangements because, as Portuguese consul, he could cross the border at will."

"He says you told him the Jewess Friedenthal had relatives in Switzerland and wanted to join them there."

"It's quite possible, Your Honor. She may even have been chosen for that reason. After all, who would suspect such a person of working for the Abwehr?"

"Not I, certainly," said Roeder, and some of the Gestapo men laughed.

Bonhoeffer waited. "I'll not deny that for me there was a Christian element in this operation," he said, as soon as they were silent. "Indeed, without it, we could not have counted on the help of the Swiss churches."

"How much did she pay to be included?"

Bonhoeffer regarded him steadily. "Fräulein Friedenthal was not permitted to work in Switzerland. This meant that the Abwehr had to provide—through Schmidhuber—the money necessary to support her and the rest of the group. If Schmidhuber has confessed to wrongdoing, then the arrangements were obviously open to abuse, but to suggest that my brother-in-law was involved, or even knew of this, is quite absurd."

"Other than as a means of escape for fourteen Jews, the entire operation was absurd," said Roeder, not much put out. "How, conceivably, could this Jewess have provided the Abwehr with information of military value?"

"Your Honor, I repeat—I knew nothing of their objectives in Switzerland. And even if I had, I am too new to this difficult business to venture an opinion. I would have thought their purpose was as much political as military, but I wasn't invited to comment. I just wrote the letter, and that was all."

"Are you so new to the business that no one told you how responsibilities are divided between the Abwehr and Reich Security Head Office?" Roeder had embarked on a lengthy addition to his notes.

"I was aware of it, yes," he said cautiously.

"You knew that by agreement between Admiral Canaris and the late Obergruppenführer Heydrich, the Abwehr was specifically excluded from the field of political intelligence?"

"Your Honor, it was clear even to me that almost any given operation might at some time fall somewhere between the two." He had made a bad slip. "No doubt that was why Admiral Canaris took the precaution of clearing Operation 7 with Reich Security in advance."

"But you still think it was political in character—that's interesting." Roeder carefully underlined the last few words he had written. "By the same reasoning, don't you see your own excursions for the Abwehr in the same light—as political rather than military?"

"By no means," said Bonhoeffer, annoyed with himself. "They were generally to assess enemy response to the Führer's victories, although sometimes there was a more specific end in view. In the spring of 1942, for example, I traveled to Norway with Count Helmut von Moltke, representing the High Command, to intervene directly in a crisis endangering our forces there."

108

"You mean the Berggrav affair?"

"There was more involved than the fate of one man, Your Honor. The entire Norwegian church under Archbishop Berggrav had strongly resisted Quisling's attempt to interfere with its ministry. At Easter, every pastor in the church resigned from office, and when the archbishop was arrested, the whole country was brought to the edge of revolt. As this obviously threatened our military position there, Moltke and I were sent to mediate, and I'm happy to say the danger was averted."

"The danger to whom?" asked Roeder. "Berggrav?"

"The High Command was concerned solely with damping down the spirit of resistance."

"I don't doubt it. But what were *you* concerned with? Did you manage to persuade Berggrav to repent his treason? Did you even try?"

"We were not allowed to see the archbishop, Your Honor. The problem was resolved successfully with his colleagues."

"You *resolved* it?" Roeder laid down his pen. "Berggrav was released, and the Quisling government forced to abandon its church reforms. You call *that* a successful resolution? We could hardly have done worse if you'd gone there to *encourage* the spirit of resistance."

As that had, indeed, been the purpose of his mission, Bonhoeffer bowed his head meekly. "The decision was not ours, Your Honor. We merely reported on our discussions with the church leaders. The archbishop was released by order of Deputy Führer Bormann."

Roeder sniffed. "It was just a coincidence, I suppose, that the Norwegian church should have adopted the pattern of resistance you'd been urging on the German church since 1933?"

"Germany was not occupied by a foreign power," said Bonhoeffer firmly. "The Norwegian situation offered no parallel."

"Well, I can't conceive of a less suitable person to send on such a mission." Roeder picked up his pen. "How would you describe your second trip to Scandinavia last year? Was it equally . . . successful?"

"I went to Sweden in May for quite a different purpose."

"So you did. You went to see your old friend Bishop Bell. You cut short another of your Swiss holidays and hurried off, with Foreign Office papers this time, to meet an envoy of the British government. What for?"

Bonhoeffer took a moment to steady himself. "Bishop Bell was in Sweden as an envoy of the Church of England, Your Honor—not of the British government. And I prepared a full report for Admiral Canaris, which I'm sure he'd be glad to show you. The idea was to take the measure of public opinion in Britain, and in particular, of government attitudes toward the course of the war."

"You mean it was another one of those missions that were more political than military in character."

"I'm not competent to judge, Your Honor. I simply carried out my orders. But I'm fairly certain that Bishop Bell would never have discussed the state of British morale with a representative of Reich Security Head Office."

This time, somebody laughed on the army side of the court, and Roeder slammed down his hand on the desk. "From whom did you receive your orders?"

"They were relayed to me from Admiral Canaris by my brother-in-law and General Oster."

"Did you discuss them with anyone?"

"Other than with my Abwehr colleagues? No, certainly not. The mission was highly confidential."

Roeder looked inquiringly at Sonderegger, who considered Bonhoeffer for a moment, chin in hand, then shook his head.

"You returned to Berlin on June 2," said Roeder, back with his notes, "and left again for Italy on the twenty-sixth with Dohnanyi. Was that connected in some way with your meeting with Bell?"

"Only in the sense that it was again to take soundings of foreign opinion, Your Honor. It was my fourth such journey abroad in four months." Sonderegger was still watching him. He had an uncomfortable feeling that the Gestapo knew or guessed more about his talks with Bell than they had told Roeder. "We spent several days in Rome talking to officials at the Vatican."

"Schmidhuber says you met him in Venice."

"That's right," he agreed warily. "We had business there *and* in Florence, but after that I'm afraid there was again a period of enforced idleness. I was to have traveled to the Balkans in the autumn and again to Switzerland, but when Schmidhuber disappeared, these plans were postponed until we knew what had happened. And sooner than wait in Munich, where I would have had nothing to do, I stayed in Berlin —on instructions from Admiral Canaris."

"I'm sure he kept you busy."

"I was frequently asked for recommendations and advice."

"Were you indeed?" Roeder smiled unpleasantly. "Recommendations and advice—well, well. And this—this enforced idleness lasted from—let me see—from July until when exactly?"

"I was on the point of leaving for Italy and the Balkans when I was arrested."

"In April. Well now, that's a further eight months, by my reckoning. For eight months your contribution to the war effort consisted of recommendations and advice—is that right?"

"Your Honor, I asked repeatedly for some other assignment—and almost every day I expected to resume my travels."

"Still, you managed to occupy yourself somehow."

"Yes."

"Living comfortably in Berlin with your parents, I dare say."

"I stayed with them, yes."

"And working on your illegal book, no doubt. Or were you too busy sending illegal circulars to your students at the front?"

Bonhoeffer looked down at his manacled hands. "Had I been a physicist like my brother, Your Honor, I don't think anyone would have thought it remarkable that I should have continued with my work between assignments."

"I think I can safely say his physics has served the Reich better than your metaphysics." Roeder seemed pleased with this, and wrote it down. "You were to have gone to Italy, I believe, with Josef Müller."

"Dr. Müller enjoys the confidence of Pope Pius. Together we hoped to influence the content of his peace message."

"Very sensible," said Roeder. "A very proper and useful assignment."

"We thought so." Bonhoeffer eyed him. "The message was bound to have a profound effect on Catholic opinion everywhere."

"Oh, I agree. What I *don't* understand is why General Oster felt it necessary to try to hide this mission from us."

"He did?" But for the book code, Roeder might have ambushed him here.

"While we were searching Dohnanyi's office, Oster attempted to conceal a slip of paper apparently authorizing the journey. Can you think of any reason why he would want to do that?"

"No," he said hesitantly. "It was a matter of exceptional delicacy, of course. Perhaps he wished to restrict all knowledge of it to those immediately concerned."

"Or *possibly* there was more to the mission than met the eye? Some hidden purpose, perhaps?"

"Not if you saw the authorization, Your Honor. The Abwehr would hardly keep secrets from itself. Slips of that sort are prepared for every mission."

Roeder looked doubtfully at Sonderegger. "Do you know what was on this particular piece of paper?"

"I've no idea. General Oster would have briefed me on it before I left. But whatever it said should not necessarily be taken at its face value. These slips are meant to indicate the best line to take in winning our informants' confidence. If you like, they're the Abwehr's playing cards."

With some satisfaction, Bonhoeffer watched Roeder add briefly to his notes and turn the page. Oster had obviously acknowledged the "O" on the slip as his initial, and everyone's story had again tallied.

"You say your plans were postponed because of Schmidhuber's disappearance in September."

"Yes, Your Honor. If he'd compromised me with my church colleagues abroad, it was obviously better to go prepared than to be suddenly confronted with it on the spot."

"Did Müller tell you about his conversations with Schmidhuber in Italy during October?"

This was more difficult. He had not thought to agree on a story with Müller and had no idea of what he might have said. "I've no doubt he told my brother-in-law. I heard later that he tried his best to persuade Schmidhuber to return home voluntarily to answer the charges against him."

"Did you know what the charges were?"

"I understood they had something to do with mishandling foreign currency."

"Were you also aware that while in Italy, he threatened to defect to the British?"

"No, Your Honor." Bonhoeffer had no trouble sounding shocked. It explained why the Gestapo had chosen to move against the Abwehr when they did, and Roeder sensed his dismay.

"He'd learned a lot about your British connections, it seems. He thought they might help him. In fact, he's implicated you, Dohnanyi, and Oster in all kinds of dubious activities."

Sonderegger coughed, and they both looked at him.

"I would have thought that was only to be expected," said Bonhoeffer. "He was simply trying to distract attention from his own crimes by making wild charges against his colleagues."

"He says he helped Dohnanyi and Oster obtain your military exemption. Is that a wild charge?"

"He attended to some of the Munich formalities, Your Honor."

"He also confirms that the real purpose of the exemption was so that you could ignore the Gestapo's restrictions and continue your church work under the Abwehr's protection."

"Your Honor, I have already dealt with that slander. I realize you couldn't let it go unexamined, but now that I know how it originated, I must say I'm surprised the court should lend such credence to it."

Roeder poured himself a glass of water. "His testimony fits the known facts," he said, with the mildness he had shown throughout this session. "You reported to Munich in January, 1941. You were arrested in Berlin on April 5 last—some twenty-seven months later. In all that time, you spent less than three and a half months traveling abroad— which does rather suggest that your principal occupation lay somewhere other than with the Abwehr."

"That's less than fair, Your Honor," Bonhoeffer protested. "The journeys took months to prepare, and each one had to be followed up with reports, discussion, and analysis. The traveling itself was just the visible tip of the iceberg."

"Then let's be generous and assume that two-thirds of this iceberg was hidden from view. That still leaves plenty of time for your illegal church activities. There's nothing implausible in Schmidhuber's evidence."

"Not, I agree, if the court is already decided upon my guilt. But I'm distressed you should prefer the word of an accused embezzler to mine."

"Well, his allegations are not *entirely* unsubstantiated." Roeder searched again through his notes. "For instance, he says that you induced Dohnanyi and Oster to procure exemptions for other members of the so-called Confessing Church so that they, too, could continue with their antiwar activities. He mentions in particular Niesel, Wolf, and Jannasch."

"Admiral Canaris took an interest in them for the same reason as he took one in me," said Bonhoeffer, retreating. "For the possible military value of their church connections."

"But you *did* intercede urgently on their behalf? And after their exemption, they *did* carry on much as before?"

He sensed a trap, but couldn't see it. "I was certainly in favor of their exemption," he agreed. "And their effectiveness, like mine, depended on their remaining men of the church. But I can think of no way in which Schmidhuber can support the charge that their exemptions were simply to save them from military service."

"You're right," said Roeder. "He can't. But *I* can. I have evidence from a source that even you will agree is unimpeachable." He held up a folded sheet of notepaper, and Bonhoeffer felt the ground lurch under his feet. "It's a letter you wrote to Dohnanyi about Wilhelm Niesel— a troublemaker with a Gestapo record as bad as your own."

Now he knew why Roeder had had no need to bluster. It was so unfair. Hans had assured him over and over again that every scrap of evidence had been purged from the files.

"You seem surprised."

"Your Honor, I'm trying to recall how the letter came to be written."

"No mystery about that." Roeder pretended to read it over. "Niesel shared your reluctance to serve with the armed forces of the Third Reich, so you asked your brother-in-law to have him exempted."

"He was a member of the Old Prussian Council of Brethren, and its director of training. If his position had been recognized by the state, as it certainly should have been, his services would have been declared indispensable to the German people."

"Recognized by the *state?* Indispensable? Did you seriously think you were doing the German people a service by sparing yourselves the dangers and discomforts of the front?"

Bonhoeffer was desperately trying to remember what the letter said. "Your Honor, I can think of no one in the Confessing Church who would not have welcomed his call-up as a blessed release from suspicion."

Roeder wagged the letter at him reprovingly. "Then why is it, in reference to Niesel, you wrote 'there is a *threat* of call-up'?"

Bonhoeffer stared at him numbly.

"Well?" Roeder made sure Sonderegger was attending to his triumph. "Haven't we got at the truth—at last? Isn't that how you *really* saw military service? Not as an honor and privilege, but as a *threat?*"

Bonhoeffer found nothing to appeal to in the faces watching him. "It was never a threat to me personally," he said. "But in Niesel's case, it *did* threaten the Confessing Church." He had not known what he would say before he spoke. "I'm shocked I should have used the word. Taken by itself, it does make a most unpleasant impression. But no one in the Confessing Church ever regarded the call-up as threatening in a personal sense. The hundreds of young ministers who volunteered testify to that. And it's precisely *because* our conscience is clear that I felt able to plead in urgent individual cases like Niesel's that a pastor should be exempted for church service at home."

Roeder frowned. "Let's be clear about this. Are you saying that Dohnanyi intervened to procure Niesel's exemption for *church* service?"

"He had no power to do that, Your Honor. It could only be justified on military grounds, which was why I sought his advice. Over the years, I've grown accustomed to consulting him in this way, to see if help could be offered in this or that difficulty."

"And I'm sure he never let you down."

"Neither of us saw it in that light, Your Honor. It would never have occurred to me to press anything on him that he thought irresponsible. I would simply set the facts before him."

"Like this threat to Niesel."

"I know I expressed myself badly, and I can see how someone

might misunderstand or take exception to it, but my brother-in-law knew quite well what I meant."

"Evidently. Niesel got his exemption."

"He knew I meant a threat to the church," said Bonhoeffer patiently. "He would never have been swayed by purely personal considerations."

"Then perhaps you can tell us the *military* considerations that induced him to intervene."

"I'm sure he could explain them better than I. But I know he shares my conviction that final victory depends on the spiritual strength of the German people, which is, after all, the special province of the church."

"A church weakened and divided by men like you and Niesel, who flout its lawful authority?"

"A church weakened and divided by men who've lost sight of the laws of God."

Dear Parents,

I'm beginning this letter today, though I hope that I shall be seeing you in person tomorrow. . . .

I see from the parcels that the whole family keeps sharing in them —and the children and Maria's family. I want them all to know how grateful I am. It is a real help. What a blessing it is, in such distressing times, to belong to a large, closely knit family, where each trusts the other and stands by him. I sometimes used to think when pastors were arrested that it must be easiest for those who were unmarried. But I did not know then what the warmth that radiates from the love of a wife and family can mean in the cold air of imprisonment, and how in just such times of separation the feeling of belonging together through thick and thin actually grows stronger. . . .

Letters from Mother and Grandmother have just come. Thank you very much. From what you say about strawberries and raspberries, school holidays and plans for travel, I begin to feel that summer has really come. Time is not of much account here. I'm glad the weather is mild. A little while ago a tomtit had its nest with ten little ones in a recess in the yard here. I enjoyed going to look at it every day till some cruel fellow went and destroyed the lot and left some of the tomtits lying dead on the ground; I can't understand it. . . .

I've just come back and have seen Maria—an indescribable surprise and joy. I knew about it only a minute beforehand. It's still like a dream—really an almost unimaginable situation—what will we think of it one day? What one can say at such a time is so trivial, but that's not the main thing. It was so brave of her to come; I wouldn't have dared suggest it to her. It's so much more difficult for her than for me. I know where I am, but for her it is all unimaginable, mysterious, terrifying. Think how things will be when this nightmare is over! And now Maria's and Mother's letters have just come, to make my joy complete and as an echo of this morning. How good things still are! Tell them that I say this to myself every day. . . .

Ever your grateful Dietrich

# 8

✢ ✢ ✢

IF ROEDER HAD HOPED to break Bonhoeffer's spirit by confronting him with Maria, he again misjudged his man. Though Bonhoeffer still mourned the past bitterly, he had taken hold of another life that in some ways suited him better than he cared to admit. God had seen fit to narrow his field of experience, but in doing so, had deepened it and changed him. As yet, he had no very clear idea of what final form this change might take, but he knew it for a movement toward simplicity. Roeder's assaults on his reserve, and the daily humiliations of imprisonment, were rasping through pride and habit down to the bare metal.

The taunts of shirking the dangers and hardships of army service had been particularly hurtful, for his students and friends at the front were rarely far from his mind. Though never doubting he had made the right decision, he was always very conscious that his particular role in the resistance had required him to stay home in relative comfort while others suffered and died, and to have Roeder attribute this to cowardly self-indulgence magnified his misgivings most painfully. But that, too, he accepted as a necessary condition for the change in him. Nothing now was external to his faith. And while Maria's soft, clear beauty had cut him to the heart, she was a past loss more than a present loss. He endured the longing for his lost life not as the man he had been, but as the man he now was, simpler in belief and gaining in purpose.

118

The confrontation was also Roeder's last serious attempt to get under his guard. As the weeks went by, Bonhoeffer's appearances before the War Court became less frequent and the questioning more perfunctory. Sonderegger again tried privately to induce him to talk about his political involvements, hinting that the Gestapo might then take a lenient view, but in general there was less talk of treason and more of "irregularities" in procedure.

Toward the middle of July, he found out why. Understandably nervous of what the investigation might uncover, their friends in the resistance had undertaken to relieve the pressure by getting rid of Roeder. Besides Canaris, who had taken full responsibility for their actions, Dohnanyi had a powerful ally in Dr. Karl Sack, chief of the army's legal department. In his progress reports on the investigation, Sack had managed to convince Field Marshal Keitel that Roeder was more interested in discrediting Canaris and the Abwehr than in pursuing the case against Dohnanyi and Bonhoeffer, and when an independent review of the court's papers confirmed this impression, Keitel ordered Roeder to drop the political charges and confine his investigations to the alleged misuse of Abwehr authority. A week later, on July 30, Roeder wound up another session with Bonhoeffer in the War Court by announcing that he would be sent for trial on the relatively minor charge of damaging the war effort. That night, Bonhoeffer celebrated what felt like a notable victory with Engel, Knobloch, Holzendorf, and Bergmann in the sick bay, accounting for rather more than his fair share of Holzendorf's last bottle of schnapps.

Next morning, he woke to a headache and the recognition that nothing had really changed. He had played his part successfully, and the tension had eased to that extent, but he had never been more than a secondary target. The final outcome of the case still depended on what happened to Hans, whose health was giving way under the strain of an interrogation far more ruthless than anything Bonhoeffer had experienced. Shortly after her release in June, his sister Christine had sent a coded message saying that Hans had contracted phlebitis in both legs. If he could continue to hold out, there was still a chance that Roeder might have to settle for minor charges against him as well, but even so, Sonderegger and the Gestapo would still be waiting.

And there was something else to worry about now. In the space of a week, from July 25 to August 2, the city of Hamburg was razed to the ground. Five massive raids by British bombers, attacking at night, and American bombers, attacking by day, touched off such an inferno that even the streets caught fire, and tens of thousands suffocated to death in air raid shelters for want of oxygen. The heat was so fierce that the buildings burned white, like gas mantles, sucking in great winds from the sea and countryside, then flinging them skyward in roaring columns of incandescence. It was a new conception in warfare. Most German cities had felt the weight of Allied bombs before, but Hamburg was the first to be lost in a firestorm.

Piecing the story together night by night from the guarded reports on the sick-bay radio, Bonhoeffer faced up grimly to the idea that Berlin might be next, a fear that Goebbels immediately confirmed by appealing to all Berliners not engaged in essential work to evacuate the city.

"I sometimes wonder whether you wouldn't do better for the immediate future to go to Sakrow in case of possible alerts," he wrote to his parents. "Maria also suggested Pätzig, but communications there are so complicated and I don't imagine that you will want to travel before my case is settled. Wouldn't it be sensible for Renate to stay awhile in the country with her mother-in-law and for her husband to try to arrange his work to fit in with that?"

Though worried about his parents, who had finally received permission to visit him a week after he had seen Maria, Bonhoeffer was particularly concerned about Renate, who was now pregnant. He hoped "her husband" would take the hint. It was frustrating not to be able to address Eberhard directly, but his letters were still being censored and he had no wish to draw Roeder's attention to another relative by marriage in the Abwehr.

He returned to the subject in his next letter; he was now allowed to send one every four days to either his parents or Maria.

I wonder if you are still very much occupied with air-raid precautions. After all that has been in the papers lately, one cannot help thinking out the whole matter afresh. I just remember that we talked once about the beams in the cellar and were rather doubtful about them; were not some alterations going to be made in the central beam? I wonder whether you are still thinking of it, and

120

whether you can get anyone to help with the work. I think it might be difficult now. How I should love to help you with it myself. Do tell me all about it; I'm interested in every detail. What plans do my brothers and sisters have for the children? Will you be going to Sakrow, at least for nights?

Half proud and half dismayed, he was soon disabused of any idea that his parents might be persuaded to join in the now general evacuation of the city. "We had such a warm and friendly invitation to the country from Maria's mother, for ourselves or any of the grandchildren," wrote his mother on August 11.

But we don't want to go until your case has been cleared up. If it gets too chaotic, we shall perhaps sleep in Sakrow. Father doesn't want to leave his work, despite his seventy-five years. . . . If the attacks come, look after yourself, too, as well as you can. Make sure that you get a helmet and have enough water to dampen a towel, which you should make into a hood and put over your head; get your blanket from your room, wet it, and wrap it round you, and wet your shoes, etc.; that is said to be the most important thing if one has to go through fire.

The frustration of not being able to see personally to his parents' safety, as the last of their children still living at home, and his impatience at the delay in setting a date for the trial had combined to blow his careful routine to the winds. On the seventeenth he wrote to his parents:

For the past fortnight I've been waiting in such uncertainty day by day that I've hardly felt equal to any serious work; but I'm going to try now to get down to some more writing. Some weeks ago I sketched the outlines of a play, but meanwhile I've realized that the material is not suitable for drama, and so I shall now try to rewrite it as a story. It's about the life of a family, and of course there is a good deal of autobiography mixed up in it.

The experiment had been prompted by the difficulty he found in discussing the world with men like Meiser, Knobloch, and Engel, who were either unconscious of the larger questions or unused to talking about them, and who, in any case, lacked the technical equipment of the philosopher and theologian. The condescension he sometimes detected in his attitude toward them seemed to him a fatal sign of hubris, of a sinful sense of being set apart as one of God's elect, an initiate of mysteries beyond the understanding of ordinary men. Christianity was not just for theologians, addressing themselves to one another in language that Christ had never used.

That was when he first thought of a play. He tried to air the questions that troubled him by contrasting the views of Christoph, a passionate young exponent of the aristocratic ideal, with those of his friend Heinrich, representing the masses. Through Christoph, Bonhoeffer defined an outlook he had known since childhood. "I argued that one should never make freedom a slogan for the masses, because that led to the most dreadful slavery," Christoph says to his father.

> Freedom was always something to be limited to the very few, the noble, the select. For the rest, law and order took the place of freedom. I also said that there had to be superiors and inferiors among men, and that anyone who did not understand this fact was introducing chaos. And finally, I even said that there were people who were noble by nature, who were destined for rule and for freedom, and that there were also people who were rabble by nature, who had to serve, and that there was nothing more fearful and more disruptive than when this order collapsed and the rabble ruled and the nobility served. The two groups of people were distinguished by the fact that the rabble only knew how to live, whereas the nobility also knew how to die.

Bonhoeffer also made Christoph voice his own attachment to the values of his class. "I hardly know the world in which you have grown up," he says to Heinrich.

> Our sort never get to know it thoroughly. But you don't know my world either. I come from a so-called good family, from an old, respected bourgeois family, and I am not one of those who are ashamed to say so. On the contrary, I know the tranquil strength that there is in a good bourgeois home. No one can know that if they have not grown up in it. It's difficult to explain. But you must know one thing. We have become great by respecting what has happened and what is given, in other words, by respecting every man. We hold mistrust to be common and low. We look for the frank word and deed of the other man and we want to accept it

without suspicion. The psychologizing and analyzing of people which has now become fashionable means the destruction of all trust, the public slander of all that is decent, the revolt of all that is common against what is true and free. . . . But you mustn't think that we are blind in our trust, that we throw ourselves straight into the arms of any man. We leave that to those who drivel about the equality and goodness of all men. We have learned to distinguish —and we will let no one stand in our way—to distinguish between authentic and spurious, true and false, noble and common, decency and exploitation.

"And is what you call authentic, true, noble, decent, something quite beyond question, something self-evident to you?" asks poor Heinrich, overwhelmed by such assurance.

"There must be some self-evident things in life," replies Bonhoeffer/Christoph, "and one must have the courage to stand by them. One cannot begin life from the beginning again every day, questioning everything that one learned and assumed the day before. . . . That is the great mistake which people keep on making today. They think that the world only began with them."

Bonhoeffer/Heinrich acknowledges the justice of this, but repudiates the suggestion that the masses are really interested in new political ideas.

We want something far simpler: ground under our feet, so that we can live. . . . You have a foundation, you have ground under your feet, you have a place in the world. For you there are self-evident values, for which you stand and for which you would gladly lay down your lives, because you know that your roots lie so deep that they will continue to sustain you. . . . We do not have this ground. So we are blown hither and thither with the storm. We have nothing for which we are able and willing to lay down our lives, and we cling to our miserable life not because we love it, but because it is the only one we have. And if you have the threat of death grinning at you daily, then it's a miracle if you are *not* frenzied with greed for life and despair, filled with hatred for everything living and a lust for wild enjoyment. . . . There *is* a mob, and this mob must be kept under. But what is the offense of those who have been thrust into life without any ground under their feet? Can you pass by them and speak over their heads without being smitten with grief?

As Bonhoeffer had told his parents, this oratorical exchange, though deeply felt, was not the stuff of drama. He was now to find his material equally intractable in the context of a novel, but before he could get very far with it, the war reached Berlin.

He had come down with flu on Sunday, August 22, and taken to his bed with a high fever. Next day, though not well enough to take his morning walk with Captain Maetz, he resolutely refused a transfer to the sick bay for fear that Roeder might hear of it and delay the trial. Instead, he stayed in his cell, and Bergmann stopped by several times with hot drinks and aspirin. That night, while dreaming fitfully of bombs falling around his parents' house, he was roused by the guard coming in and cursing softly as he struggled with the window catch. Bonhoeffer had slept through a red alert, when by order of the captain, all windows were to be fastened open to reduce the risk of injury by flying glass.

It was the start not only of an Allied bombardment that in eighteen months would reduce Berlin to rubble, but of a prison legend about Bonhoeffer's imperturbability under fire that led many to think he enjoyed God's special protection. They felt safer when they were near him, and as there were no shelters at Tegel, even for the guards, he never lacked for company during the raids. Even on the first night, as he stood at the open window, wrapped in his blanket, the guards on his floor wandered in and out in ones and twos to stand in silence at his elbow as the attack developed.

But they were in no particular danger. With his grandstand view from the third floor, he soon saw that the attack was concentrated on the south side of the city, and although it was much heavier than anything he had seen before, it was not as bad as the raids on Hamburg had led him to expect. On the whole, he thought the bomber crews had more to be frightened of. Hundreds of guns had been added to the city's defenses since last time, in preparation for this new offensive, and they were ripping the night to pieces.

The noise was too great for them to hear the approach of aircraft engines, and too confusing to allow much of what they saw to be linked to particular sounds. The first indication of a new bombing run was always a silent blossoming of ice-white Christmas tree flares over the target, a glare so unearthly that the searchlights turned pallid and groped about feebly. Then the horizon would twitch with continuous summer lightning as the heavier guns fired, and lazy fountains of orange tracer hosed down the sky, swaying gently before curling over and falling back spent. Above them the shells burst matter-of-factly in carpets of twinkling bronze sparks.

It looked impossible for even a bird to survive, but as the flares drifted lower, the bombs would start to hit in clumps, their shock waves lit by evil winks of light that burst like bubbles forced up through the ground. The whole world then trembled with a resonance that went beyond the compass of the human ear. Small fires started to burn, but the British were after military targets, not the city itself, and losing remarkably few of their aircraft. Three or four times only did Bonhoeffer see what might have been a hit, once when a dozen or more searchlights locked into a cone that abruptly fell apart when a sudden orange glow flared at its apex, and twice when, through the gathering smoke, a ball of yellow light declined from view like a slow comet. Then abruptly it was over. The last flares flickered out, the guns stopped uncertainly, and a black silence rushed back singing in their ears. It was so quiet they fancied they could hear the crackle of the fires.

So far as he could tell, very little had fallen in the neighborhood of Charlottenburg, but he was very relieved next morning when Captain Maetz sent word that his parents were safe; he had arranged with the commandant that they should call the guardroom after a raid so as to set his mind at rest. His fever had also subsided, which spared him any further anxiety about being fit to stand trial, and a surprise visit from Maria next day put the finishing touch to his recovery.

He was so grateful to see her that he hardly minded the constraint of having a guard present. He had never been able to discuss anything really personal in front of strangers, and so long as his imprisonment prevented their giving real expression to what lay between them, he thought it no bad thing that they should confine themselves to family gossip, which in any case he craved. It was only in his letters to her that he could speak of his true feelings. His longing for a life with her was anchoring his faith ever more firmly in the world, and the very fact that they had found each other at such a black time he took as evidence that they should trust in the future.

"This is where faith belongs," he wrote in his next letter.

> May God give it to us daily. And I do not mean the faith which flees the world, but the one that endures the world and which loves and remains true to the world in spite of all the suffering which it holds for us. Our marriage shall be a yes to God's earth; it will strengthen our courage to act and accomplish something. I fear that Christians who stand with only one leg on earth also stand with only one leg in heaven.

His spirits stayed high after her visit. "For the last few days, I've been able to work well and write a good deal," he told his parents on the last day of August.

> When I find myself back in the cell after a few hours of complete absorption in my work, it takes a moment or two to get my bearings again. The fact of my being here is hard to credit even now, however much I get used to the external conditions. I find it quite interesting to watch this gradual process of accustoming and adapting myself. A week ago I was given a knife and fork for my meals —a new provision—and they seemed almost unnecessary, as it had become so much a matter of course for me to use a spoon for spreading my bread and so on. On the other hand, I think there are some things that are so irrational, for example, the actual state of being in prison, that it is impossible, or at least very difficult, to get used to them. That kind of thing needs a conscious effort if it is to be accepted.

The next night, the nervousness of those around him in the sick bay meant that he had to watch impassively while hundreds of British bombers pounded Charlottenburg, ten kilometers away. The antiaircraft barrage, if anything, was heavier than before, but wave after wave of planes droned through unscathed, dropping so many flares that the whole city lay bare to the rain of bombs that followed them down. Though experience told him the damage would not be as great as the thundering impact suggested, Bonhoeffer knew somehow that all had been lost. It was not just his helpless fear for the family, as a huge pall of smoke and dust rolled slowly outward and upward, twitching insanely with light; Germany itself was going down. He knew, with finality, that whatever else might happen, the Germany that had made him could never be called back. The ideals he shared with Hans and the others might survive, but the mold those ideals had shaped for generations was being shattered forever.

Linke brought word early next morning that his parents were safe. "By chance, we were spending the night at Christel's, in Sakrow," his mother explained in a letter on September 3.

> We saw that our neighborhood was in great danger round the Heerstrasse, but we were really quite composed in the face of what couldn't be altered. When we went home the next morning, we saw many fine houses destroyed in the Heerstrasse; the station was burning, and there were some fire bombs in Lötzenerallee. There was blast damage in Soldauer, Kurländer and Marienburgerstrasse, windows and roofs broken in two. We only lost a kitchen window, and there was some damage to the ceiling in the baggage room next to your room. It has been worse in Charlottenburg and Moabit, and I expect they're what we saw burning. Unfortunately, there's been the same damage at Susi's as before, if not worse, with damage to the windows and doors that was caused by a high-explosive bomb which came down on the Sehrings' house. We were there the whole morning helping to move things so that one could at least get in and out. Then we packed up some more things and took them with us in a station wagon, as this neighborhood is almost always getting it.

That same night, September 3, as though to mark the fourth anniversary of the war, the British mounted a still heavier attack, their bombers swarming over the city in such numbers that they confused and finally swamped its defenses. Only a few hours earlier, on Captain Maetz's orders, Bonhoeffer had been moved down from the third floor to the comparative safety of the first, and at the time he had felt a perverse regret at having to leave what amounted to home. But now, as the church towers he could see from the window of his new cell were etched ever more sharply against the gaudy horizon, and sticks of bombs clumped incessantly across the city, rattling his cell door and jingling the cutlery, he was suddenly grateful for the two extra floors between him and the sky, although he felt like a traitor to the men left up there alone in the dark.

For the first time in the five months he had spent in Tegel, bombs were falling nearby. There was a new and uglier note in the background noise of the prison. The guards at least were free to work off the tension by stamping and banging about, pretending to be busy, but the prisoners were entombed. As the raid went on, their nerves gave way. A man would start beating on his door with a metal cup or mess tin, clamoring to be let out, and hysteria would flare suddenly from cell to cell until a whole section was in a panicky uproar. A squad of guards would then clatter upstairs at the double to silence them, and when threats and abuse failed to work, they would open up a few cells at a time and go in swinging their clubs until all was quiet.

Now expert in translating prison sounds, Bonhoeffer stood listening to this and praying that someone would let him out. There had to be something useful he could do. The guards on this floor had obviously not been told that he was supposed to report to the sick bay during an alert, and from the mounting savagery of the bombardment outside, his services might soon be needed. Time and again, a chain of explosions would head in their direction, and as the prison's edgy murmuring died away, he would hear the rising, plummeting screech of bombs slanting in, then a split second's silence before each detonation. As the last one fell in each stick, the prison would let go its breath in a new babel of terror and shouting.

After almost an hour of this, Holzendorf unlocked his cell, cursing the guards for not doing it sooner.

"I put out the flag," said Bonhoeffer, hurrying along beside him. "Nobody took any notice."

"You should have banged on the door."

"I was afraid they'd bang back on my skull."

Holzendorf held him away from a window as another bomb burst nearby, then urged him on again. "There's a few broken heads in the sick bay," he said. "See what you can do, Pastor. It's a madhouse down there."

He was not exaggerating. Watched by two nervous guards, Bergmann and another orderly were dealing swiftly and calmly with a line of men with head or arm injuries, but the ward beyond was in bedlam. As Bonhoeffer went on through, he found Engel, dressed for once, trying to hold one frantic prisoner in bed while he headed off another, who was sobbing with pain as he hobbled about on a heavily bandaged foot. On the opposite side of the room, with his back to Bonhoeffer, a second man in uniform was also struggling to hold a patient down with one hand as he groped under the adjoining bed for someone else, and all the while, except for one or two staring rigidly at the ceiling, the rest kept up an animal keening that filled Bonhoeffer with as much anger as compassion. He had never seen men reduced to this. He wanted to slap them, to make them pull themselves together before they shamed their creator. He stood for a moment, silent and immovable, blocking the way of the man with the injured foot, then patted his cheek and gently led him back to bed.

"You shouldn't be doing this, Max," he said. "You'll hurt yourself."

"I'm all right." Engel pushed the other man flat and sat down beside him, out of breath. "I'll take care of this one. You go and help your friend Meiser."

"Meiser?" Bonhoeffer looked across the ward in surprise. "What's *he* doing here?"

"Passing blood again. But he's kept his head—I'll give him that."

Bonhoeffer walked down the center aisle, pausing at the foot of each bed. There was nothing he could say to these men that they would hear, or want to hear, but he hoped they might catch a little of his unconcern.

"Let me give you a hand," he said, taking over from Meiser. "I think if you tuck the blanket in tightly on your side, that should hold him. What's going on under there?" He nodded at the adjoining bed.

"It's Klaus," said Meiser, straightening his back with a grimace. His face was the color of wet sand. "He won't come out."

"What's wrong with him?"

"What's *wrong* with him?" Meiser groaned comically. "He's frightened."

"They don't send a man to the sick bay because he's frightened."

"They do after they've beaten him for it. After they've broken his ribs and split his head open."

"When did it happen?" He would have something to say to Maetz in the morning.

"I don't know. Half an hour ago. Bergmann patched him up, but he needs a doctor."

"I'll see to it. Is he a friend of yours?"

"I know him." Meiser sat down heavily, on the point of collapse.

"All right. I'll try to get him out. Now, which is *your* bed?"

He shook his head, closing his eyes. "I think I'll stay here."

Bonhoeffer just managed to catch him as he fell awkwardly sideways. Lifting his legs onto the bed, he pulled off his boots and covered him with the blanket.

"Now, you lie there quietly while I talk to your friend."

Meiser turned his face away. "Let him die," he said. "They're going to hang him anyway."

Bonhoeffer stood up with a sigh. There was a lull in the attack, and the ward had quieted down a little. The only man still out of bed was Engel, with whom he exchanged a rueful shrug before squatting on his haunches. Klaus was very young. He lay on his side against the back wall with his knees drawn up to his chin, holding his face in his hands, and so still that for a moment Bonhoeffer thought he *was* dead. But as he leaned under to shake him by the shoulder, the eyes snapped open in alarm and Klaus squirmed out of reach.

Bonhoeffer sat back on his heels. His father would have known what to do. He propped himself against the wall and began to talk. Just the sound of a voice might help, he thought—just that simple human connection. So he talked about his brother Klaus, hesitantly at first but then, as self-consciousness seemed absurd, with a growing ease that led him on to his other brothers and sisters, and their life together as children. There was no response from the huddled figure under the bed, but he seemed to be listening, and he had stopped flinching at the now occasional explosions outside.

Then Bonhoeffer found himself explaining how, as a boy, he had been fascinated with the idea of eternity. He and his twin sister, Sabine, had sometimes stayed awake at night, holding their breath until they were dizzy, trying to imagine what eternity felt like. He had been obsessed then by thoughts of death, not as something grievous or alien, but as a glorious thing, to be welcomed. He had seen himself, still young, dying a fine, devout death with his family and friends at his bedside, and had even composed little speeches for the occasion. But one day, a great disgust came over him. It was vanity, not piety, that inspired these thoughts. His infatuation with eternity was the devil's work, sinful self-love, and as he recognized it for what it was, he had been seized by such an overpowering fear of death that he had not been able to think of it again for many years. It was like an incurable illness. No one could cure him of it because his fear was simply a recognition of reality, of the unalterable.

He turned his head, and caught Klaus looking at him. Meiser, too, had rolled over on his side to face him. "It took a long time before I got it right," he said cheerfully. "Before I came to understand death for what it truly was."

The ward was quiet now, and the guns sounded far away.

"You know I'm not religious," said Meiser. "Klaus isn't either."

"Then don't think of death in that way. Think of it as an unavoidable fact. Think of life leading to it for a reason."

"A reason?" He smiled pityingly. "What reason?"

"To fulfill itself? To free itself? It couldn't be to *deny* itself. If death were anything other than fulfillment, life would be absurd. There'd be no sense or meaning or hope in anything, and we know that isn't so."

"We do?"

"Klaus does. If life has no meaning for him, why is he hiding under the bed?"

"Instinct. Being alive means trying to stay alive. Just being alive is enough."

"For a dog. But you and I can't live as men until we accept that we're going to die." He smiled at Klaus. "And death comes to fulfill us when God wills it—no matter where we hide."

Klaus turned on his back, gasping with pain.

"Leave him alone," said Meiser. "He doesn't want to be fulfilled."

Bonhoeffer struggled to his feet. There was no bridge between them, and the guilt fell on him. It was not their fault if the church proclaimed the living truth in ways that had no meaning and no comfort for them.

An hour or so before dawn, Holzendorf took Bonhoeffer back to his cell. He ached in every joint. With a curiously empty mind, he stood at the window watching the fires burn until daylight bleached them out. The morning air stank of smoke and destruction.

"It's remarkable how we think at such times about the people that we should not like to live without, and almost or entirely forget about ourselves," he wrote to his parents.

> It is only then that we feel how closely our own lives are bound up with other people's, and in fact how the center of our own lives is outside ourselves, and how little we are separate entities. The "as though it were a part of me" is perfectly true, as I have often felt after hearing that one of my colleagues or pupils had been killed. I think it is a literal fact of nature that human life extends far beyond our physical existence.

# 9

✠ ✠ ✠

ON SEPTEMBER 25, 1943, a warrant was sworn out for Bonhoeffer's arrest on a charge of antiwar activity. No date was set for the trial, but he was so elated by this sign of movement, and so confident of being acquitted, that he closed his mind to the Gestapo threat and took it for granted that release was a matter of course. "So it seems that the apparently purposeless waiting will soon be over," he wrote that day. "At the same time, being in custody for so long has brought me experiences that I shall never forget. . . . Much as I long to be out of here, I don't believe a single day has been wasted. What will come out of my time here it's still too early to say; but something will come of it."

Word had also reached him via the book code of new preparations for a *Putsch*. The resistance had regrouped during the summer around General Friedrich Olbricht and Colonel Count Claus von Stauffenberg of the Reserve Army in Berlin. Bonhoeffer knew of Stauffenberg through his friend Fabian von Schlabrendorff, a cousin of Maria's, who had himself planted a bomb on board the Führer's aircraft in March, and with great daring had managed to retrieve it after the detonator failed. As liaison officer between General Henning von Tresckow, Chief of Staff of the Central Army Group on the Eastern front, and the Abwehr conspirators, Schlabrendorff had helped establish the new center of resistance in the Reserve Army after Dohnanyi's arrest, and was now working closely with Olbricht and Stauffenberg in the race to bring down Hitler and make peace while there was still something left of Germany to save.

In the east, the Russians were massing for a new winter offensive after their victory at Stalingrad. In Africa, the war was over; a quarter of a million German troops had laid down their arms. To the south, Italy had surrendered to the Allies and was about to declare war on Germany. To the west, the Atlantic had been cleared of U-boats, and preparations were well advanced for an Allied landing in France. At home, the new Allied strategy of massed bombing around the clock was steadily reducing Germany's principal cities to rubble. It was shameful that the generals should have wavered so long that the world would now see the *Putsch* as a sordid maneuver to stave off total defeat rather than as a vindication of Germany's essential decency, but the humiliation would have to be borne as part of their national atonement. All that counted was a return to sanity.

Daily expecting the date to be set for his trial, Bonhoeffer contrived to keep busy through October. Maria and his parents were allowed to visit him, and he spent some time with Kurt Wergin, a lawyer friend of his brother Klaus, going over his defense. For most of the month, the Allied bombers concentrated on the Ruhr and other industrial targets, leaving Berlin more or less in peace, but he still found it hard to sleep. Besides fretting over the continuing delay, he was very worried about Dohnanyi. Hans had so far used his ill health with great skill against Roeder, whose methods had taken a still more vicious turn after Keitel's order to drop the political charges, but his condition was now really alarming the family. Not only was his own life at risk, but every man in the resistance still depended on his holding out, including Klaus, Rüdiger, and several of Bonhoeffer's dearest friends. But during the day, at least, Bonhoeffer could still generally manage to distract himself.

"I've again been doing a good deal of writing lately," he told his parents on October 13,

> and for the work I have set myself to do, the day is often too short,
> so that sometimes, comically enough, I even feel that I have "no

time" here for this or that less important matter! After breakfast in the morning (about 7 o'clock) I read some theology, and then I write till midday; in the afternoon I read, then comes a chapter from Delbruck's *World History,* some English grammar, about which I can still learn all kinds of things, and finally, as the mood takes me, I write or read again. Then in the evening I am tired enough to be glad to lie down, though that does not mean going to sleep at once.

He was also spending an hour or more with his friends in the sick bay every day, but he could hardly tell his parents that without telling Roeder as well. With half a year in Tegel behind him, he was now treated by guards and prisoners alike as a kind of auxiliary chaplain, and he took both pride and pleasure in his unofficial ministry.

Very few of the men were Christian in any meaningful sense. He shared their circumstances, but his reality was not theirs. They lived without God, and without thinking of God. The idea embarrassed them, as though it were unmanly or in any case irrelevant to life as they knew it. They were rarely disrespectful, but it was practical help they wanted, not spiritual guidance. The guards talked to him mainly about their personal or family problems, and the prisoners about the way they were treated and what was likely to become of them. Some of the younger ones, like Meiser's friend Klaus, were being tried and condemned to death without ever hearing a word of legal advice—an outrage so extreme that Bonhoeffer again seriously questioned how complete his view of life had been. Whenever he came across such a case, he would either get the family to help, or else ask his own lawyer, Kurt Wergin, to look into the matter.

Prison was unsettling many of his old assumptions. He could now see that what had always been real and immediate to him was academic and remote to most of those outside his own circle. In itself, this was no reflection on the value of his work, but it did begin to seem narrow —as though Christian scholarship had become detached from ordinary human experience, and was falling behind the rush of events.

Above all, he wished he could talk to Eberhard Bethge about it. Since their earliest days together at Finkenwalde, he had relied on Bethge, not just as a sounding board, but as a partner in his intellectual life. Each knew so well how the other's mind worked that in their interplay Bonhoeffer's thinking would always come into sharper focus. Bethge never allowed their friendship to weaken his independence. He was cautious in his opinions, and although this occasionally irritated Bonhoeffer in his more cavalier moments, he relied heavily on the other's judgment. Bethge was never carried away, as he sometimes was, by the broad sweep of an idea or the sudden promise of a new insight. When they talked, he had to advance his position step by step and test his reasoning link by link, but in collaboration rather than argument. Bonhoeffer missed this exchange. He was less sure of himself without it. And now that Bethge had wisely renounced his exempt status in the Abwehr, and allowed himself to be called into the army, there seemed no further need for elaborate caution. On learning he was stationed nearby at Spandau, Bonhoeffer was filled with such longing to reestablish contact that he made up his mind to work on Corporal Linke until he agreed to carry a letter out. He would have asked the faithful Knobloch to do it, except that he was already smuggling his correspondence with Maria back and forth, and anything more would have been to take advantage of his friendship.

The suspense of waiting for a trial date was now almost unbearable, and with the colder weather, he had again been crippled by rheumatism. On Reformation Day, October 31, his despondency showed through even the calculated calm of a letter to his parents:

> One wonders why Luther's action had to be followed by consequences that were the exact opposite of what he intended, and that darkened the last years of his life, so that he sometimes even doubted the value of his life's work. He wanted a real unity of the church and the West—that is, of the Christian peoples—and the consequence was the disintegration of the church and of Europe; he wanted the "freedom of the Christian man," and the consequence was indifference and licentiousness; he wanted the establishment of a genuine secular social order free from clerical privilege, and the result was insurrection, the Peasants' War, and soon afterward the gradual dissolution of all real cohesion and order in society. . . . As long as a hundred years ago, Kierkegaard said that today Luther would say the opposite of what he said then. I think he was right—with some reservations. . . .
>
> A short time ago my rheumatism was so bad that for a few

hours I couldn't get up from my chair without help, or even lift my hands to feed myself. But they at once gave me electrical treatment in the sick bay and it's much better now, though I haven't been entirely free of it since May. Is there anything I can do about it later?

For once, even a visit from Maria failed to lift his spirits. She looked tired, and a dreadful suspicion that she might be finding the strain too great to bear haunted him for days and nights on end.

A week later, on November 17, he cheered up a little when he saw his sister Ursula for the first time since his arrest. Assured and matter-of-fact as ever, she came well primed with family gossip and he pumped her greedily, not only about Maria and the family's impressions of her, but in particular about Renate, now six months pregnant, and Eberhard, who was home on leave. He was still more delighted when Ursel went on to say that Eberhard had applied for permission to see him.

That evening, he happened to mention to Engel and Knobloch in the sick bay how much this friendship meant to him, and what a blow it would be if the War Court refused to allow Bethge's visit.

"Why don't you ever write to him?" asked Knobloch casually, gathering in the cards. "Send him a letter. I'll take it out the next time you write to Fräulein von Wedemeyer. Or Holzendorf can do it. . . ."

"Dear Eberhard." It was hard to know where to start. Could everything still be the same?

> And now, after these long months without worship, penitence, and eucharist, and without the *consolatio fratrum*—once again be ᵤ, pastor as you have so often been in the past, and listen to me. . . . During this time I have been preserved from any serious spiritual trial. You are the only person who knows how often *accidie, tristitia,* with all its menacing consequences, has laid in wait for me; and I feared at the time that you must be worrying about me on that account. But I told myself from the beginning that I was not going to oblige either man or devil in any such way. . . .
>
> At first, I wondered a great deal whether it was really for the cause of Christ that I was causing you all such grief, but I soon put that out of my head as a temptation, as I became certain that the

duty had been laid on me to hold out in this boundary situation with all its problems; I became quite content to do this, and have remained so ever since.

I've reproached myself for not having finished my Ethics (parts of it have probably been confiscated), and it was some consolation to me that I had told you the essentials, and that even if you had forgotten it, it would probably emerge again indirectly somehow. Besides, my ideas were still incomplete. . . .

As soon as it was possible, apart from my daily work on the Bible (I've read through the Old Testament two and a half times and learned a great deal), I began to do some non-theological work. . . . I began to write the story of a contemporary middle-class family . . . but I haven't yet got much further than the beginning, mainly because the repeated false forecasts of my release have made it difficult for me to concentrate. But the work is giving me great pleasure. Only I wish I could talk it over with you every day; indeed, I miss that more than you think. I may often have originated our ideas, but the clarification of them was completely on your side. I only learned in conversation with you whether an idea was any good or not. . . .

To be on the safe side, I've made my will and given it to my lawyer. In it, I've left almost everything I have to you. But first Maria must be allowed to look for something that she would like in remembrance. If this should happen, please be very good to Maria, and if possible, write to her in my stead from time to time, just a few kind words, as you can do so well, and tell her gently that I asked you to. . . .

I'm now praying quite simply for freedom. There is such a thing as a false composure which is quite unchristian. As Christians we needn't be at all ashamed of some impatience, longing, opposition to what is unnatural, and our full share of desire for freedom, earthly happiness, and opportunity for effective work. I think we entirely agree about that.

Well, in spite of everything, or rather because of everything that we are now going through, each in his own way, we shall still be the same as before, shan't we?

He went on adding page after page to the letter for the next several days, ending it more than once, only to begin again as another thought struck him or out of the sheer joy it gave him to express his

138

feelings without constraint. It also helped him over his bewilderment when he asked about Meiser, whom he had not seen for some time, and was told offhandedly that he had been tried, convicted, and sentenced to death.

"My cell is being cleaned out for me," he told Bethge on November 20,

> and while it's being done, I can give the cleaner something to eat. One of them was sentenced to death the other day; it gave me a great shock. One sees a great deal in seven and a half months, particularly what heavy consequences may follow trivial acts of folly. I think a lengthy confinement is demoralizing in *every* way for most people. . . . Why does the Old Testament law never punish anyone by depriving him of his freedom?

That night, he once more finished the letter. Then he added a lengthy postscript, and the next morning started in again:

> Today is Remembrance Sunday. . . . Then comes Advent, with all its happy memories for us. Life in a prison cell may well be compared to Advent; one waits, hopes, and does this, that, or the other—things that are really of no consequence—the door is shut, and can be opened only *from the outside.* That idea is just as it occurs to me; don't suppose we go in very much for symbolism here! But I must tell you . . . I've found that following Luther's instructions to "make the sign of the cross" at our morning and evening prayers is in itself very helpful. There is something objective about it, and that is what is particularly badly needed here. Don't be alarmed; I shall not come out of here a *homo religiosus!* On the contrary, my fear and distrust of "religiosity" have become greater than ever here. The fact that the Israelites *never* uttered the name of God always makes me think, and I can understand it better as I go on.

He was no more willing to part with the letter on Monday.

> November 22nd.
> If there is anything that would help Renate in her present condition, and you need money for it, please simply take as much as you need without saying any more about it. . . . There is really no point in the money rotting in my account.

Just tell me how you get on with the soldiers. . . . Two or three times here I've given people a quite colossal dressing down for indulging in only the slightest rudeness, and they were so disconcerted that they have behaved very correctly since then. I thoroughly enjoy this sort of thing, but I know it's really an impossible over-sensitiveness that I can hardly get rid of. . . . It makes me furious to see quite defenseless people being unjustly shouted at and insulted. . . .

You see, I am always thinking of things that I want to talk over with you, and when I start again after such a long time, I find it difficult to stop. . . . We really must meet again soon. This really is the end. Love to you and Renate.

Your Dietrich

In fact it was not the end. Half an hour before lights out, the sirens sounded the alert and almost at once the guns began firing in the distance, sporadically at first, but then, as the other flak batteries joined in, mounting such a stupefying barrage that Bonhoeffer turned away from the window with his hands to his ears. The Propaganda Ministry had been boasting for weeks that the city's defenses were now impregnable, and he was prepared to believe it.

Having complained at length to Captain Maetz about being left in his cell last time, he had not finished dressing before the door was unlocked. When ready, he walked, unescorted, to the sick bay, where Bergmann and the other medical orderlies were already laying out their equipment. In the ward, those patients who could walk were sitting on the edge of their beds, wrapped in blankets. The rest lay silent, looking this way and that, as though trying to see through the walls. They were like blind men caught in a battle. They could hear death around them, but had no way of steeling themselves against it.

As he stood in the middle of the ward, nodding at those who met his eye and trying to decide whom to talk to first, the floor began to shake. It was not the momentary tremor of a nearby bomb—that he was used to—but continuous, more like an earthquake shock. And it grew in intensity. Bottles started to jingle together and instruments to rattle sympathetically against their trays, until a dozen tiny alarms were ringing in the ward. Then the noise came, a slow swelling thunder rolling toward them that Bonhoeffer felt in his legs and bowels. Somebody started to whimper, and he looked around distractedly to see who it was, but there was no time to move before this monstrous assault would engulf them. It was close enough now to pick out the jolting bursts before their shock waves merged into one all-destructive, encompassing roar.

Then it stopped. The floor was still again, the echoes died, and there was just the barrage, banging away at the sky. He let go of his breath and walked down the aisle, still smiling and nodding. He was not being brave. To be brave was to overcome fear, and he was not afraid. He thanked God for it, but it was no virtue. He felt guilty when the man who had whimpered hung his head. Bonhoeffer sat on the edge of his bed for a time, not talking, and then with others as the raid went on. For nearly two hours, the bombers droned back and forth, laying carpets of high explosive on the city, but none came so close again and the ward stayed quiet till the all-clear.

Dawn was late next morning. Unable to sleep, Bonhoeffer had kept watch at his window, still trying to grasp God's purpose in the course his life had taken. As the fires burned down, a suffocating blackness settled on the city, and it was slow to lift. After breakfast, a yellowish light at last broke through a vast umbrella of smoke and dust arching overhead from horizon to horizon, billow on dirty billow mounting up to stupendous heights.

Sick with worry, he sat down to write out another will, but then abandoned it in disgust. There was little point in arranging for the disposal of his possessions until he was sure that the British had not done so already, and that the would-be beneficiaries were still alive to receive them. He tried to read instead, forcing down his dismay as the morning wore on and no word came from his parents. When the guard raised his hopes by unlocking the door some time before the midday meal was due, only to announce the self-evident fact that his exercise period had been canceled, he was unforgivably curt.

Then came a miracle. In the early afternoon, the guard returned, still offended, and led him across the yard to Captain Maetz's outer office, where he found his parents waiting for him. After such a night, he had not for a moment expected a visit, but they had made up their minds to bring him the news in person. His trial had been set for December 17. In a great gust of elation, he paced his cell for hours after they had gone, making plans. If he was given a couple of months before his call-up, then he and Maria would get married right away. If not, if it was only two or three weeks, then he would wait till the end of the war rather than deny her a family wedding. He dashed off a loving note. Then he finished his marathon letter to Bethge, completed the will, sealed both in an envelope, and handed everything over to Knobloch that night when Holzendorf took him to the sick bay to listen to a concert on the radio. Engel joined them later—he was now a trusty —and they were just settling down to a mild celebration when the sirens went.

The raid was heavier than that of the night before. They knew from the news broadcasts that the industrial suburbs had taken the brunt of the attack, and while no one mentioned it, they were painfully conscious of the Borsig locomotive works next door. Again, the growling, elemental thunder of carpet bombing shook the prison for almost an hour, but only once did anything fall closer than two or three kilometers away, and the ward stayed calm. There were even a few jokes about it. Exhausted by a sleepless night and the excitement of the day, Bonhoeffer fell into bed around midnight and woke next morning to another swirling black sky.

That night the bombers came back again. The British were clearly bent on leveling Berlin, and although nothing worse than a few fire bombs dropped around the prison, Bonhoeffer knew from the guards that huge areas of the city were already a wilderness of rubble. No one knew how many Berliners were buried beneath it, and by the third day, tens of thousands of homeless were sheltering as best they could in the ruins. Whole districts were without water, gas, and electricity; public transport had all but broken down, and food was running short. And yet, paradoxically, morale had rarely been higher—in the prison as well as outside. Sharing in this unimaginable catastrophe, people had for once found more to unite than divide them.

Now that his trial was only three weeks off, Bonhoeffer contrived to spend as much time out of his cell as in it. He was determined to do all he could for the prisoners while he still had the chance, and each morning, he had a new list of grievances to discuss with Captain Maetz as they strolled around the yard. That Thursday his parents were due, but until Holzendorf came for him in the late afternoon, he had seriously doubted if they would get through. When he strode eagerly into the visitors' room to greet them, he found Maria and Eberhard there as well.

"So it really came off!" he wrote next morning, beginning another long letter to Bethge in the aftermath of the fourth consecutive nightly raid.

> Only for a moment, but that doesn't matter so much; even a few hours would be far too little, and when we are isolated here we can take in so much that even a few minutes gives us something to think about for a long time afterwards. It will be with me for a long time now—the memory of having the four people who are nearest and dearest to me with me for a brief moment. When I got back to my cell afterwards, I paced up and down for a whole hour, while my dinner stood there and got cold, so that at last I couldn't help laughing at myself when I found myself repeating over and over again, "That was really great!"

The one brake on his delight had been the news that Hans was now in the Charité Hospital. He had suffered a slight stroke when an incendiary bomb struck his cell in the Lehrter Strasse prison during the first night's raid. His speech and vision had been affected, though not seriously, and Dr. Sack had seized the chance to get him out of Roeder's hands. As his father was not unduly alarmed, Bonhoeffer allowed himself to be reassured, and even began to see some advantage in it to Hans if it meant he would be better treated.

Exhausted by four disturbed nights in a row, he put aside his letter to Bethge and went to bed early. But he had hardly stretched out, or so it seemed, before the sirens were going again. Half asleep, he struggled back into his clothes, and waited by the door as the barrage began. He was too used to it now to pay much attention, but a sudden premonition took him to the window just as the night dissolved in a harsh silver radiance that stripped the prison bare. Craning his neck, he saw the Christmas trees burning right overhead.

The guard saw their light when he opened the door. He turned and ran down the gallery. Bonhoeffer followed more sedately, but his heart was beating fast as he entered the ward. There was a brutal rising shriek, and in the split second left he opened his arms, transfixed. The windows burst in through the blackout screens in a storm of splintered wood and glass. The room rocked with a singing concussion that knocked him off his feet and set the lights dancing. Before the last of them shattered, he saw cracks open in the ceiling and flicker across it like lightning, raining lumps of plaster down in a blossoming cloud of dust. Picking himself up, he brushed at his shoulders mechanically, coughing and spluttering, with a frieze of terrified faces imprinted across his sight.

They had to have light. There were kerosene emergency lamps in the dispensary. He stumbled out of the ward, crunching glass and debris underfoot, and found Bergmann already handing them out to the orderlies. Grabbing one, he rounded up several patients blundering about in a daze and set them to pulling blankets off the beds to black out the gaping windows. But the bombs were shrieking down all around them now, and every time they got a few blankets secured, the blast would rip them away again. It was hopeless. Barely able to make himself heard in the din of explosions and screaming, he got those on their feet to help the rest take cover under the beds. So far as he could tell in the last evil light from the flares, nobody had suffered much worse than a few cuts and bruises.

He turned to go and help Bergmann, and as he reached the door, there was a flash so icy bright that even though his eyes closed involuntarily against the sudden blinding image of the ward, it still seemed to burn through the lids. A huge force flung him against the end of a bed, held him there, then let him fall back winded to the floor. Instinctively he curled up, crossing his wrists on his head to protect himself against the battering roar of the explosion and another avalanche of plaster. Though his ears buzzed from the blast, he could hear masonry falling outside, and between other splitting bomb bursts, a thin wailing of dread from the cells.

Choking on the dust, he waited until it seemed safe to move, then levered himself up on his hands and knees. The man under the bed was sobbing, "Oh God, oh God," over and over to himself. Bonhoeffer shook him by the shoulder. "It's all right," he said. "It's all right. It'll be over in a minute."

"Meanwhile we've had the expected large-scale raid on Borsig," he wrote next morning, resuming his letter to Bethge.

144

The shouting and screaming of the prisoners in their cells was terrible. We had no dead, only injured, and we had finished bandaging them by one o'clock. After that, I was able to drop off at once into a sound sleep. People here talk quite openly about how frightened they were. I don't quite know what to make of it, for fright is surely something to be ashamed of. . . . I wonder whether fright is not one of the *pudenda*, which ought to be concealed. I must think about it further.

The second bomb had struck the prison wall about twenty-five yards away and demolished it. As Captain Maetz explained when he came around next day on a tour of inspection, this meant no more outdoor exercise until it could be repaired, but Bonhoeffer was more concerned to find out what he meant to do to protect the prisoners in future raids. The commandant seemed surprised, but invited his suggestions, and Bonhoeffer worked till nightfall on a report recommending the construction of a hospital bunker and the digging of slit trenches. After the first peaceful night in almost a week, he sent it along to the captain's office next day, but the experience was not so easily exorcised.

> . . . a sick bay with no lights or windows [he wrote to Bethge]. Prisoners screaming for help, with no one but ourselves taking any notice of them; but we, too, could do very little to help in the darkness, and one has to be cautious about opening the cell doors of those with the heaviest sentences, for you never know whether they will hit you on the head with a chair leg and try to get away. . . . Nearly every window in the place has been blown out, and the men are sitting in their cells freezing. Although I had forgotten to open my windows when I left the cell, I found at night to my great surprise that they were undamaged. I'm very glad about that, although I'm terribly sorry for the others.

He came back to it again on the following day.

> Usually on Monday mornings the shouting and swearing in the corridors is at its fiercest, but after the experiences of last week even the loudest shouters and bullies have become quite subdued —a most obvious change. Now there's something I must tell you personally: the heavy air raids, especially the last one, when the

windows of the sick bay were blown out by the land mine, and bottles and medical supplies fell down from the cupboards and shelves, and I lay on the floor in the darkness with little hope of coming through the attack safely, led me back quite simply to prayer and the Bible. More about that later when I see you. In more than one respect, my time of imprisonment is being a very wholesome though drastic cure.

But for his restlessness, which now only the sternest self-discipline could overcome, and the distractions of the life he had made for himself in Tegel, which he half welcomed, half resented, he would have settled down to examine the nature of this "cure" more systematically. Knowing that Eberhard was so close and yet not being able to talk things over with him was particularly galling.

"My thoughts and feelings seem to be getting more and more like those in the Old Testament," he wrote, beginning a new letter to him on December 5.

It is only when one knows the unutterability of the name of God that one can utter the name of Jesus Christ; it is only when one loves life and the earth so much that without them everything seems to be over that one may believe in the resurrection and a new world; it is only when one submits to God's law that one may speak of grace; and it is only when God's wrath and vengeance are hanging as grim realities over the heads of one's enemies that something of what it means to love and forgive them can touch our hearts. In my opinion, it is not Christian to want to take our thoughts and feelings too quickly and too directly from the New Testament. We have already talked about this several times, and every day confirms my opinion. One cannot and must not speak the last word before the last but one. We live in the last but one and believe the last, don't we? Lutherans (so-called!) and pietists would shudder at the thought, but it is true all the same. . . . Why is it that in the Old Testament men tell lies vigorously and often to the glory of God (I've now collected the passages), kill, deceive, rob, divorce, and even fornicate (see the genealogy of Jesus), doubt, blaspheme, and curse, whereas in the New Testament there is nothing of all this? "An earlier stage" of religion? That is a very naïve way out; it is one and the same God.

146

It was less than two weeks to the day of the trial. As the days went by, a simmering excitement kept breaking through his guard, and he would have to remind himself sharply that behind Roeder stood Sonderegger, who had as good as said the Gestapo would never let him go. But the thought was intolerable. His whole being rejected it. After his acquittal, the army would take him. Even so, enough caution remained to temper his hopes, and he was profoundly grateful for it when Dr. Wergin called for what Bonhoeffer had assumed would be the final rehearsal of his defense. He seemed curiously vague about the trial, as though it were still far off rather than in a few days' time. Sick with apprehension, Bonhoeffer demanded to know why.

Wergin hesitated. "I saw Dr. Sack yesterday," he said, with a warning glance at Holzendorf, who was trying hard to efface himself in the corner of the visitors' room.

"He's a friend," said Bonhoeffer. "What did Sack say?"

"He's worried. The Gestapo are taking too close an interest. He's not sure it's wise for you to stand trial alone."

"But I have to." His bewilderment hurt. "Hans is ill."

"Exactly," said Wergin, avoiding his eye. "So it may be safer to wait."

Bonhoeffer tried to collect his thoughts. "Until he's better, you mean."

Wergin nodded. "And I do see Sack's point."

"Yes, but does he see *mine?* After eight months in here, I'm in no mood for legal niceties. I want this over and done with."

"Of course. We all do. If there was nothing more to this business than the charge against you, we'd have you out in a week. But there *is* more." He glanced again at Holzendorf.

"I'm sorry." Bonhoeffer rubbed his forehead. "I don't mean to be critical. But if I got through the interrogation, I can get through the trial. I'm not afraid of Roeder."

"No one thinks so. You've handled him beautifully. But you know what's behind it. The charge isn't political, but their motives are. Once you're in court, there's no telling how it may go."

"I'm willing to risk that."

Wergin sighed. "There's Dohnanyi to consider, Dietrich—among others. What if you jeopardize *his* defense?"

"I haven't so far."

"I know that. So does Sack. But it's not *you* they'll be trying —it's the Abwehr."

Bonhoeffer stared at him miserably. "I was only on the fringe of it. Roeder knows that. I've pleaded ignorance all along."

"That just makes it easier for him. If he can get at Dohnanyi through you, and Dohnanyi isn't there to head him off . . . I'm sorry, Dietrich. I know how hard this must be."

"Never mind that. Sack doesn't think I'm up to it, and you agree."

"I think you and Dohnanyi together could beat Roeder handsomely. So does Sack. But knowing how much is at stake"—he let this sink in—"I'm inclined to think he's right. You may be risking more than a few more weeks of detention if you go to trial alone. There are too many imponderables."

Bonhoeffer took off his glasses. Wergin was right, of course. He should have recognized what Hans's illness meant from the start. Having come so far and endured so much, it would be absurd to run an unnecessary risk just to gratify a sentimental yearning for Christmas at home. Half Europe would be yearning for the same thing, and in worse situations than his.

"What does Sack want us to do?"

"Nothing," said Wergin. "He doesn't want us to press for trial on the seventeenth. We should be ready—in case Roeder insists on it— but Sack has openly assumed that Dohnanyi's illness means a postponement, and so far no one has contradicted him." He leaned forward, hiding his face from Holzendorf. "He also seems to think there's a good chance of getting Roeder off the case altogether, if he's given more time."

"Good," said Bonhoeffer mechanically. "Good."

"What's more, I'm told that events may soon overtake the whole affair."

It was this hint of an imminent *Putsch* that helped him over the next few days. He began another letter to Bethge cheerfully enough on December 15, but there was no hiding his desolation for long.

> I imagine the two of us sitting together as we used to in the
> old days after supper . . . discussing the day's events. And then at

last I should have to start telling you that, in spite of everything that I've written so far, things here are revolting, that my grim experiences often pursue me into the night and that I can shake them off only by reciting one hymn after another, and that I'm apt to wake up with a sigh rather than a hymn of praise to God. It's possible to get used to physical hardships, and to live for months out of the body, so to speak—almost too much so—but one doesn't get used to the psychological strain; on the contrary, I have the feeling that everything I see and hear is putting years on me, and I often find the world nauseating and burdensome. . . .

I often wonder who I really am—the man who goes on squirming under these ghastly experiences of wretchedness that cries to heaven, or the man who scourges himself and pretends to others (and even to himself) that he is placid, cheerful, composed, and in control of himself, and allows people to admire him for it. . . . In short I know less than ever about myself, and I'm no longer attaching any importance to it. I've had more than enough psychology, and I'm less and less inclined to analyze the state of my soul. . . . There is something more at stake than self-knowledge.

Then I should discuss with you whether you think that this trial, which has associated me with the Abwehr (I hardly think that has remained a secret), may prevent me from taking up my ministry again later on. . . . Please think it over and give me your candid opinion.

Finally, I couldn't talk about anything else with you but Maria. We've now been engaged almost a year, and so far we haven't spent even an hour alone together. Isn't that mad! We have to talk and write about things which in the end aren't the most important for the two of us; every month, we sit upright for an hour, side by side, as on a school bench, and then we're torn apart again. . . . Isn't that an impossible situation? And she bears up with such great self-control. It's only occasionally that something else comes through, as on the last visit, when I told her that even Christmas wasn't certain yet. She sighed and said, "Oh, it's too *long* for me." I know full well that she won't leave me in the lurch; it isn't "too long" for her to hold out, but for her heart, and that's much more important. The only thing that I keep saying to myself is that it has all come about without our doing and so will probably make sense one day. As long as I don't do her wrong by asking too much of her. . . .

I sometimes feel as though my life were more or less over, and as if all I had to do now were to finish my Ethics. But you know, when I feel like this, there comes over me a longing (unlike any other that I experience) to have a child and not to vanish without a trace—an Old Testament rather than a New Testament wish, I suppose.

He finished the letter next day while waiting for Wergin to come with the final word on his trial. He knew what it would be, but went on hoping against all reason. Some intransigent streak in his nature simply rejected every circumstance and argument he could muster for continuing in a situation that so outraged every instinct, and he was by no means certain which was the higher rationality. When Wergin arrived at last, he confirmed the postponement but was otherwise so vague that Bonhoeffer cut him short and went back to his cell. He stayed there all day on December 17, but managed to write, if not a cheerful, then at least a calm Christmas letter to his parents.

An alert that evening got him going again. The saturation bombing had been followed by a series of hit-and-run raids that caused relatively little damage but great disruption, for no one could be sure that each was not the prelude to another massed attack. To counter these new tactics, the radio warning system had been extended to include the estimated numbers and likely targets of all enemy aircraft over Germany at any given moment. In this way, the civil defense authorities were better able to judge when and where to send people underground and thus avoid unnecessary losses in production—but at some cost to civilian morale, for the Propaganda Ministry had previously been at pains to disguise the scope and weight of Allied attacks. After listening to the broadcast for almost an hour while the night's offensive built up, Bonhoeffer went to bed in a grim but more positive mood. *Putsch* or no *Putsch*, the war could not last much longer.

18 December 1943

Dear Eberhard,

You, too, must at least have a letter for Christmas. I'm no longer expecting to be released. As far as I could see, I should have been released on 17 December, but the jurists wanted to take the safe course, and now I shall probably be kept here for weeks if not months. The past weeks have been more of a strain than anything before that. There's no changing it, only it's more difficult to adapt oneself to something that one thinks could have been prevented than to something inevitable. . . .

A few times in my life I've come to know what homesickness means. There is nothing more painful, and during these months in prison I've sometimes been terribly homesick.

. . . on the Christian aspect of the matter, there are some lines that say

> ". . . that we remember what we would forget,
> that this poor earth is not our home."

That is indeed something essential, but it must come last of all. I believe that we ought so to love and trust God in our *lives,* and in all good things that he sends us, that when the time comes (but not before) we may go to him with love, trust and joy. But, to put it plainly, for a man in his wife's arms to be hankering after the other world is, in mild terms, a piece of bad taste, and not God's will. . . . God will see to it that the man who finds Him in his earthly happiness and thanks Him for it does not lack reminder that earthly things are transient, that it is good for him to attune his heart to what is eternal, and that sooner or later there will be times when he can say in all sincerity, "I wish I were home."

It was not the kind of Christmas letter he had meant to write. He held it over and continued next day in a less painfully personal vein. But that, too, went wrong, and he was on the point of scrapping it when Maria came to see him on the twenty-second. She had brought his Christmas present—the watch her father had been wearing when he was killed—and the news that Bethge had at last received permission to visit him again. It was hard to say which pleased him more. When she had gone, he read through the letter again and decided to finish it anyway.

> I do want to convey to you somehow tomorrow that my attitude toward my case is unquestionably one of faith, and I feel that it has become too much a matter of calculation and foresight. I'm not so much concerned about the rather artless question

whether I shall be home for Christmas or not; I think I could willingly renounce that if I could do so "in faith," knowing that it was inevitable. I can (I hope) bear all things "in faith," even my condemnation, and even the other consequences I fear, but to be anxiously looking ahead wears one down. Don't worry about me if something worse happens. Others of the brethren have already been through that. But faithless vacillation, endless deliberation without action, refusal to take any risks—that's a real danger. I must be able to know for certain that I am in God's hands, not in men's. Then everything becomes easy, even the severest privation. . . .

Now I want to assure you that I haven't for a moment regretted coming back in 1939—nor any of the consequences either. I knew quite well what I was doing, and I acted with a clear conscience. I've no wish to cross out of my life anything that has happened since, either to me personally . . . or as regards events in general. And I regard my being kept here . . . as being involved in Germany's fate, as I was resolved to be. I don't look back on the past and accept the present reproachfully, but I don't want the machinations of men to make me waver.

# 10

✛ ✛ ✛

HE SOMEHOW KEPT his life in order. He still rose at six to have a cold wash-up before prayers, and after sharing his breakfast with the trusty who cleaned his cell, he would emerge as usual, smiling and unruffled, to join the other privileged prisoners in the yard, as he had done every day since the wall was repaired. There he would chat for half an hour with his new Italian friend, Professor Gaetano Latmiral, who had been lodged in Tegel since Italy's declaration of war on Germany, and then return to his cell to read and to write letters until the midday meal and his afternoon rheumatism treatments in the sick bay. He was also seeing more of the prison chaplains, Pastors Dannenbaum and Poelchau, and in addition to practicing his Italian in the mornings, aired his English whenever he could with the British officer in the next cell. But it was all pretense. He felt totally disengaged, even from Knobloch and Engel, whom he still saw most evenings when the air raid alerts sent him back to the sick bay. He would talk, play chess or cards, analyze their handwriting to keep them amused, listen to the radio, and try to comfort those who needed it, but his life hung motionless. He could neither work nor concentrate well enough to read for long, not even the Bible. And though certain that none of this showed, he was by no means sure how long he could keep it up.

In mid-January, Rüdiger Schleicher came to see him. Knowing he would report back in full to his parents—Rüdiger was incapable of

153

lying, even diplomatically—Bonhoeffer made a special effort to seem in full command, and was rewarded with news of both Dohnanyi and Bethge. Officially, no one was allowed to visit Hans except Christine and the children, but Bonhoeffer already knew from the book code that Dr. Sauerbruch and his staff at the Charité Hospital had turned a blind eye to a steady stream of callers, including Rüdiger, Klaus Bonhoeffer, his Abwehr friends Justus Delbrück and Baron Guttenberg, and other leading members of the resistance, like Friedrich Justus Perels and Otto John. Among them, they had brought Hans up to date with the progress of the conspiracy under Stauffenberg's leadership, and as it now seemed from Rüdiger's hints, persuaded him that his best course was to follow Sack's advice—to let matters lie and avoid going to trial.

Encouraged by Rüdiger's optimism, Bonhoeffer then learned that Eberhard had been sent to the Italian front, and resigned himself to the thought that only censored letters could now pass between them. But Knobloch that evening had other ideas. They could use his house, or Holzendorf's, as an accommodation address, and one or the other of them would carry the letters in and out as before.

Bonhoeffer sent one to both Renate and Eberhard on January 23.

> It's a strange feeling [he wrote] to see a man whose life has in one way or another been so intimately bound up with one's own for years going out to meet an unknown future about which one can do virtually nothing. . . . As long as we ourselves are trying to help shape someone else's destiny, we are never quite free of the question whether what we're doing is really for the other person's benefit—at least in any matter of great importance. But when all possibility of cooperating in anything is suddenly cut off, then behind any anxiety about him there is the consciousness that his life has now been placed wholly in better and stronger hands. For you, and for us, the greatest task during the coming weeks, and perhaps months, may be to entrust each other to those hands. . . . Whatever weaknesses, miscalculations, and guilt there is in what precedes the facts, God is in the facts themselves. If we survive during these coming weeks or months, we shall be able to see quite clearly that all has turned out for the best. The idea that we could have avoided many of life's difficulties if we had taken things more cautiously is too foolish to be entertained for a mo-

ment. . . . To renounce a full life and its real joys in order to avoid pain is neither Christian nor human.

He was coming alive again. Knowing that Hans agreed with the tactic of delay had done something to reconcile him to it, and Wergin had also helped when, on his first visit in two weeks, he reported that Sack's long campaign to get Roeder off the case was within days of success. But Roeder still had a card to play. On January 22, in Dr. Sauerbruch's absence, he had arrived at the Charité with an army doctor and ambulance and moved Hans to the prison hospital at Buch, with the obvious intention of having him declared fit to stand trial. When Bonhoeffer heard the news a few days later, he was torn between concern for Hans, now back in the hands of his enemies, and his own guilty relief at the thought of a new date being set.

"Am I wrong, Max?" he asked Engel that night, as another nuisance raid straggled noisily over the city.

"To want to get out of here?"

"To pin so much on it."

"Well, it's out of your hands, isn't it?"

"You mean we should just trust in God," he said slyly.

"Why not? He's doing *me* a favor. I'm getting out tomorrow."

"Getting *out?*"

Engel laughed. "Don't look so pleased for me, Dietrich. It's just for the day. I'm due for a medical."

"I'm sorry. It sounded so final."

"Don't be sorry. I take it as a compliment." A particularly loud explosion jangled the medicine bottles, and they both ducked involuntarily.

"Are they getting ready to try you?"

"They want to see if I'm fit enough."

"I'm sorry to hear that." Bonhoeffer pulled a face. "You look a lot better these days."

"Don't worry. I feel a relapse coming on." He winked at Bergmann. "You'd be amazed what a little insulin can do."

"Oh, Max." He, too, looked at Bergmann. "Isn't that dangerous?"

"Not half as dangerous as a firing squad," said Engel cheerfully, and Bergmann shrugged. "The pallor—you should see the pallor.

Enough to melt an MP's heart. Last time, they were so impressed I talked them into taking me home for a last goodbye to my grieving family." He smiled. "I think I'll try that again."

Bonhoeffer was not reassured. "You be careful. I'll pray you don't get the same escort."

"That's it. Use your influence. With any luck, I'll get caught in a raid and have to spend the night there."

It was the last time Bonhoeffer saw him. The following evening, January 27, Engel was killed in the city by a direct hit.

The raid was the first of a new series of mass attacks. "I must talk to you sometime about prayer in time of trouble," he wrote to Bethge two days later.

> It's a difficult matter, and yet our misgivings about it may not be good. Psalm 50 says quite clearly, "Call upon me in the day of trouble; I will deliver you, and you shall glorify me." The whole history of the children of Israel consists of such cries for help. And I must say that the last two nights have made me face this problem again in a quite elementary way. While the bombs are falling like that all round the building, I cannot help thinking of God, His judgment, His hand stretched out, and His anger not turned away, and of my own unpreparedness. . . .
>
> I'm sorry to say that I suffered a severe loss the night before last. The man who was, to my mind, by far the most intelligent and attractive in the place was killed in the city by a direct hit. I should certainly have put you in touch with him later, and we already had plans for the future. . . . I was very much distressed by his death.

On January 30, the British bombers returned for the second night running to attack the Borsig locomotive works. As Bonhoeffer lay on the floor of the sick bay, trying to pray but continually distracted by the shriek of bombs planing in over the prison roof, he heard one that he somehow knew was falling short and in the moment before it hit, thought of Engel. Once again, the night burst in on the ward in a hellish uproar, and once again, choking on the dust and fumes, Bonhoeffer labored to his feet as soon as the plaster stopped falling to see to those around him. He heard later that the bomb had exploded by the guardroom, killing Holzendorf.

"Those who had been bombed out came to me the next morning for a bit of comfort," he wrote to Bethge.

> But I'm afraid I'm bad at comforting. I can listen all right, but I can hardly ever find anything to say. But perhaps the way one asks about some things and not about others helps to suggest what really matters; and it seems to me more important actually to share someone's distress than to use smooth words about it. . . . I sometimes think that real comfort must break in just as unexpectedly as the distress.

And, unexpectedly, comfort broke in on his thirty-eighth birthday, February 4, beginning with a bunch of spring flowers from the trusties who worked in the prison greenhouse. There was white bread for breakfast, spread with honey, and letters from his parents and Renate. Then he settled down to write again to Bethge, upon whom he now depended utterly for the freedom of being able to speak his mind without causing pain or offense. He began by recalling some of the eight previous birthdays they had celebrated together, and he had just written, "I think that we, who have become more exacting than most people with regard to friendship, have more difficulty in finding what we miss and are looking for," when Knobloch came to fetch him for an hour with Maria. And for once, he returned to his cell afterward not feeling hollowed out by her departure.

> When I was in the middle of this letter, I was called downstairs, where the first thing with which Maria greeted me was the happy news: "Renate has a little boy, and his name is Dietrich!" Everything went well; it took an hour and a half, and Mother acted as midwife, with Christel's help! What a surprise, and what a delight! I'm happier than I can tell you. . . . So now you have a son, and all your thoughts will turn towards the future, full of hope. . . . I should be insincere if I didn't say that I'm immensely pleased and proud that you've named your first-born after me. The fact that his birthday comes one day before mine means, no doubt, that he will keep his independence vis-à-vis his namesake uncle, and will always be a little ahead of him. . . . Thank

you both very much for deciding to do this, and I think the others will be pleased about it, too.

Yesterday, when so many people were showing such kindly concern for me, I completely forgot my own birthday, as my delight over little Dietrich's birthday put it right out of my head. . . . The day couldn't possibly have brought me any greater joy. It wasn't till I was going to sleep that I realized that you've pushed our family on by one generation—3 February has created great-grandparents, grandparents, great-uncles and great-aunts, and young uncles and aunts! That's a fine achievement of yours; you've promoted me to the third generation! . . . My head and my heart are so overflowing with good and happy thoughts that I simply can't put them all on paper. But you know how I think about you and try to share your joy with you. . . . Now I hope I shall soon follow your example. Goodbye, keep well; God keep and bless you both, and the little boy.

Faithfully, your Dietrich

He had started work again with the renewed prospect of going to trial, and the birth of young Dietrich helped him over the empty aftermath of Max Engel's death, but otherwise the news was very black. The Gestapo were closing in. From his latest consignment of books, he learned that Helmut von Moltke had been arrested, along with the whole resistance group centered around Anna Solf, widow of the former ambassador to Japan. Closer to home, and bearing more immediately on his own situation, Josef Müller had managed to detach his case from Dohnanyi's and it was to be tried separately, but Reich Security Head Office had already threatened to rearrest him if he was acquitted.

Bonhoeffer had a sudden vision of Sonderegger, shutting out the light, and he was not at all reassured when Wergin came a day or two later to tell him that Hans had been declared fit enough to stand trial in eight to ten days.

"Dear Eberhard," he wrote on February 12,

I've been in bed for a few days with slight influenza, but I'm up again; that's a good thing because in about a week's time I shall need to have all my wits about me. Till then I shall go on reading

158

and writing as much as I can; who knows when I shall have another chance? . . .

Are you having a taste of spring yet? Here the winter is just beginning. In my imagination I live a good deal in nature, in the glades near Friedrichsbrunn, or on the slopes from which one can look beyond Treseburg to the Brocken. I lie on my back in the grass, watch the clouds sailing in the breeze across the blue sky, and listen to the rustling of the woods.

In quiet moments, he often retraced in his mind the long country walks he had taken as a boy with his father, who was a keen naturalist —much keener than his son, whose interest in those days of food shortages during and after the Great War had been more practical than aesthetic. He had made his father teach him how to distinguish the edible wild fruits and fungi from the poisonous ones, and had remained a great berry and mushroom collector ever since.

It's remarkable how greatly these memories of my childhood affect one's whole outlook; it would seem to me impossible and unnatural for us to have lived either up in the mountains or by the sea. It is the hills of central Germany, the Harz, the Thuringian forest, the Weserberge, that to me represent nature, that belong to me and have fashioned me.

Then two things happened that effectively settled the issue of whether or not he should go to trial, although he did not see this at once. The first was the departure of Manfred Roeder. Having revived the case by virtually abducting Hans von Dohnanyi from the Charité, he left Berlin to take up a new post as Luftwaffe judge in the Balkans just as Dohnanyi was pronounced fit to be tried. Thanks to Sack, Roeder's successor was Otto Kutzner, a lawyer known to Dohnanyi since his days at the Ministry of Justice. Coming fresh to the investigation, Kutzner was in no particular hurry. He had none of Roeder's political zeal—his first visit to Buch had convinced him that Dohnanyi was in no state even to be questioned, let alone tried—and he needed time to study the documents in the case. When Sack pressed him for his best estimate of how soon he might be ready, Kutzner thought it would be Easter at least.

On the heels of this development came the second and finally conclusive reason for letting things rest as they were. The Führer dismissed Admiral Canaris.

After the arrest of Helmut von Moltke, two of his friends, Erich and Elizabeth Vermehren, had been ordered back to Germany from Turkey, where Canaris had sent them to assist the Abwehr's chief intelligence officer in Ankara. Fearing for their lives, they had instead defected to the British, and thereby provided Reich Security Head Office with the pretext they had hoped to find in the investigation of Dohnanyi, Bonhoeffer, and Müller. Canaris was relieved of his post for recruiting unreliable agents, and on February 18, Hitler signed a decree authorizing Reichsführer Himmler to take over the Abwehr and establish a unified secret intelligence service. Now shorn of the admiral's protection, what was left of the resistance group within the Abwehr finally collapsed, and with it, much of the defense based on references to higher authority upon which Dohnanyi and Bonhoeffer depended.

"I'm sorry to have to tell you that I'm not likely to be out of here before Easter," he wrote to Bethge on February 21, after Wergin had brought him the news.

> As long as Hans is ill, no changes can be taken in hand. I can't completely rid myself of the feeling that something has been too contrived and imagined and that the simplest things haven't happened yet. I'm fully convinced of the best will of all concerned, but one all too easily takes a conversation, a fancy, a hope for an action. I keep noting with amazement that in fact nothing has happened for six months, although a great deal of time and even sleep has been spent in considerations and discussion; the only thing that would have happened of itself, namely the clarification before Christmas, has been prevented.

Meanwhile, the air raids continued with mounting savagery, the Americans continuing by day the British assaults by night. On March 6, a large force of Flying Fortresses bombed the city for the first time, and returned to the attack two days later as though to prove that nothing could now save Germany from systematic, around-the-clock destruction. On March 9, while Bonhoeffer was in the sick bay writing to Eberhard, they came again.

The radio is just announcing the approach of strong contingents of aircraft [he wrote]. We could see a good deal of the last two daylight raids on Berlin; there were fairly large formations flying through a cloudless sky and leaving vapor trails behind them, and at times there was plenty of flak. The alert was on for two and a half hours yesterday, longer than at night. Today the sky is overcast. I'm very glad that Renate is in Sakrow; also thinking of you. The siren is just going, so I must break off and write more later.

It lasted two hours. "Bombs were dropped in all parts of the city," says the radio. In my time here, I've been trying to observe how far people believe in anything "supernatural." Three ideas seem to be widespread, each being partly expressed in some superstitious practice: (1) Time after time, one hears "Keep your fingers crossed," some sort of power being associated with the accompanying thought: people do not want to feel alone in times of danger, but to be sure of some invisible presence. (2) "Touch wood" is the exclamation every evening when the question is discussed "whether they will come tonight or not"; this seems to be a recollection of the wrath of God on the hubris of man, a metaphysical, and not merely a moral, reason for humility. (3) "If it's got your number on, you'll get it," and therefore everyone may as well stay where he is. On a Christian interpretation, these three points might be regarded as a recollection of intercession and community, of God's wrath and grace, and of divine guidance. To the last-mentioned, we might add another remark that is very often heard here: "Who knows what good may come of it?" . . .

This is my second Passiontide here. When people suggest in their letters that I'm "suffering" here, I reject the thought. It seems to me a profanation. These things mustn't be dramatized. I doubt very much whether I'm "suffering" any more than you, or most people, are suffering today. Of course, a great deal here is horrible, but where isn't it? Perhaps we've made too much of this question of suffering, and been too solemn about it. I've sometimes been surprised that the Roman Catholics take so little notice of that kind of thing. Is it because they are stronger than we are? Perhaps they know better from their own history what suffering and martyrdom really are, and are silent about petty inconveniences and obstacles. . . . I must admit candidly that I sometimes feel almost ashamed of how often we've talked about our own sufferings. No, suffering must be something quite different, and have a quite different dimension, from what I've so far experienced.

He now accepted that only a successful *Putsch* could release him from Tegel. He was also increasingly preoccupied with the idea that his imprisonment was meant to serve a particular purpose, and he was struck again by the effect he seemed to have on those around him, particularly during the raids. "Isn't it characteristic of a man, in contrast to an immature person, that his center of gravity is always where he actually is?" he wrote to Bethge on March 19.

> There is a wholeness about the fully grown man which enables him to face an existing situation squarely. He may have his longings, but he keeps them out of sight, and somehow masters them; and the more he has to overcome in order to live fully in the present, the more he will have the respect and confidence of his fellows, especially the younger ones, who are still on the road that he has already traveled. . . . I think that even in this place we ought to live as if we had no wishes and no future, and just be our true selves. It's remarkable then how others come to rely on us, confide in us, and let us talk to them. . . .
>
> Once again I'm having weeks when I don't read the Bible much; I never know quite what to do about it. I have no feeling of obligation about it, and I know too that after some time I shall plunge into it again voraciously. May one accept this as an entirely "natural" mental process? I'm almost inclined to think so. . . . I'm curious as to how the future will lead us on, whether perhaps we shall be together again in our work—which I should very much like —or whether we shall have to be content with what has been. They really were quite wonderful years.

Despite the brave words about living fully in the present, only his belief that it held a hidden meaning kept him from retreating into the past. Everything he valued belonged to the life that had ended in suspense a year ago, and the dread that he could never resume it, that he had stood still while the people he loved had moved on and Germany had been destroyed, tormented him at times unbearably. Certainly, the future held no comfort. The raids were getting worse, and the odds against surviving them had lengthened. He was in Tegel for a reason—a *present* reason.

162

The British mounted another all-out attack on the night of March 24. When it became clear that this time they were concentrating on the eastern side of the city, Knobloch grew suddenly restless, and suggested to Bonhoeffer that they go up and watch from the roof. As they left the sick bay, Bonhoeffer told Bergmann where they were going, and to their surprise, he said he would join them.

With the whole arena of the sky overhead and the smoke-tainted wind in their faces, the appalling spectacle of Berlin collapsing into fire and ruin could be mourned for its own sake. Downstairs in the dark, they were victims, each oppressed by the threat to his own life. Up here, they were witnesses to tragedy on such an epic scale that it dwarfed their fears, the air rocking under the weight of bombs and aircraft engines, as bursting bubbles of light flickered continuously over the burning ground.

"Can you look at that and believe in God?" asked Bergmann in his halting voice.

Bonhoeffer knew him now as the gentlest of men. "Would you have us believe in ourselves instead?"

"But how could a loving father let this happen?"

"Ask yourself, how could we let this happen to a loving father?"

Bergmann looked up as another cluster of Christmas trees flared in the sky. "Then that's all we can expect from heaven?"

"He didn't give us life to live it for us. If we choose to live without Him, we can't expect to summon Him in the last extremity to do *our* will. But He *is* merciful."

Bergmann looked out over the city. "Then why doesn't He save us from ourselves?"

"He did. On the cross."

A huge flash lit the belly of a cloud, and seconds later, the sound of the explosion rolled over all the others.

"Big one," said Knobloch uneasily.

"I would like to believe," said Bergmann.

"If you look for Him, He'll find you."

"But if you look for Him in that, there's nothing to make you believe."

"If He made us believe, we'd be puppets."

Bergmann turned to go, but Bonhoeffer touched his arm.

"You're asking me, how is God possible?—and that's already a godless question. God is given us. He revealed Himself in His son as the final reality. If you think of Him existing out there in some mysterious way beyond our understanding, then the more we learn, the farther we push Him away. The true God stands at the center. We're not asked to believe beyond reason, because faith reveals Him in everything."

Another formation of bombers labored overhead, and they watched in silence until the salvos began to fall. "Not to me," said Bergmann. "Not in that."

Bonhoeffer weighed the answers he could make, and let it be. "Sometimes we try to understand more than we can," he said. "These are not the last things."

The dissatisfaction which had plagued him for months had crystallized. What he had at first taken for doubt and trampled on was in fact new ground to explore. In his year at Tegel, he had stepped from one life into another that he had always sensed running parallel to his but had never experienced directly. All he knew and felt had to be reexpressed in terms of this other life or remain unintelligible to Bergmann and the rest. And as the idea took hold, it suddenly linked up with the certainty that his imprisonment had a purpose.

The two came together in a shock of recognition and excitement that he doused at once in professional caution. The body of Christian thought was not to be transfigured by a single arresting insight. Mistrusting his nature, he waited some days before starting to think it through. More than ever he needed Bethge, who was the only one who might be able to tell him if his hardening conviction that God had prepared him for this work was truly a recognition of God's will or just another self-serving delusion. Once or twice he hinted at what was on his mind to Pastor Poelchau and Professor Latmiral, but they seemed hardly to grasp what he was saying, and he knew it was unreasonable in the circumstances to expect them to. What he needed was a sign. The naïveté of the idea amused him.

But then he received one. From the next delivery of books he learned that the Gestapo had carried out its threat to rearrest Josef Müller, whose trial in March had resulted in acquittal. And at a meeting with Wergin a few days later, he was given a final message from Sack that he should no longer expect any change in his situation. It was

164

indeed a sign. There was a purpose to being in prison, and now time to fulfill it. Released at last from self-questioning, he settled to work with a calmness of mind that filled him with thankfulness.

"You've no need to worry about me at all," he wrote to Bethge on April 30,

as I'm getting on uncommonly well—you would be surprised, if you came to see me. People here keep on telling me (as you can see, I feel very flattered by it) that I'm "radiating so much peace around me," and that I'm "always so cheerful"—so that the feelings I sometimes have to the contrary must, I suppose, rest on an illusion (not that I really believe that at all!).

You would be surprised, and perhaps even worried, by my theological thoughts and the conclusions that they lead to. . . . What is bothering me incessantly is the question what Christianity really is, or indeed who Christ really is, for us today. The time when people could be told everything by means of words, whether theological or pious, is over, and so is the time of inwardness and conscience—and that means the time of religion in general. We are moving toward a completely religionless time; people as they are now simply cannot be religious anymore. . . . If therefore man becomes radically religionless—and I think that that is already more or less the case . . . —what does that mean for "Christianity"? . . . If our final judgment must be that the western form of Christianity, too, was only a preliminary stage to a complete absence of religion, what kind of situation emerges for us, for the church? How can Christ become the Lord of the religionless as well? Are there religionless Christians? . . .

How do we speak of God—without religion, i.e., without the temporally conditioned presuppositions of metaphysics, inwardness, and so on? How do we speak (or perhaps we cannot now even "speak" as we used to) in a "secular" way about "God"? . . . In what way are we the *ekklesia*, those who are called forth, not regarding ourselves from a religious point of view as specially favored, but rather as belonging wholly to the world? In that case, Christ is no longer an object of religion but something quite different, really the lord of the world. But what does that mean? . . .

Religious people speak of God when human knowledge (perhaps simply because they are too lazy to think) has come to an end, or when human resources fail—in fact, it is always the *deus ex machina* that they bring on to the scene, either for the apparent solution of insoluble problems, or as strength in human failure— always, that is to say, exploiting human weakness or human boundaries. Of necessity, that can go on only until people can by their own strength push these boundaries somewhat further out, so that God becomes superfluous as a *deus ex machina.* I've come to be doubtful of talking about any human boundaries (is even death, which people now hardly fear, and is sin, which they now hardly understand, still a genuine boundary today?). It always seems to me that we are trying anxiously in this way to reserve some space for God; I should like to speak of God not on the boundaries but at the center, not in weakness but in strength; and therefore not in death and guilt but in man's life and goodness. As to the boundaries, it seems to me better to be silent and leave the insoluble unsolved. . . . God is beyond in the midst of our life. The church stands not at the boundaries where human powers give out, but in the middle of the village.

# 11

✠ ✠ ✠

IT WAS A MATTER OF SUBSTANCE, not form. He was not simply concerned with a method of presenting Christ to nonreligious people; he was examining the way in which Christ was lord in their world.

"We are once again being driven right back to the beginnings of our understanding," he wrote in a sermon for young Dietrich's baptism.

> Reconciliation and redemption, regeneration and the Holy Spirit, love of our enemies, cross and resurrection, life in Christ and Christian discipleship—all these things are so difficult and so remote that we hardly venture any more to speak of them. In the traditional words and acts we suspect that there may be something quite new and revolutionary, though we cannot as yet grasp or express it. That is our own fault. Our church, which has been fighting in these years only for its self-preservation, as though that were an end in itself, is incapable of taking the word of reconciliation and redemption to mankind and the world. . . . Our being Christians today will be limited to two things: prayer and righteous action among men. All Christian thinking, speaking, and organizing must be born anew out of this prayer and action. . . . It is not for us to prophesy the day (though the day will come) when men will once more be called so to utter the word of God that the world will be changed and renewed by it. It will be a new language,

perhaps quite non-religious, but liberating and redeeming—as was Jesus' language; it will shock people and yet overcome them by its power; it will be the language of a new righteousness and truth, proclaiming God's peace with men and the coming of his kingdom. . . . Till then the Christian cause will be a silent and hidden affair, but there will be those who pray and do right and wait for God's own time.

The baptism would take place as soon as Bethge arrived home on leave from the Italian front. Bonhoeffer was still writing to him every few days, but Holzendorf's death had broken the incoming connection and he had heard nothing in reply for some time, which was doubly disturbing because he knew from the afternoon radio bulletins that the Allies were pounding the German lines in preparation for a new offensive. Despite this, however, and despite his constant concern for Maria and the family as the demolition of Berlin from the air went on, he faced each day with an underlying serenity he had seldom felt since leaving Finkenwalde. He was not even ruffled when the War Court recalled him on May 4 to be questioned by Kutzner for the first time.

Accompanied by Wergin, he spent that afternoon and the next going quietly over the ground he had already covered with Roeder, but nothing seemed to hinge on it. With Sonderegger absent and only a scattering of observers in court, he had the impression that Kutzner was merely going through the motions of continuing the investigation. "The result has been quite satisfactory," he wrote to Bethge on the seventh. "But as the question of the date is still unresolved, I am really losing interest in my case; I often quite forget it for weeks on end."

He had shelved his Ethics and abandoned the novel. The past was gone and the mold smashed. A new setting for life would have to be pieced together when the time came, and in an effort to free himself from the wreck, he tried his hand at verse after a visit from Maria:

O happiness beloved, and pain beloved in heaviness,
you went from me.
What shall I call you? Anguish, life, blessedness,
part of myself, my heart—the past?
The door was slammed;
I hear your steps depart and slowly die away.
What now remains for me—torment, delight, desire?

This only do I know: that with you, all has gone.
But do you feel how I now grasp at you
and so clutch hold of you
that it must hurt you?
How I so rend you
that your blood gushes out,
simply to be sure that you are near me,
a life in earthly form, complete?
Do you divine my terrible desire
for my own suffering,
my eager wish to see my own blood flow,
only that all may not go under,
lost in the past?

It came easily, which made him suspicious of its quality, but he pushed on while the impulse lasted, through page after page of angry lament.

Evil comes into my eye and soul;
what I see, I hate;
I hate what moves me;
all that lives, I hate, all that is lovely,
all that would recompense me for my loss.
I want my life; I claim my own life back again,
my past, yourself . . .

His vehemence surprised him. By giving rein to his feelings, he had hoped to master them, but all he had done was distance himself a little. Finishing the poem on a more submissive note, he put it away and said nothing about it to anyone.

On May 16, Linke brought him a letter from Bethge posted in Italy eleven days earlier, and a message from Renate saying that she expected him to arrive in Berlin that very morning, the first anniversary of their wedding day. Bonhoeffer's relief was immense; the Wehrmacht bulletin of the fifteenth had announced the start of the Allied offensive. "For once, I was almost ready to talk about 'providence' and 'an answer to prayer,' " he said in a note to welcome his friend home, and he was readier still when he heard two days later that Bethge and Renate would be coming to see him in place of his parents on the nineteenth.

They arrived from Sakrow just as another air raid alert was sounding. Bonhoeffer was afraid that Maetz would cancel the visit because of it, but "providence" remained on his side. Leaving Linke in charge, the captain stayed in his newly built bunker until the all-clear went ninety minutes later, and only then ventured out to end a reunion that would otherwise have lasted an hour. Even so, it was not nearly long enough. While Bonhoeffer's circumstances had hardly changed in the five months since their last meeting, Bethge had been lucky to get out of Italy alive. Most of the talk was about his experiences there, with Bonhoeffer insisting on every detail of the merciless bombing and strafing his unit had suffered before the Allied advance began.

> I must say to begin with [he wrote next morning] that every-thing you told me has moved me so much that I couldn't stop thinking of it all day yesterday. . . . I'm infinitely grateful to you for it, for it was a confirmation of our friendship, and moreover reawakens the spirit for life and for battle, and makes it stubborn, clear, and hard. But I can't completely escape the feeling that there is a tension in you which you can't get rid of completely, and so I would like to help you as a brother. Accept it as it is intended. If a man loves, he wants to live, to live above all, and hates everything that represents a threat to his life. You hate the recollection of the last weeks, you hate the blue sky, because it reminds you of them, you hate the planes. You want to live with Renate and be happy, and you have a right to that. And indeed you must live, for the sake of Renate and the little—and also the big—Dietrich.

He had sworn off self-analysis, but listening to Bethge had aroused a passionate longing to stand in his place and spare him these trials. It was almost as though he resented Bethge undergoing the experience without him, and in chiding himself for it, Bonhoeffer realized that a good part of his frustration in the past year had probably been due to this. He felt so much better equipped to shoulder the burdens of those he loved than they were themselves—though whether this was from vanity or strength he was not sure. But instead of being there to take them upon himself, he had himself become a burden.

"Perhaps you were surprised that yesterday's letter was on the one hand intended to say something to *you,* but on the other was itself so helpless," he wrote on May 21, during another raid.

170

But isn't this what happens? One tries to help and is oneself the person most in need of help. . . .

The photographs that you brought I have put in front of me, and I'm looking at the baby who is being baptized today. . . . I think he's lovely, and if he is to take after me at all physically, I only hope he will have my freedom from toothache and headache, and my leg muscles and sensitive palate (though the latter is not an unmixed blessing). For other things he can do better elsewhere. . . .

I'm still completely under the influence of your story. If only we could experience all this together!

The one thing he was determined they should share was the new ground he was breaking in his work. As they had barely touched on it during the visit, he urged Bethge to apply for permission to come again, and at the same time, set about using his influence with Maetz to see if something could be arranged unofficially. But a week passed by with no word, and then Maetz went on leave.

"At first I was a bit disconcerted, and perhaps even saddened, not to have a letter from anyone this Whitsuntide," he wrote on the twenty-ninth.

Then I told myself that it was perhaps a good sign, as it meant that no one was worrying about me. It's a strange human characteristic that we like other people to be anxious about us—at least just a trifle anxious.

Weizsäcker's book *The World-View of Physics* is still keeping me very busy. It has again brought home to me quite clearly how wrong it is to use God as a stop-gap for the incompleteness of our knowledge. If in fact the frontiers of knowledge are being pushed further and further back (and that is bound to be the case), then God is being pushed back with them, and is therefore continually in retreat. We are to find God in what we know, not in what we don't know; God wants us to realize His presence, not in unsolved problems but in those that are solved. That is true of the relationship between God and scientific knowledge, but it is also true of the wider human problems of death, suffering, and guilt. It is now possible to find, even for these questions, human answers that take no account whatever of God. In point of fact, people deal with these problems without God (it has always been so), and it is simply not true to say that only Christianity has the answers to them. As to the idea of "solving" problems, it may be that the Christian answers are just as unconvincing—or convincing—as any others. Here again, God is no stopgap; he must be recognized at the center of life, not when we are at the end of our resources; it is His will to be recognized in life, and not only when death comes; in health and vigor, and not only in suffering; in our activities, and not only in sin. The ground for this lies in the revelation of God in Jesus Christ. He is the center of life, and He certainly didn't "come" to answer our unsolved problems.

On the thirtieth, there was again no word from anyone, and Bethge's leave was running out. "I'm sitting alone upstairs," Bonhoeffer wrote, resuming the letter.

> Everything is quiet in the building; a few birds are still singing outside, and I can even hear the cuckoo in the distance. I find these long, warm evenings, which I'm now living through here for the second time, rather trying. . . . When you've deliberately suppressed every desire for so long, it may have one or two bad results: either it burns you up inside, or it all gets so bottled up that one day there is a terrific explosion. . . . Perhaps you will say that one oughtn't to suppress one's desires, and I expect you would be right. But look, this evening, for example, I couldn't dare to give really full rein to my imagination and picture myself and Maria at your house, sitting in the garden by the water, and talking together into the night, etc., etc. That is simply self-torture, and gives one physical pain. So I take refuge in thinking, in writing letters, in delighting in your good fortune, and curb my desires as a measure of self-protection. . . . Just now I happened to hear Solveig's Song on the radio in the sick-bay. It quite got hold of me. To wait loyally a whole lifetime—that is to triumph over the hostility of space, i.e., separation, and over time, i.e. the past.

In Italy, the Wehrmacht was in full retreat, and the thought of Bethge going off to meet chaos and death without him, without even seeing him first, was almost more than he could bear. He said as much one evening to Linke, who was getting to know Bethge quite well from delivering Bonhoeffer's letters, but Linke just shrugged with the offhanded air he always assumed when people told him their problems.

It was not indifference; Bonhoeffer had caught him out in too many kindnesses for that. It was just that, if he wasn't sure he could help, he would pretend not to hear rather than raise false hopes. But on the morning of June 4, as Bonhoeffer was strolling in the yard with his English neighbor, Richard Jones, Knobloch came to take him to the sergeant major's office, where he found Linke on the telephone, arguing with the operator. As he waited to be connected, Linke covered the mouthpiece with his hand and observed confidentially that there would be no one in the prison that afternoon above the rank of sergeant.

"Herr Bethge?" he said, before he could explain how this concerned Bonhoeffer. "Corporal Linke. No, no—nothing's wrong. I have a call for you. Hold on, please." Covering the mouthpiece again, he held out the phone to Bonhoeffer. "Don't identify yourself. Get him here at three, and we'll see what we can do."

Bethge arrived from Sakrow promptly at three, and what Linke did was lock him in for an hour with Bonhoeffer so that they could talk privately. In spite of himself, the chance to talk about Maria and the family with no one else listening was too tempting for Bonhoeffer to spend much time discussing his work. He was just beginning to tell Bethge about it when Linke interrupted apologetically to say that the night duty officer was expected any minute. As usual, neither lingered over their parting. "God be with you, Eberhard," said Bonhoeffer. "It can't possibly last much longer."

It was June 4, 1944. Forty-eight hours later, the Allies landed in Normandy. He sent a note to Bethge, just to feel he was sharing the day with him, and suddenly full of confidence, picked up their interrupted conversation in a long letter on June 8, the day Bethge left for the front.

> You now ask so many important questions on the subjects that have been occupying me lately that I should be happy if I could answer them myself. But it's all very much in the early stages; and as usual I'm being led on more by an instinctive feeling for questions that will arise later than by any conclusions that I've already reached about them. . . .
>
> Man has learned to deal with himself in all questions of importance without recourse to the "working hypothesis" called "God." In questions of science, art, and ethics this has become an under-

stood thing at which one now hardly dares to tilt. But for the last hundred years or so it has also become evident that everything gets along without "God"—and, in fact, just as well as before. . . .

Christian apologetic has taken the most varied forms of opposition to this self-assurance. Efforts are made to prove to a world thus come of age that it cannot live without the tutelage of "God." Even though there has been surrender on all secular problems, there still remain the so-called "ultimate questions"—death, guilt —to which only "God" can give an answer, and because of which we need God and the church and the pastor. So we live, in some degree, on these so-called ultimate questions of humanity. But what if one day they no longer exist as such, if they, too, can be answered "without God"?

Of course, we now have the secularized offshoots of Christian theology, namely existentialist philosophy and psychotherapists, who demonstrate to secure, contented, and happy mankind that it is really unhappy and desperate and simply unwilling to admit that it is in a predicament about which it knows nothing, and from which only they can rescue it. . . . They set themselves to drive people to inward despair and then the game is in their hands. That is secularized methodism. And whom does it touch? A small number of intellectuals, of degenerates, of people who regard themselves as the most important thing in the world, and who therefore like to busy themselves with themselves. The ordinary man, who spends his everyday life at work and with his family, and of course with all kinds of diversions, is not affected. He has neither the time nor the inclination to concern himself with his existential despair, or to regard his perhaps modest share of happiness as a trial, a trouble, or a calamity.

The attack by Christian apologetic on the adulthood of the world I consider to be in the first place pointless, in the second place ignoble, and in the third place unchristian. Pointless, because it seems to me like an attempt to put a grown-up man back into adolescence, i.e., to make him dependent on things on which he is, in fact, no longer dependent, and thrusting him into problems that are, in fact, no longer problems to him. Ignoble, because it amounts to an attempt to exploit man's weakness for purposes that are alien to him and to which he has not freely assented. Unchristian, because it confuses Christ with one particular stage in man's religiousness, i.e., with a human law.

Until he knew for certain that Bethge had rejoined his unit, Bonhoeffer was reluctant to send any further letters of this sort to his old field post number. In three weeks, the Wehrmacht had pulled back from Rome to the Tuscan hills, harried all the way by Allied aircraft, and there was no telling where Bethge might find himself eventually. Bonhoeffer soon heard he had broken his journey at Munich to find out if the Abwehr office there, with its radio links to the front, had any news of his unit, and on June 21 received a letter from him, dated five days earlier, saying that he still had no idea of its whereabouts, but was leaving for Italy in any case.

That same day, Berlin suffered the heaviest daylight attack of the war. "For several hours my room was so dark with the cloud of smoke that hung over the city that I almost switched the light on," he wrote to Bethge, acknowledging his letter.

> I've just heard that all is well at home. I expect that Renate is continuing to stay in Sakrow with the little boy; she could do any shopping that she needed in Potsdam. Nothing has happened there yet. I'm not pleased that my parents are coming back at just this moment. They, too, ought to go to Sakrow for the time being. . . . I'm waiting daily for news of your whereabouts and am always with you in my thoughts.

While he waited, he wrote some more poetry. After talking to Bethge, he had sent him his first attempt at verse to see what he would make of it. In parting with Renate and his son, Bethge shared the feelings he had tried to express. The medium fascinated Bonhoeffer, with its strictness of form and freedom of imagery.

> Sorrow and joy,
> striking suddenly on our startled senses,
> seem, at the first approach, all but impossible
> of just distinction one from the other,
> even as frost and heat at the first keen contact
> burn us alike.

He completed a long, ambitious poem called "Night Voices in Tegel," in which he sought to catch the terror and wretchedness of prison life, and several shorter ones, including:

Who am I? They often tell me
I would step from my cell's confinement
calmly, cheerfully, firmly,
like a squire from his country house. . . .
Who am I? They also tell me
I would bear the days of misfortune
equably, smilingly, proudly,
like one accustomed to win.
Am I then really all that other men tell of?
Or am I only what I know of myself,
restless and longing and sick, like a bird in a cage . . .
weary and empty at praying, at thinking, at making,
faint, and ready to say farewell to it all? . . .
Who am I? They mock me, these lonely questions of mine.
Whoever I am, thou knowest, O God, I am thine.

Maria came to see him on June 27. He pined for her visits, and was always trying to picture their life together, but Bethge was still the only one he could speak to without having first to calculate what effect his words might have. He was in Verona, she said, still looking for his unit.

Back in his cell, Bonhoeffer decided to write to him anyway—the illusion of contact was better than nothing.

Unlike the other oriental religions, the faith of the Old Testament isn't a religion of redemption. It's true that Christianity has always been regarded as a religion of redemption. But isn't this a cardinal error, which separates Christ from the Old Testament and interprets him on the lines of the myths about redemption? . . . Israel is delivered out of Egypt so that it may live before God as God's people on earth. The redemption myths try unhistorically to find an eternity after death. . . .

The decisive factor is said to be that in Christianity the hope of resurrection is proclaimed, and that that means the emergence of a genuine religion of redemption, the main emphasis now being on the far side of the boundary drawn by death. But it seems to me that this is just where the mistake and the danger lie. Redemption now means redemption from cares, distress, fears, and longings, from sin and death, in a better world beyond the grave. But is this really the essential character of the proclamation of Christ in the gospels and by Paul? I should say it is not. The difference between the Christian hope of resurrection and the mythological hope is that the former sends a man back to his life on earth in a wholly new way which is even more sharply defined than it is in the Old Testament. The Christian, unlike the devotees of the redemption myths, has no last line of escape available from earthly tasks and difficulties into the eternal, but, like Christ himself ("My God, why hast thou forsaken me?"), he must drink the earthly cup to the dregs, and only in his doing so is the crucified and risen Lord with him, and he crucified and risen with Christ. The world must not be prematurely written off; in this the Old and New Testaments are one. Redemption myths arise from human boundary-experiences, but Christ takes hold of a man at the center of his life.

You see how my thoughts are constantly revolving round the same theme.

Three days later, the question of redemption took a more concrete turn. Bonhoeffer was settling down to work after his morning exercise when the normal background murmur of the cell block was suddenly shattered by an uproar of shouting, banging, and clattering boots. No alert had sounded, so he went to the door, now rarely kept locked, to see what was happening and found the guard about to turn the key. It was a prison inspection, he explained apologetically. Some officers had arrived from Berlin Command. Satisfied, Bonhoeffer went back to his books. An inspection usually meant that the prisoners would get their full day's rations for a change. But then the tramp of a marching party approached down the gallery and halted outside his cell. When he heard Sergeant Major Weber order the guard to open up, he ground out his cigarette with a stab of disquiet. Unless there was some unpleasant duty to perform, Weber generally stayed out of his way.

"What's this, Sergeant Major?" he asked, looking past him. "A firing squad?"

"You're to see the commandant immediately," said Weber, clearly wishing it were. "Will you come with us, please?"

It was unmistakably a request, and Bonhoeffer folded his arms. "I left Captain Maetz not fifteen minutes ago," he said. "I don't understand."

"Not the captain." Weber worked his jaw. "General von Hase."

"Uncle *Paul?*" He was not so taken aback that he failed to enjoy Weber's flinch. *"Here?"*

"In the captain's office."

Weber stood aside, ready to follow him through the door, but Bonhoeffer was in no hurry. "Well, that *is* a surprise. How very nice of him." He stood up to put on his coat. "But you can dismiss your men, Herr Weber. I'm not going across under guard."

The sergeant major hesitated, and Bonhoeffer sat down again. Weber then went out to send them away, and when Bonhoeffer was ready, followed him across the yard several paces behind. It was a small victory, but a useful one. As they walked through the administration building, the guards stared as though they had never seen him before, and when the duty corporal outside Maetz's office saw them coming, he knocked over his chair in his eagerness to open the door and announce him.

"My dear Dietrich," said his uncle, and Maetz and another officer stood aside. Coming forward to meet him, he took Bonhoeffer's hand between his and drew him in, kicking the door shut. "It's good to see you. My God, how long has it been?" He held him at arm's length and then, evidently satisfied with what he saw, clapped him affectionately on the shoulder and turned to the others. "Come and meet Colonel Maas. Commandant of the Lehrter Strasse prison."

Bonhoeffer shook hands with him gladly. "I know what you did for Hans while he was there. I'm very grateful."

"It was little enough, I'm afraid," said Maas. "Poor Dohnanyi had a bad time."

"Yes, he did," agreed Hase. "But let's not get into that now. Accounts will be settled in full. Very soon." He held Bonhoeffer's eye for a moment. "It's my nephew I want to hear about—and that's a pleasure I've denied myself too long. Sit down, Dietrich. Let me look at you. I'm to give your mother a full report."

"You've seen her?" he asked, not yet daring to believe what his uncle seemed to be saying.

"I spoke to her yesterday on the telephone. I'm afraid events this past year have conspired to keep me away from the family. You know how it is. With so much going on, it didn't seem wise—to stray far from my office, I mean."

Bonhoeffer glanced at Maetz, who was not completely stupid. "I quite understand," he said. "And I'm sure she does, too. The raids must keep you very busy."

"Among other things. But I think we can expect a radical change in a matter of days."

Bonhoeffer blinked at him foolishly. "Thank God," he said.

Maetz coughed to draw their attention. "You mean the Führer's V-weapons, sir?" he said brightly. "You think they'll relieve the pressure?"

"What?" said Hase, his eyes still on Bonhoeffer.

"The V-weapons, sir. You think the bombers will concentrate on the launching sites now?"

"Why, yes. Naturally. I must say you're looking well, Dietrich. A little pale, perhaps. What do you think, Maetz?"

"A little, sir, yes." He laughed uncomfortably.

"Why's that? How much time does he spend outside?"

"Half an hour a day, sir. As laid down in the regulations."

"Well, damn the regulations. See that he gets more sun."

"I will, sir."

"And send someone out to my driver, will you? I've got something in the car that should bring a bit of color back."

"Very good, sir."

Thinking he would leave the room, Hase beckoned Bonhoeffer closer, but Maetz shouted his order from the doorway and returned at once.

"It won't take a moment, sir."

Hase grunted. "Got any decent glasses? I'll be damned if I'll drink champagne out of a chipped cup."

Maetz stared, then pulled himself together. "I have some in my quarters, sir—if you'll excuse me." This time he did go outside, but only just beyond the door, to speak to one of the clerks, and judging him still to be in earshot, Hase sat back with a good-humored shrug.

"*Champagne,* Uncle?" said Bonhoeffer. "How subversive."

"All the more appropriate, then. God knows, we've waited long enough for this. You've done well, Dietrich. It's been hard on you."

"I wonder. When I'm tempted to think so, I try to imagine how many there are who'd be glad to change places."

"Well, don't include *me* among them." His uncle offered him a cigarette and took one himself. "You get that from your mother. There's a self-denying streak in the Hases that I'm glad to say I escaped." He accepted a light from Colonel Maas, nodding his thanks. "Privation is bad for the character."

"Privation? I've books to read, and time to think. No responsibilities to speak of. No decisions to make. And now there's champagne in the morning," he added, as a guard appeared at the door and handed the bottle to Maetz.

"Not so loud," said his uncle. "If this gets about, Maetz'll have the whole Wehrmacht clamoring to get in—from the High Command downward."

Bonhoeffer laughed. "If I could be sure of that, Uncle, I can think of one or two I'd willingly give up my place to make room for. And I wouldn't even think of it as self-denial."

Hase chuckled, with his eye on Maetz, who smiled rather tentatively. "Then I think we might let him do it, don't you, Maetz?" he said. "Is that cold enough, d'you think?"

"I think so, sir." He held out the bottle for him to feel, but Hase shook his head.

"I rely on your judgment, Maetz. Just as you seem to rely on the judgment of *your* subordinates."

"Yes, sir," he said, sensing trouble. "Although not as confidently as I would wish, I'm afraid. The caliber of men available for prison duty these days leaves a lot to be desired. Except for a few reliable NCOs, the rest need constant supervision."

"When have they not? But it may help if you let them know that any breach of the regulations, particularly in their treatment of prisoners, will mean an automatic posting to the Eastern front."

180

Despite his easy tone, there was an edge on it, and Maetz stiffened to attention. "Yes, sir."

"Good man." Hase nodded, and allowed him to fetch a tray of glasses from the corporal standing in the doorway. "I'll have no bullying or corruption in *my* command. And I'm confident my officers are as anxious as I am to stamp it out."

To mark the completion of a year in prison, Bonhoeffer had sent his uncle a report on conditions at Tegel. Now he smiled at him gratefully, but the general seemed not to notice. It was a professional matter.

"You can count on me, sir." Maetz set down the tray on the desk and stood back.

"I do, Maetz. I do." Hase began to unbutton his tunic. "I'm also counting on you to open that bottle without squirting it all over the office. You know, the last time I drank champagne with you, Dietrich, was at your father's seventy-fifth birthday party?"

With great good humor, he then told several family anecdotes that Bonhoeffer had never heard before about his Hase ancestors, and these reminded him of others, and once launched on his reminiscences, he kept his nephew royally entertained for the rest of the morning and well into the afternoon. Three times, he had Maetz send out to the car for further bottles of *Sekt,* and he was on the point of calling for yet another when he caught Maas's eye and consulted his watch.

"Good God, is that the time? I'd better get back before the High Command thinks it can run the war without me."

Maetz laughed immoderately, having accounted for the best part of a bottle himself, and the general's smile faded. He started to do up his buttons.

"I'd intended to have a look around while I was here, Maetz, but I'm afraid I'll have to forgo the pleasure."

"You'd have found everything in order, sir," said Maetz, struggling to his feet. "You have my assurance on that. With your permission, I'll stand the men down, and send someone to fetch your driver."

"One moment." Hase looked at Bonhoeffer thoughtfully. "I wouldn't want them to think it had been for nothing. If Colonel Maas doesn't mind, perhaps you'll take him around while I have a last word with my nephew."

The idea of his prisoner having a private talk with his commanding officer sobered Maetz instantly, but under Hase's eye and with Maas at his elbow, he dared not hesitate. "I'd be honored, sir," he said unhappily.

"Poor Maetz," said Bonhoeffer, as the door closed behind them. "He's not a bad fellow. A bit overanxious, perhaps."

Hase drained the bottle into his glass. "Then his next batch of prisoners will really give him something to worry about."

Bonhoeffer leaned forward eagerly. "When is it to be, Uncle Paul?"

"The next time Stauffenberg is ordered to a conference with the Führer—preferably with Himmler or Göring in attendance."

"A bomb, then?"

"He's got two more of those British things with the silent fuses. And I hope he has better luck with them than young Schlabrendorff did last year."

"You mean Stauffenberg will plant it himself?"

"He must. No one else can get near. They've made him Fromm's chief of staff with the Reserve Army. Besides, who'd suspect a man with only three fingers?" Hase held up his left hand with the thumb and index finger folded down. "It'll be in his briefcase."

Bonhoeffer shivered involuntarily. "Will he be able to save himself?"

"He must. It'll probably be at Berchtesgaden. Once he's carried it in, he'll make some excuse to leave the room—a phone call or something. Then as soon as Olbricht gets the signal, he'll order out the Reserve Army to secure the capital. The planning's a bit sketchy, to my mind, but it should work."

"It *must* work. There's no more time."

"It will. Don't worry." His uncle downed the last of the champagne. "Too bad we couldn't have pulled it off before the landings in France. We might have patched up an armistice in the West and thrown everything we've got against the Bolsheviks—that's Rommel's idea. But you're right—it's too late for that now."

Bonhoeffer looked at him in amazement. "It was never possible.

182

If anything, there's a better chance of making a separate peace with the Russians than with the West. It's ridiculous. What does Hassell say? Surely Beck and Goerdeler never agreed to such a thing?"

"I think they'd agree with anybody at this point if it helped to get things moving. Revolution is a damned untidy business. But once we're rid of this gang, they'll sort themselves out."

Bonhoeffer was suddenly full of misgivings. They had always accepted that it would be fatal to Germany if a new government took over without a definite program to act on. Indecision was the surest prescription for total defeat.

"What about the Gestapo?"

"Too close for comfort. Himmler obviously knows. Not about Stauffenberg, I don't think, but he's got most of the other names. If I were Goerdeler or one of his Socialist friends, I think I'd make myself scarce. It's the usual cat and mouse. Only this time, the mouse must spring first."

Bonhoeffer shook his head. "Can you imagine what Hans would say? After planning everything so carefully? Does he know about this?"

"I doubt it. Hans is very ill."

The last tremor of elation died away. "What have they done to him now?"

"He's in quarantine at Potsdam. They say it's scarlet fever and diphtherial paralysis."

"Will Father be able to see him?"

"I'm trying to arrange that. The one good thing about it is that Kutzner has asked Keitel to suspend the case indefinitely. Hans will probably stay in a sanatorium till the end of the war—and that shouldn't be long." Hase patted his arm sympathetically. "Cheer up, Dietrich. It won't happen exactly the way you both wanted—these things never do—but don't worry. We'll have you out of here soon."

"Thank you, Uncle—but that's really not the point."

Thinking about it later, he was afraid he had sounded churlish. But he had not risked his liberty and everything dear to him just so that a pack of vacillating generals could rearrange the war to suit their convenience. On the other hand, his uncle was obviously right in thinking that the last chance had come to get rid of the Führer, and it was probably idle to question the motives of the only people who could do it. It would be up to Beck and Goerdeler to assert their authority when the time came and to see that the true aims of the resistance were carried out.

He started another letter to Bethge to distract himself.

> I will try to go on with the theological reflections that I broke off not long since. I had been saying that God is being increasingly pushed out of a world that has come of age, out of the spheres of our knowledge and life, and that, since Kant, He has been relegated to a realm beyond the world of experience. Theology has on the one hand resisted this development with apologetics, and has taken up arms—in vain—against Darwinism, etc. On the other hand, it has accommodated itself to the development by restricting God to the so-called ultimate questions as a *deus ex machina;* that means He becomes the answer to life's problems, and the solution of its needs and conflicts. So if anyone has no such difficulties, or if he refuses to go into these things, to allow others to pity him, then either he cannot be open to God; or else he must be shown that he is, in fact, deeply involved in such problems, needs, and conflicts, without admitting or knowing it. . . .
>
> You see, that is the attitude that I am contending against. When Jesus blessed sinners, they were really sinners, but Jesus did not make everyone a sinner first. . . . Jesus claims for Himself and the Kingdom of God the whole of human life in all its manifestations.

A week passed. It was suffocatingly hot in Berlin. The raids continued day and night; no serious reverses were reported from any of the fronts, and the propaganda ministry continued to blanket the press and radio with glowing accounts of the V-weapons, whose destructive power would soon decide the war.

"I will try to squeeze a few thoughts out of my sweating brain and let you have them," he wrote to Bethge on the eighth.

> Who knows—it may be that it won't have to be too often now, and that we shall see each other sooner than we expect. . . .
>
> The displacement of God from the world, and from the public part of human life, led to the attempt to keep His place secure at least in the sphere of the "personal," the "inner," and "the private." And as every man still has a private sphere somewhere, that

is where he was thought to be the most vulnerable. The secrets known to a man's valet—that is, to put it crudely, the range of his intimate life, from prayer to his sexual life—have become the hunting ground of modern pastoral workers. In that way they resemble (though with quite different intentions) the dirtiest gutter journalists. . . . In the one case it's social, financial, or political blackmail and in the other, religious blackmail. Forgive me, but I can't put it more mildly.

From the sociological point of view this is a revolution from below, a revolt of inferiority. . . . Anything clothed, veiled, pure, and chaste is presumed to be deceitful, disguised and impure; people here simply show their own impurity. A basic anti-social attitude of mistrust and suspicion is the revolt of inferiority.

Regarded theologically, the error is twofold. First, it is thought that a man can be addressed as a sinner only after his weaknesses and meannesses have been spied out. Secondly, it is thought that a man's essential nature consists of his inmost and most intimate background; that is defined as his "inner life," and it is precisely in those secret human places that God is to have his domain! . . .

I therefore want to start from the premise that God shouldn't be smuggled into some last secret place, but that we should frankly recognize that the world, and people, have come of age, that we shouldn't run man down in his worldliness, but confront him with God at his strongest point, that we should give up all our clerical tricks, and not regard psychotherapy and existentialist philosophy as God's pioneers. . . .

9 July. That's all. I think that we shall meet again soon. . . .

But another week went by, and the fortunes of the resistance slipped backward. As his uncle had feared, the Gestapo arrested Julius Leber, leader of the Socialist group, who was to be a member of the new government, and Adolf Reichwein, one of Leber's closest associates. Spending most of his days now within earshot of the sick-bay radio, Bonhoeffer was very conscious of an ugly race in the dark between the Gestapo and the conspirators, a race he could do nothing to influence and whose progress he could only guess at.

"There's not much to report about myself," he wrote to Bethge on the sixteenth.

I'm only gradually working my way to the non-religious interpretation of biblical concepts; the job is too big for me to finish just yet.

On the historical side: There is one great development that leads to the world's autonomy. In theology one sees it first in Lord Herbert of Cherbury, who maintains that reason is sufficient for religious knowledge. In ethics, it appears in Montaigne and Bodin, with their substitution of rules of life for the commandments. In politics, Machiavelli detaches politics from morality in general and founds the doctrine of "reasons of state." Later, and very differently from Machiavelli, but tending like him towards the autonomy of human society, comes Grotius, setting up his natural law as international law, which is valid *etsi deus non daretur*, "even if there were no God." The philosophers provide the finishing touches: on the one hand we have the deism of Descartes, who holds that the world is a mechanism, running by itself with no interference from God; and on the other hand the pantheism of Spinoza, who says that God is nature. In the last resort, Kant is a deist, and Fichte and Hegel are pantheists. Everywhere the thinking is directed toward the autonomy of man and the world. . . .

And we cannot be honest unless we recognize that we have to live in the world *etsi deus non daretur*. But this is just what we do recognize—before God. God himself compels us to recognize it. So our coming of age leads us to a true recognition of our situation before God. God would have us know that we must live as men who manage our lives without Him. The God who is with us is the God who forsakes us (Mark 15:34). The God who lets us live in the world without the working hypothesis of God is the God before whom we stand continually. Before God and with God we live without God. God lets Himself be pushed out of the world on to the cross. He is weak and powerless in the world, and that is precisely the way, the only way, in which He is with us and helps us. Matt. 8:17 makes it quite clear that Christ helps us not by virtue of His omnipotence, but by virtue of His weakness and suffering.

Here is the decisive difference between Christianity and all religions.

He resumed the letter on the eighteenth. The Allies had broken through the German positions on both fronts, and Rommel was in

186

hospital with a fractured skull. His car had been forced off the road in France by a low-flying aircraft. It was almost too late.

Jesus asked in Gethsemane, "Could you not watch with me one hour?" That is a reversal of what the religious man expects from God. Man is summoned to share in God's suffering at the hands of a godless world.

He must therefore really live in the godless world, without attempting to gloss over or explain its ungodliness in some religious way or other. He must live a "secular" life, and thereby share in God's sufferings. He *may* live a "secular" life (as one who has been freed from false religious obligations and inhibitions). To be a Christian does not mean to be religious in a particular way, to make something of oneself (a sinner, a penitent, or a saint) on the basis of some method or other, but to be a man—not a type of man, but the man that Christ creates in us. It is not the religious act that makes the Christian, but participation in the sufferings of God in the secular life. That is *metanoia;* not in the first place thinking about one's own needs, problems, sins, and fears, but allowing oneself to be caught up into the way of Jesus Christ, into the messianic event. . . . There is nothing of religious method here. The "religious act" is always something partial; "faith" is something whole, involving the whole of one's life. Jesus calls men not to a new religion, but to life. . . .

Just one more point for today. When we speak of God in a "non-religious" way, we must speak of Him in such a way that the godlessness of the world is not in some way concealed, but rather revealed, and thus exposed to an unexpected light. The world that has come of age is more godless, and perhaps for that very reason nearer to God than the world before its coming of age. Forgive me for still putting it all so terribly clumsily and badly, as I really feel I am. . . . We're getting up at 1:30 almost every night here; it's a bad time, and it handicaps work rather.

# 12

✛ ✛ ✛

IN THE EARLY MORNING of July 20, Claus von Stauffenberg flew north from Berlin with his aide, Werner von Haeften, to attend a conference in the Führer's headquarters at Rastenberg in East Prussia. Each of them carried a bomb in his briefcase.

On reporting to Keitel, Stauffenberg learned that the conference had been brought forward half an hour to 12:30 P.M. because Mussolini was expected that afternoon. It was to take place not in the underground concrete bunker, where the blast would have killed everyone present, but in the map room, a comparatively flimsy wooden hut.

As Keitel led his officers across the compound shortly before 12:30, Stauffenberg hung back and activated the silent ten-minute fuse of his briefcase bomb. He then followed them into the conference, where he found Hitler sprawled across the table examining a map of the Eastern front. Setting the briefcase down by the plinth of the table, close to the Führer's feet, he then excused himself on the pretext of having to take a telephone call from Berlin, and left the hut to rejoin Haeften, who was waiting for him with a car between the inner and outer perimeter fences. As he opened the door to get in, there was a bellowing explosion behind him, and the guards started running toward the smother of smoke and dust among the trees. It was 12:42.

Certain that no one could have lived through such a blast, Stauffenberg and Haeften bluffed their way past the outer-perimeter guards, drove to the airport, and took off for Berlin at 1:15, confident that they would arrive there to find that the Reserve Army had taken over the capital. But only moments before the bomb went off, someone had kicked the briefcase and moved it out of the way to the other side of the heavy plinth, so that Hitler was shielded from it as he leaned across the table. Lurching out of the wreckage with a stiff right arm, his hair singed, and eardrums bleeding, he ordered the SS to seal Rastenberg off from the outside world until the cause of the explosion was known.

With this, the plot began to unravel. The officer in charge of communications was General Erich Fellgiebel, who was supposed to send word for the *Putsch* to begin as soon as he knew that Hitler was dead. But before he could send anything, the SS took over, and the conspirators awaiting his signal in General Olbricht's office in Berlin were left high and dry, not daring to order out the troops until Hitler's death had been confirmed. Still, it was clear from the fact that communications *were* cut that something momentous had happened at Rastenberg, and shortly after 4 P.M., Olbricht decided he could wait no longer. In the name of his commanding officer, General Fromm, who knew nothing of what was happening, he instructed units of the Reserve Army to take up positions in the city.

With nothing but rumors to go on, however, and lacking firm direction, the army responded hesitantly. At 4:30, Olbricht confronted Fromm with news of the revolt, and allowed him to try to reach Keitel on the telephone. To their surprise, Fromm got through without difficulty, and was at once told that the Führer was very much alive. When Stauffenberg arrived from Rastenberg half an hour later, he found the whole enterprise on the point of collapse. Though he arrested Fromm and the Gestapo officers whom Himmler had sent to detain him, the Reserve Army units were already withdrawing to their barracks.

By 6:45, it was all over. Even as General Beck, the putative president, was trying to persuade the army group commander in France to join the revolt, Goebbels himself went on the air in Berlin to announce officially that the attempt on Hitler's life had failed. In their confusion, the conspirators had omitted to arrest him and seize the radio station. Suddenly remembering their loyalty to the Führer, the fence-sitters at the War Office then released Fromm, who by now was as anxious as they were to demonstrate his innocence. He had the known conspirators rounded up, convened a summary court-martial, and sentenced them to death.

Out of consideration for his age and rank, Beck was given an opportunity to shoot himself, but he bungled it twice, and a sergeant had to finish him off with a bullet through the head. As for Stauffenberg, Olbricht, and Haeften, they were taken down to the courtyard and shot—much to the annoyance of the SS and Gestapo men who arrived shortly after, for they had wanted to question them about their accomplices.

When Knobloch brought word of Goebbels's broadcast, Bonhoeffer heard him out, thanked him politely, and lay down on the bed with his face to the wall.

Next morning, he wrote what he thought might be his last letter to Bethge:

> All I want to do today is to send you a short greeting. I expect you are often with us here in your thoughts and are always glad of any sign of life. . . .
>
> During the last year or so I've come to know and understand more and more the profound this-worldliness of Christianity. . . . I don't mean the shallow and banal this-worldliness of the enlightened, the busy, the comfortable, or the lascivious, but the profound this-worldliness characterized by discipline and the constant knowledge of death and resurrection. . . .
>
> I remember a conversation that I had in America thirteen years ago with a young French pastor. We were asking ourselves quite simply what we wanted to do with our lives. He said he would like to become a saint (and I think it's quite likely that he did become one). At the time I was very impressed, but I disagreed with him, and said, in effect, that I should like to learn to have faith. For a long time I didn't realize the depth of the contrast. I thought I could acquire faith by trying to live a holy life, or something like it. . . .
>
> I discovered later, and I'm still discovering right up to this moment, that it is only by living completely in this world that one learns to have faith. One must completely abandon any attempt to make something of oneself, whether it be a saint, or a converted sinner, or a churchman (a so-called priestly type!), a righteous man or an unrighteous one, a sick man or a healthy one. By this-worldli-

ness I mean living unreservedly in life's duties, problems, successes and failures, experiences and perplexities. In so doing we throw ourselves completely into the arms of God, taking seriously not our own suffering, but those of God in the world—watching with Christ at Gethsemane. That, I think, is faith. . . . How can success make us arrogant or failure lead us astray when we share in God's sufferings through a life of this kind?

I think you see what I mean, even though I put it so briefly. I'm glad to have been able to learn this, and I know I've been able to do so only along the road that I've traveled. So I'm grateful for the past and present, and content with them. . . .

May God in His mercy lead us through these times; but above all, may He lead us to Himself.

July 21 was the first day since his uncle's visit that Maetz failed to join him for his morning walk. Glad to spend it alone for once, he abandoned himself to the air and sunlight as mindlessly as a cat. Afterward, he worked on his poetry, read a little, and made some notes for the book he was planning. That evening, Knobloch took him to the sick bay as usual, and as they pushed through the swing doors, Bergmann went quickly to the radio and turned it down. Somebody was saying, "Holy anger and measureless wrath fill us today over the criminal attack that was supposed to have cost the life of our beloved Führer. . . ."

"Who's that?"

Bergmann hesitated. "Grand Admiral Doenitz."

"An admiral?" Bonhoeffer eased himself into his usual chair. "They must be short of generals today."

"They are," said Knobloch. He cleared his throat. "Have you heard about General von Hase?"

"Dead?"

"Not yet."

Bonhoeffer nodded. The one hope for them now was that defeat might come sooner than the hangman. He turned up the volume control on the radio.

"If these blackguards and henchmen of our enemies, whom they assist with unprincipled, dastardly, and false cleverness—in reality, their stupidity is unlimited—believe that by removing the Führer they can free us from our hard but inexorable and fateful struggle, they do not see in their fearful and blind limitation that their criminal act would have thrown us into terrible chaos, and would deliver us unarmed into the hands of our enemies."

"Shut it off," shouted someone from the ward, and Bonhoeffer turned it low again.

"There's been nothing else all day," said Bergmann, offering him a cigarette.

"Never mind them," said Knobloch as he leaned over to light it. "If you want to listen."

"No, it's all right. I heard enough."

Knobloch stared at Bergmann until he took the hint, and went about his business.

"So what now?" he asked. "A purge?"

"Oh, yes. Trials. Executions. Spontaneous demonstrations of loyalty and affection. The usual circus."

"Is there any way they can connect *you* with it?"

Bonhoeffer looked at him blankly.

"I mean, you've been sitting here over a year. You're not really involved. Nor is Herr Dohnanyi."

It was a moment before he grasped what Knobloch was saying. "You don't understand. There are papers. Hans kept records. Everything we did. Every foul atrocity we came across. The Jews. The camps. Terrible things. I don't know where they are, these files, but the Gestapo are sure to find them now."

Knobloch struggled for something polite to say. "Perhaps they've been destroyed."

"I doubt it. Hans asked Beck to burn everything after we were arrested, but he wouldn't."

"Why didn't he just send a signed confession to Reichsführer Himmler and have done with it?"

Bonhoeffer managed a smile. "He wanted to show that some of us had resisted Hitler from the start—for reasons of decency and honor. It was important for Germany."

Knobloch gestured impatiently, but his mind was on something else.

"We also had to justify a *Putsch* to the German people—to show

192

them the crimes committed in their name. If it failed, Beck knew that sooner or later the Gestapo would take us all in any case."

"Right," said Knobloch, as though glad they agreed on something. "So what are you going to do?"

"Do?"

"Are you going to sit in your cell and wait for them?" He turned up the volume of the radio. "Or are we going to walk out of here and lie low till it's over?"

Bonhoeffer released a long breath. Knobloch was no fool.

"We'll need some help from your family, of course. Clothing, papers, food coupons. And a set of overalls. There are workmen in and out all the time. Nobody'll look twice if we go through the gate together some night. Specially if there's an alert on."

Bonhoeffer regarded him in silence.

"The war's lost," said Knobloch irritably. "How much longer can it last? Three months? Four? God wouldn't want you killed for nothing, would He? He'd want you to save yourself if you could."

"Not at your expense, my friend." Bonhoeffer gripped his hand awkwardly. "Don't you know what the Gestapo would do to you?"

"I certainly wouldn't want to wait and find out. Once through that gate, we disappear and stay disappeared."

"You'll desert? After eighteen years?"

"If the Führer wants to fight to the last man, he can do it without me."

Bonhoeffer smiled. "You mean you're going in any case—whether I join you or not?"

"I've been thinking about it. I wouldn't have gone just yet, not if I'd been going alone. I'd have waited a few more weeks. But the way things are"—he shrugged—"I don't mind bringing it forward a bit."

He said this with dignity, expecting to be taken as he chose to present himself, and not to be doubted, patronized, or embarrassed by any more questions.

"You've considered the possibility of reprisals?"

"I'm not worried. There's just my sister. Besides, who's going to get excited about a missing corporal? You're the one who's got to think about that."

"Yes." Bonhoeffer remembered how frail his parents had looked on their last visit, and his heart turned over.

"I know," said Knobloch. "It's hard. It's hard to know which is worse for a family—to have someone on the run or someone just sitting in here, waiting for the chop."

"That's not quite the point. The question is, what will the Gestapo do to them if I go with you?"

"I don't know that it makes much difference if you go or stay—not when it comes to treason." He avoided his eye. "They're not going to leave them alone in any case."

Bonhoeffer sat frozen. "I must think about that."

Knobloch ground out his cigarette abstractedly. "I've got a twenty-four-hour pass tomorrow. Would you like me to have a word with your family? Just to sound them out?"

"I don't think so. Not yet." He touched Knobloch's arm. "I'm not clear in my mind. There's still Hans to consider."

"All right." He yawned, and reached for the pack of cards. "It'll take a few days to fix things up, but you're the best judge of what time we've got."

There was another heavy raid that night. Bonhoeffer returned to his cell too restless to sleep, and worked at his verses for a while to calm himself. Knobloch was right. He had not returned home from America to die uselessly, but to share in the misfortunes of his people and in building a new Germany. If that was God's purpose for him, then God would preserve him for it, perhaps in the way that Knobloch proposed. But until he was sure, even to think of taking steps to preserve his own life at the risk of others' was a dangerous self-indulgence. He was all too conscious of his own will always to be at the center of things, and, after sixteen months in Tegel, of a longing to be free at almost any price.

In the morning, he read over the poem he had written, and decided to send it to Bethge in the rough:

STATIONS ON THE ROAD TO FREEDOM

*Discipline*
If you set out to seek freedom, then learn above all things
to govern your soul and your senses, for fear that your passions
and longing may lead you away from the path you should follow.

Chaste be your mind and your body, and both in subjection,
obediently, steadfastly seeking the aim set before them;
only through discipline may a man learn to be free.

### Action

Daring to do what is right, not what fancy may tell you,
valiantly grasping occasions, not cravenly doubting—
freedom comes only through deeds, not through thoughts taking wing.
Faint not nor fear, but go out to the storm and the action,
trusting in God, whose commandment you faithfully follow;
freedom, exultant, will welcome your spirit with joy.

### Suffering

A change has come indeed. Your hands, so strong and active,
are bound; in helplessness now you see your action
is ended; you sigh in relief, your cause committing
to stronger hands; so now you may rest contented.
Only for one blissful moment could you draw near to touch freedom;
then, that it might be perfected in glory, you gave it to God.

### Death

Come now, thou greatest of feasts on the journey to freedom eternal;
death, cast aside all the burdensome chains, and demolish
the walls of our temporal body, the walls of our souls that are blinded,
so that at last we may see that which here remains hidden.
Freedom, how long we have sought thee in discipline, action, and
    suffering;
dying, we now may behold thee revealed in the Lord.

It was his epitaph for the resistance. He knew from the radio that
hundreds were being rounded up by the SS and Gestapo, and, from the
next delivery of books, that Uncle Paul had been hanged. He also
learned that Sonderegger had called on his parents in person at 7:30
A.M. on the morning after the abortive *Putsch* to ask questions about
Hans, who, perhaps luckily, was still very ill and in quarantine. The only
man Bonhoeffer knew for certain had escaped was Otto John, who had
simply boarded a Lufthansa flight to Madrid. But John's brother Hans
was Rüdiger Schleicher's legal assistant, which forged yet another link
between the conspiracy and the family.

On July 28, Bonhoeffer managed to spend almost an hour in the yard talking to his youngest sister, Susanne Dress, who had cycled over from Dahlem with his weekly parcel. Knowing that he sometimes took his morning walk as soon as it arrived, in the hope of seeing who had brought it, she dawdled over repacking her suitcase with his dirty laundry, and was reluctantly making her way to the gate when she saw him emerge from the cell block with Knobloch.

Propping her bicycle against the wall, she let the air out of both tires and pretended to have trouble pumping them up. Knobloch gallantly offered his assistance, and as thcy both bent over the machine, she quickly brought Bonhoeffer up to date.

Klaus was still free, and so was Rüdiger, but Bonhoeffer's friend Hans von Haeften and his wife had been arrested, presumably because Haeften's brother had been with Stauffenberg on July 20. Almost everyone else they knew who had been in any way connected with the resistance was dead or in prison or on the run, like Goerdeler. It was such a grim recital, confirming the very worst of his fears, that it almost extinguished Bonhoeffer's pleasure at seeing her. And a few hours later he learned that Hassell had been arrested.

Knobloch said nothing—with an effort. After hearing about the Haeftens, Bonhoeffer was still less inclined to do anything that might draw the Gestapo's attention to the family while Klaus and Rüdiger remained free—and certainly not while there was still the chance of a sudden military collapse that might save them all.

In the east, the Russians had crossed the Polish border, and to the north, were approaching the Gulf of Riga. By the beginning of August, they had reached the outskirts of Warsaw, where the Polish underground had already risen against the German garrison. In the west, the entire front had been ripped open by a massive breakout from the Allied bridgehead that threatened to encircle the bulk of the German army in France, and to the south, the retreat continued in Italy, the last German divisions south of the Arno falling back toward the Gothic Line on August 3.

Bonhoeffer wrote to Bethge that day. Since the failure of the *Putsch,* he had kept his letters brief and innocuous for fear the Gestapo might now be taking a closer interest in his affairs. He was particularly worried about compromising Linke and Knobloch, although when he suggested to them that it might be wise to break off his illicit correspondence, at least for the time being, Knobloch grew quite angry and insisted that Bonhoeffer continue with it, exactly as before. Not that he needed much urging. The link with Bethge, however tenuous, kept him anchored in a wider reality than that enclosed by his cell; it was a link he needed, not only to sustain himself, but also to validate his work—and he had at last managed to contain his thoughts in a scheme for a new book.

I'm enclosing the outline of a book that I've planned. I don't know whether you can get anything from it, but I think you more or less understand what I'm driving at. I hope I shall be given the peace and strength to finish it. . . . How very useful your help would be! But even if we are prevented from clarifying our minds by talking things over, we can still pray, and it is only in the spirit of prayer that any such work can be begun and carried through. . . .

### Outline for a Book

I should like to write a book of not more than 100 pages, divided into three chapters:
  1. A Stocktaking of Christianity.
  2. The Real Meaning of Christian Faith.
  3. Conclusions.

*Chapter 1* to deal with
  (a) The coming of age of mankind (as already indicated) . . . Nature was formerly conquered by spiritual means, with us by technical organizations of all kinds. Our immediate environment is not nature, as formerly, but organization. But with this protection from nature's menace there arises a new one—through organization itself.
  But the spiritual force is lacking. The question is: What protects us against the menace of organization? Man is again thrown back on himself. He has managed to deal with everything, only not with himself. He can insure against everything, only not against man. In the last resort, it all turns on man.
  (b) The religionlessness of man who has come of age. 'God' as a working hypothesis, as a stop-gap for our embarrassments, has become superfluous (as already indicated).
  (c) The Protestant church: Pietism as a last attempt to main-

tain evangelical Christianity as a religion . . . 'Jesus' is disappearing from sight. Sociologically: no effect on the masses—interest confined to the upper and lower middle classes. A heavy incubus of difficult traditional ideas. The decisive factor: the church on the defensive. No taking risks for others.

(d) Public morals—as shown by sexual behavior.

*Chapter 2*
(a) God and the secular.

(b) Who is God? Not in the first place an abstract belief in God, in His omnipotence, etc. That is not a genuine experience of God, but a partial extension of the world. Encounter with Jesus Christ. The experience that a transformation of all human life is given in the fact that 'Jesus is there only for others.' His 'being there for others' is the experience of transcendence. It is only this 'being there for others,' maintained till death, that is the ground of His omnipotence, omniscience, and omnipresence. Faith is participation in this being of Jesus (incarnation, cross and resurrection). Our relation to God is not a 'religious' relationship to the highest, most powerful and best Being imaginable—that is not authentic transcendence—but our relation to God is a new life in 'existence for others,' through participation in the being of Jesus. The transcendental is not infinite and unattainable tasks, but the neighbor who is within reach in any given situation. God in human form—not, as in oriental religions, in animal form, monstrous, chaotic, remote, and terrifying, nor in the conceptual forms of the absolute, metaphysical, infinite, etc., nor yet in the Greek divine-human form of 'man in himself,' but 'the man for others,' and therefore the Crucified, the man who lives out of the transcendent.

(c) Interpretation of Biblical concepts on this basis. (Creation, fall, atonement, repentance, faith, the new life, the last things.)

(d) Cultus . . .

(e) What do we really believe? I mean, believe in such a way that we stake our lives on it? . . . 'What *must* I believe?' is the wrong question; antiquated controversies, especially those between the different sects; the Lutheran versus reformed, and to some extent the Roman Catholic versus the Protestant, are now unreal. . . . To say that it is the church's business, not mine, may be a clerical evasion, and outsiders always regard it as such. It is much the same with the dialectical assertion that I do not control my own faith, and that it is therefore not for me to say what my faith is. There may be a place for all these considerations, but they do not absolve us from the duty of being honest with ourselves. We cannot, like the Roman Catholics, simply identify ourselves with the church. . . .

### Chapter 3
Conclusions: The church is the church only when it exists for others. To make a start, it should give away all its property to those in need. The clergy must live solely on the free-will offerings of their congregations, or possibly engage in some secular calling. The church must share in the secular problems of ordinary human life, not dominating, but helping and serving. It must tell men of every calling what it means to live in Christ, to exist for others. In particular, our own church will have to take the field against the vices of *hubris*, power-worship, envy, and humbug, as the roots of all evil. It will have to speak of moderation, purity, trust, loyalty, constancy, patience, discipline, humility, contentment, and modesty. It must not underestimate the importance of human example (which has its origin in the humanity of Jesus and is so important in Paul's teaching); it is not abstract argument but example that gives its word emphasis and power. . . .

All this is very crude and condensed, but there are certain things I'm anxious to say simply and clearly—things that we so often like to shirk. Whether I shall succeed is another matter, especially if I cannot discuss it with you. I hope it may be of some help for the church's future.

Bonhoeffer saw little chance of saving himself now, whether he fell in with Knobloch's plan or not. Goerdeler was caught by the Gestapo on August 12, which did not augur well for a successful disappearance, and the remaining conspirators were being brought before the People's Court in Berlin to be abused and condemned to death by Roland Freisler, the Nazi zealot who had secured Dohnanyi's dismissal from the Ministry of Justice in 1938. Any chance there might have been of surviving a trial had gone for good. In his fury, Hitler had sworn to eliminate not only those directly concerned in the plot against him, but the entire German aristocracy—and Freisler was chief executioner. "Degenerate to their very bones, blueblooded to the point of idiocy, nauseatingly corrupt, and cowardly like all nasty creatures—such is the aristocratic clique which the Jew has sicked on National Socialism," wrote Reichsleiter Robert Ley in the party newspaper *Angriff* three days after the Rastenberg explosion. "We must exterminate the entire breed."

Nor was there now any real likelihood of defeat intervening swiftly enough to prevent it. The Russian advance had stalled unaccountably on the outskirts of Warsaw, where the Wehrmacht was slowly but ruthlessly suppressing the partisan uprising, and although a major disaster was looming up in France, there was no reason to suppose it would be decisive when it came. The most Bonhoeffer felt he could hope for was enough time to finish his new book. He started clearing out the cell, sending home his accumulated papers, letters, and notes for safekeeping and retaining only the books and manuscripts he was working on.

With no hopes for the future to sustain him, he had turned again to the past, and the residual warmth of his family ties. "There is hardly anything that can make one happier than to feel that one counts for something with other people," he wrote on August 14 in a letter for Bethge's birthday.

> What matters here is not numbers but intensity. In the long run, human relationships are the most important thing in life; the modern "efficient" man can do nothing to change this, nor can the demigods and lunatics who know nothing about human relationships. God uses us in His dealings with others. Everything else is very close to *hubris*.

Four days later, Hans John was arrested. The Gestapo's line of inquiry now pointed straight to Rüdiger Schleicher, and through him, to Bethge and Klaus Bonhoeffer. "All that we may rightly expect from God, and ask Him for, is to be found in Jesus Christ," he wrote on the twenty-first.

> The God of Jesus Christ has nothing to do with what God, as we imagine Him, could do and ought to do. If we are to learn what God promises, and what He fulfills, we must persevere in quiet meditation on the life, sayings, deeds, sufferings, and death of Jesus. It is certain that we may always live close to God and in the light

of His presence, and that such living is an entirely new life for us; that nothing is then impossible for us, because all things are possible with God; that no earthly power can touch us without His will, and that danger and distress can only drive us closer to Him. It is certain that we can claim nothing for ourselves, and may yet pray for everything; it is certain that our joy is hidden in suffering, and our life in death; it is certain that in all this we are in a fellowship that sustains us.

Maria came to visit him on the twenty-third. She was as tranquil and assured as he had ever seen her, not, he soon saw, from resignation or consciously to spare him worry, but from a trusting acceptance that matched his own. He was the more grateful for it because the news she brought was very bad. The previous day, Sonderegger had called at the Potsdam military hospital where Dohnanyi had been quarantined since June and removed him by ambulance to Sachsenhausen concentration camp.

When the time came for her to leave, they parted as they always did, quickly, almost shyly, with a last searching look to print the other's face on their minds, and then he went back to his cell to write to Bethge.

> I am so sure of God's guiding hand that I hope I shall always be kept in that certainty. You must never doubt that I'm traveling with gratitude and cheerfulness along the road where I'm being led. My past life is brim-full of God's goodness, and my sins are covered by the forgiving love of Christ crucified. I'm most thankful for the people I have met, and I only hope they will never have to grieve about me, but that they, too, will always be certain of, and thankful for, God's mercy and forgiveness. Forgive my writing this. Don't let it grieve or upset you for a moment, but let it make you happy.

It did not make Knobloch happy. Under cover of that night's raid, they heard over the BBC that the battle for France was virtually over. Eight German divisions had been cut to pieces near Falaise, Paris was expected to fall at any moment, and Allied troops put ashore on the Riviera five days earlier were already threatening Avignon and Grenoble. In the east, the Russians were still waiting at the gates of Warsaw for the German garrison to complete its slaughter of the Polish underground, but farther south, their armored columns were stabbing deep into Rumania.

"It's time to get out," said Knobloch, when he heard about Hans. "With a gun at your head, you don't leave it to God to deflect the bullet."

"Nor do you drag anyone else into the line of fire."

"You don't have to. They're standing beside you—in plain sight. Nothing you do or don't do can change that. They've taken Herr Dohnanyi. Do you doubt that you're next? Or your brother? Or Herr Schleicher? You must all save yourselves while you can."

"Our families, too? The children? My parents? Or do we leave them to the Gestapo?"

Knobloch threw up his hands. "They're already at risk. Look what happened to Hassell. He was like you—he waited. He thought the Gestapo would leave his family alone if he gave them no trouble. He was wrong."

"There's a difference, I think," said Bonhoeffer. "When they've done with poor Hassell, they'll surely release them. But if he'd gone into hiding . . ." He shook his head. "I must wait till I'm sure."

"There's no *way* to be sure. If you see someone aiming to kill you, you get out of the way. And you thank God for letting you see it in time. At least let me speak to your family."

Bonhoeffer realized Knobloch was in a mood to do so whether he gave his consent or not, and reluctantly agreed. But he made it clear that flight was to be the very last resort, when no possibility remained of saving any member of the family from the Gestapo's attentions, and as the days went by, Knobloch gave up trying to impress upon him the dangers of delay. Bonhoeffer was working well, between raids, and although Maetz had avoided his company since the execution of General von Hase, nothing had been done to cramp his freedom of movement. He came and went much as he pleased, visiting prisoners in their cells, interceding for them with the guards, and taking particular pleasure in his friendship with Professor Latmiral, whom he met in the yard every morning.

Disturbed by his apparent indifference, Knobloch made sure that Bonhoeffer listened regularly to the news, with its daily list of conspirators tried and executed. By mid-September, most of those he had known by name or in person had appeared before Freisler, been sentenced and hanged, including Field Marshal Erwin von Witzleben, Generals Karl Heinrich Stuelpnagel and Helmut Stieff, Counts Wolff Heinrich Helldorf, former chief of Berlin police, and Peter Yorck von Wartenburg, to whom Bonhoeffer was distantly related on his mother's side, Adam von Trott du Solz, of the Foreign Office, and, on September 8, Ulrich von Hassell. As Knobloch pointed out almost every night, the likelihood of anyone connected with the plot remaining undetected was extremely remote.

So, too, now was the hope of salvation through military collapse. The Allies were well into Holland, had liberated Luxembourg, and, farther south, were reaching into the Vosges Mountains, but their advance had slowed almost to a halt. In Italy, it was the same story. The Gothic Line had been breached, but German troops were contesting every yard of ground and had stabilized the front. Even the Russians were bogged down, regrouping in Poland and the Balkans for a new winter offensive. The Wehrmacht was fighting back as though it really believed the lie that Goebbels had been pressing upon the country since July 20—that its military reverses had all been due to the treachery of an officer class now paying dearly for its crimes against the Reich. Though there was no doubt in Bonhoeffer's mind about the final outcome, it seemed clear that the war would last at least through the winter, and probably well into 1945, and this, he argued, was another reason to wait. It would be quite impossible to keep out of sight for six months or more, with no resources and no one to take them in. Already two months had gone by with no sign of Gestapo interest. To run now might well give them a reason to suspect him that they would otherwise have lacked. Indeed, Bonhoeffer was beginning to think that eighteen months in prison had been the best protection he could have had when the blow fell.

On September 22, Sonderegger found Dohnanyi's secret files at army headquarters in Zossen.

Next day, Knobloch was called to the telephone to take a message for Bonhoeffer: "The books you were anxious about have been found. Expect all to be moved to safekeeping shortly."

"Well, that settles it," he said, when Bonhoeffer explained what it meant. "I just hope there's still time."

"There can't be much against Klaus and Rüdiger," said Bonhoeffer. "They weren't that deeply involved before Hans and I were arrested."

Knobloch appealed to heaven. "It doesn't *matter*," he said, as though to a child. "Now they *know* you're guilty. They've got proof. The Gestapo will question your family, whether you're in here or not."

"They may not. There's no proof against *them*."

"They don't *need* it." He punched his palm in exasperation. "They'll want to know how much your brother and the others knew about these trips you made—who you met, who your friends were, how you spent your time. It's routine. Staying here won't stop them."

"But they already *know* all that." Bonhoeffer pulled off his glasses. "Why would they want to go over it again?"

"Because then it was Roeder and a charge of evading military service," said Knobloch patiently. "Now it's the Gestapo investigating a plot to murder the Führer. I'm going to talk to Herr Schleicher."

"And what will you say to him?" Bonhoeffer put back his glasses. "That his brother-in-law presents his compliments and invites him to become a party to high treason?"

"He is already."

"He has a family of his own to think of."

"And you are part of it. He told me that." Knobloch looked at him earnestly. "There's nothing to discuss so far as he's concerned. He said if *he* was in trouble, he knew the family would do everything it could to help *him*, no matter what the cost. That's why it was such a privilege to belong to it—those were his very words."

Bonhoeffer turned his head away. "If the worst should happen," he said, "I hope he'll also be lucky enough to find as good a friend as you have been to me. But I should never have let you talk to him about it. It's not just a privilege to belong to this family, it's a real responsibility. When people are willing to give everything, you must be careful not to ask it of them."

"No one need know they're involved," said Knobloch. "The stuff's all ready—clothes, money, food coupons, everything. I'll get it tomorrow."

"Tomorrow?" Bonhoeffer dropped his cigarette in surprise.

"Well, we can't *go* tomorrow. I've only got the day. But I'll hide the things somewhere, and we'll go as soon as I can wangle a weekend pass."

"How soon will that be, do you think?"

"I don't know. A week? Ten days?" He scratched his head. "Is that too long?"

"I shouldn't think so. They'll have names enough in those files to keep them busy for months."

They sat quiet with their thoughts.

"In any case, a few extra days may be useful," said Bonhoeffer. "If we stay in Berlin, they're sure to find us. But as we've got a little time, Rüdiger might want to look into the question of passports. It might also be an idea for someone to have a word with the chaplain at the Swedish embassy."

There was nothing connected with the plan that he had not already thought through to the point of revulsion, so that afterward, he put the whole affair out of his mind with no great difficulty. Sunday the twenty-fourth passed like any other day, and when Knobloch reported on Monday that Rüdiger, Ursula, and Renate had driven out to meet him at Niederschönhausen with the things needed for the escape, Bonhoeffer was more interested in hearing how they were and the latest news of the family. He was not ungrateful to Knobloch or the Schleichers for what they were doing—indeed, he was touched to tears by their willingness to run such risks on his account—but at heart, he simply could not bring himself to believe in the plan.

On Wednesday, Knobloch came to see him in his cell with such a nonchalant air that Bonhoeffer guessed at once that he had a pass.

"When is it to be?" he asked, ready to play the game out for Knobloch's sake.

The corporal made sure no one on the gallery was close enough to overhear. "I've got forty-eight hours from six o'clock Saturday."

"So soon?"

"I collected a favor." He was absurdly pleased. "So what do you think?"

"I think I owe you more than I've any right to."

"No." He shook his head emphatically. "I thank you for your company. And I've only got a minute, so this is what I thought." He again looked over his shoulder. "I'll go to Herr Schleicher's on Saturday night to see if he's had any luck with the passports. Then I'll come back here late on Sunday, when you're all locked up for the night, and bring the overalls."

"Won't the guards be surprised to see you? If you're not due back before Monday?"

"Oh, no. They're used to that. They know I don't have a family. So I'll take the overalls down to the sick bay and meet you there when the raid starts. And as soon as they're really banging away, out we go."

Bonhoeffer played with his glasses. "What if there isn't a raid that night?"

"Then we'll wait till about eleven-thirty, and I'll tell Bergmann I'm taking you back to your cell. If anybody on the gate wants to know, I'll say you've been working late in the motor pool—you'll just have to keep out of the light. But they won't care, if they see you're with me. We'll get a good six or seven hours' start before anyone knows you're gone."

He looked so triumphant and yet so utterly dependent on his approval that Bonhoeffer could not deny him. He took Knobloch's hand and shook it between both of his, trying to convey a warmth of feeling too complicated to express. He had been shown the way out he had craved for eighteen months—and a chance of survival in hiding was infinitely to be preferred to a sentence of death in prison. But what was still not clear was whether, by escaping, he would go out to meet God's purpose or turn his back on it. He could only be sure that God willed men to live in Christ, and thus to live for others. Pared down to that certainty, he awaited the coming of Sunday without anxiety, confident that God would make His purpose plain.

Nothing had changed by Saturday afternoon. When Knobloch came up after supper for a final word before leaving to see the Schleichers, Bonhoeffer was ready. Despite his reservations, the arguments for escape were persuasive. In the absence of a sign, to refuse to save himself when the chance was offered might well be to flout the will of God, and for all he knew, the consequences might bear as hard on the family as anything the Gestapo could do if he *did* escape. Though uneasy about the burden he would lay on them, he accepted that it had to be so, and was content to follow the course that had opened to him. He worked on his book until it was too dark to see. Then he composed himself to sleep and woke at six, quite calm, with everything out of his hands.

Knobloch came back earlier than expected, soon after three o'clock, and they looked at each other in silence.

"You mustn't grieve about it," said Bonhoeffer.

"I'm not grieving." He sat down on the bed. "I'm trying to think of a way to make you see that nothing has really changed."

"Rüdiger has been arrested."

"No. Your brother Klaus."

Bonhoeffer flinched. "When did it happen?"

"This morning. But he knew about it yesterday, when he came home from work. There was a Gestapo car waiting at the gate. So he went to Frau Schleicher's instead."

"What about his wife?"

"She's away. Visiting the children."

Bonhoeffer covered his face with his hands. "How did my brother seem?"

"He was . . . upset." Knobloch stared at his boots. "I didn't stay long. He was with your sister, trying to decide what to do. He was talking about doing away with himself—Herr Schleicher told me. But I said he ought to make a run for it—and I still think that's right."

"There are the children to think of."

"That's what your brother said. But they've got him for treason. To stay here now is just throwing your life away."

Bonhoeffer went to the window and looked out over the prison wall. "You said nothing about why you were there?"

"Well, no. It didn't seem right."

"Thank you. That was wise."

"Herr Schleicher said he needed more time, but we couldn't really talk, not with all that going on. General von Hase's widow was there as well. They'd just let her out."

"Let her out?"

"They arrested her when they took the General."

"But why was she at Ursula's? I don't understand. Why didn't she go to her own family?"

"She did. They were too frightened to take her in."

Bonhoeffer turned again to the window. Poor Ursel. Such a load to carry. "Perhaps Klaus was mistaken. We can't be certain they've got him."

There was no immediate answer, which was answer enough. "I knew you'd want to be sure," said Knobloch hesitantly, "so I kept watch."

"All night?"

"No one saw me. They came for him this morning."

"Just Klaus?"

He nodded. "You can't hurt him now. So all things considered, I think it's best not to wait for the passports. Everything's ready—the clothes and the money. I think we ought to go tonight, like we agreed."

Bonhoeffer could tell from his voice that he knew it was useless. And he was so full of pain, he prayed Knobloch would spare him further argument. He sat down heavily beside him on the bed.

"You are a good and true friend. I cherish what you've done for me, and I thank you humbly with all my heart."

Knobloch would have interrupted, but Bonhoeffer laid a hand on his arm. "Don't, please. You'll demolish me with kindness. Besides, I've another favor to ask."

"Anything." He fidgeted with embarrassment.

"I ask you, as my friend, not to press me any more. I can't go with you. I thought I could, but it's not possible."

"It'll mean your death."

"If God wills it. And if God wills it, I'm content. I'll go where He leads me."

Knobloch grunted. "How can you be sure He's not leading you out of here?"

"I am sure He wouldn't have me leave my family, Maria, and my friends to pay for my escape. Klaus is arrested, and a few hours later I disappear. What if the Gestapo see that as cause and effect? What if they think my brother knows something so damaging about me that I had to run for it? The truth is he can tell them nothing they don't already know, but what if they don't believe him? What if they torture him because of it? What if they arrest Maria to see if *she* knows? Or my parents? Do you see? I can prevent that. While I'm here, I protect them. If there's anything the Gestapo want to know, they can ask *me*. I'm here to answer for myself."

"None of that may happen."

"Can you promise me it won't?"

Knobloch struck both thighs with his fists and got up. He stopped irresolutely at the door, fidgeting with the lock.

"I *am* content," said Bonhoeffer. "Be glad for me."

Knobloch stood there scowling. "Can I do anything for you?"

"I'd be very grateful if you could spare the time to see the Schleichers again and tell them what I've decided."

On October 4, the Gestapo arrested Rüdiger. Bonhoeffer heard about it the next day, and also that Bethge was being brought back from Italy for questioning. In the evening, he wrote a poem about Jonah.

> In fear of death they cried aloud and, clinging fast
> to wet ropes straining on the battered deck,
> they gazed in stricken terror at the sea
> that now, unchained in sudden fury, lashed the ship.
>
> "O Gods eternal, excellent, provoked to anger,
> help us, or give a sign, that we may know
> who has offended you by secret sin,
> by breach of oath, or heedless blasphemy, or murder,
>
> who brings us to disaster by misdeed still hidden,
> to make a paltry profit for his pride."
> Thus they besought. And Jonah said, "Behold,
> I sinned before the Lord of hosts. My life is forfeit.
>
> Cast me away! My guilt must bear the wrath of God;
> the righteous shall not perish with the sinner!"
> They trembled. But with hands that knew no weakness
> they cast the offender from their midst. The sea stood still.

On October 8, Sergeant Major Weber came smiling to his cell and ordered him to get his things together. He was then taken downstairs and handed over to two Gestapo men. As they drove away from Tegel, Bonhoeffer wished he could have said goodbye to Knobloch.

# 13

✢ ✢ ✢

CELL 19 IN THE CELLARS of Gestapo headquarters, Prinz-Albrecht-Strasse 8, was about eight feet long, five feet wide, and windowless. It held a table, a stool, and a folding bed propped against the wall. In the yellow light of a low-power bulb, the air hung stale, warm, and motionless, prickling the eyes. But Bonhoeffer thanked the SS guard who led him there as though it were a suite at the Adlon, and, having missed supper, coaxed him into coming back with two slices of bread and preserves and a mug of ersatz coffee. He was then escorted to and from the washroom at the end of the corridor and locked in for the night, having learned no more, for all his attempts to lure the man into conversation, than that the main meal of the day was served at noon, that there was no outdoor exercise, and talking was strictly forbidden.

As he started to unpack his suitcase, the sirens sounded a preliminary alert. Though below ground, he had not been much impressed by the solidity of the building above him—Tegel was a fortress by comparison—and they were now in the heart of Berlin. Driving in, sandwiched between the two Gestapo men, he had been shocked by the devastation. Great tracts of the city had been smashed and ripped up into wasteland. Streets he remembered with buildings as sturdy as this one now ran through canyons of rubble. When the sirens howled the full alert, he sat down on the floor by the doorjamb, but almost at once he was ordered out to join the other prisoners emerging from their cells.

As casually as he could, he looked up and down the corridor, hoping to see Klaus or Rüdiger, but the open doors obstructed his view and a guard told him to stand still, shouting in his face. The only prisoner he knew—and neither betrayed the slightest sign of recognition—was Fabian von Schlabrendorff.

When all were accounted for, they marched off in single file, descended a flight of steps to a lower level of cells, and caught up with another line of prisoners threading their way through a warren of passageways to the prison kitchen and out into the courtyard. As the raid was now in full swing, stippling the night sky with flak, the guards forced them into a trot, down the zigzag ramp of a massive concrete bunker into a large, square, brightly lit underground room half full of Gestapo and SS men, most of them in uniform and some with their families. Leading off it at the far end was a corridor connecting a series of offices, where Gestapo officials were still at work, and the prisoners were spaced out along the wall on both sides, just far enough apart to prevent any whispering.

There was no sign of Klaus or his brother-in-law, but Bonhoeffer found himself in distinguished company. Besides Schlabrendorff, he exchanged stares with his friend Josef Müller, Admiral Canaris and General Oster; Hjalmar Schacht, Hitler's former Minister for Economic Affairs; Carl Goerdeler, and—the only one to acknowledge his existence—Pastor Hans Böhm, head of ecumenical affairs in the Confessing Church. The rest just leaned against the wall, shifting from foot to foot, withdrawn and indifferent, while the guards stalked back and forth.

Next morning, when Bonhoeffer was taken to the washroom, he found Schlabrendorff there, shaving, and again they ignored each other. But the moment the guard turned his back, Schlabrendorff jerked his head at the communal shower in the corner. As Bonhoeffer stepped under it, the icy shock of the water crushed his body so painfully that he almost cried out. He had to force himself upright against it, gasping for breath and uncramping his muscles to let the blood flow. But then, as he surrendered to it, stamping and swinging his arms, the slashing cold began to sluice away the crust of an airless night, and by the time Schlabrendorff joined him, to stand back to back under the rushing spray, he felt almost newborn.

"Don't I know you?" he whispered, not moving his lips.

"We never met." Schlabrendorff soaped himself vigorously. "You're looking well."

"And you." The guard was watching, but without suspicion. "I thought you were still in the East."

"Tresckow's dead. I've been back six weeks."

"Bad?"

"Not good."

Bonhoeffer jumped up and down. His body was turning to stone. "They took Klaus. Have you seen him?"

"No. I'm sorry. And Maria?"

"Safe." The guard was looking at his watch.

Schlabrendorff turned up his face to the shower, blew like a grampus, and slicked back his hair. "Go now. Play for time. And good luck."

They managed to exchange a few more words that day—on the way to the bunker during an early-afternoon alert, and again in the washroom before lights out. As at Tegel, everything depended on the guards. Discipline was tighter, but already Bonhoeffer could tell the zealots from the merely strict. Schlabrendorff had told him that those on duty at night were generally more approachable than those on the day shift, and so it proved. When the guard who came around to lock up produced a pair of handcuffs, Bonhoeffer asked him politely by whose orders he was to be shackled, since they had left him free the previous night. The guard scratched his chin. It was routine, he said doubtfully. To prevent suicide. He would have to ask. He went away, taking the handcuffs with him. Later, when they returned from the bunker after another alert, Bonhoeffer wished him good night, and the guard locked him in without a word. He evidently told his relief as well, for the next night, when a new man came on, he shackled every prisoner along the corridor but Bonhoeffer.

By the end of the first week, he was on speaking terms, more or less, with six of the eight men who rotated the guard duties in his section of the prison, and had exchanged a few words with all the prisoners he knew except Admiral Canaris, who, for some reason, was kept confined to his cell in chains. To his delight, he had also been moved across the corridor to cell No. 24, which made him Schlabren-dorff's neighbor. In addition to their conversations in the shower, they could now talk every evening through the gap between the hinges of the door that separated them as they stood waiting for the other prisoners to return from the washroom. It was another standing order that all doors should remain open until everyone was in his cell and accounted for.

He had also, on the Wednesday after his arrival, received a parcel from his family, and the fact that they knew where he was meant as much as the clean laundry, cigars, bread, and apples it contained, although the food was a godsend. Gestapo meals had turned out to be even worse than the Wehrmacht's—two slices of bread and preserves morning and night, and some watery soup at midday. They also sent writing paper, which he badly needed, for he had started work again, and two books he had asked his father to get for him. From these he learned that Klaus, Rüdiger, and Eberhard were being interrogated by the Gestapo in a civil prison on Lehrter Strasse.

His own turn came late Sunday night. He was asleep, but dressed in anticipation of the inevitable air raid alert. When he heard the key in the lock, he assumed he had slept through it, but instead of the night guard, there were two uniformed SS men in the doorway, and he sat up abruptly, wide awake. Ignoring his questions, they pushed him along the corridors that led to the yard, and it crossed his mind that they might be about to shoot him, although that hardly seemed likely without at least confronting him first with the evidence found at Zossen. It was not, he decided, a fair test of composure. They marched down the ramp to the bunker, across the main hall, and along the now familiar office corridor to a heavy, unmarked door. The leading guard rapped on it sharply, and without waiting for a response, bundled him inside.

Sonderegger was sprawled in a chair at one end of a table littered with papers, talking to a slightly built man of about Bonhoeffer's own age, who sat opposite. They were both in civilian clothes and, from the layers of cigarette smoke hanging motionless beneath the shaded lamp above the table, they had been there for hours. Between them, and directly under the lamp, was a vacant chair.

Sonderegger finished the story he was telling—it had to do with

Canaris pumping the guards for news of the war and being given false information that within hours was common knowledge among the other prisoners—and as they both laughed, he looked up and pointed to the chair.

"Sit down, Pastor. I don't believe you've met SS Section Leader Walter Huppenkothen."

"No, Herr Commissar." Seated under the light, he could scarcely make out their faces in the shadows.

"The section leader holds a special commission from the Führer to investigate the criminal conspiracy against the state that came to light on July 20."

Bonhoeffer inclined his head politely. "How can I help you, Herr Section Leader?"

"Allow me to finish," said Sonderegger. "The commission results from the discovery of certain files at Wehrmacht headquarters which prove that you and Dohnanyi, along with Canaris, Oster, and others of the former Abwehr, have been plotting against the Reich since 1938. You're here to help us make certain that no traitor escapes. It's the only reason you're still alive."

Bonhoeffer looked from one to the other. "I'm sorry," he said hesitantly. "The Herr Commissar knows I had no connection with the Abwehr until 1941. After that, I simply carried out my orders." The silence lengthened, and he went on out of politeness more than anything else. "I cannot pretend I was fully employed in this way, or even fully aware of the precise significance of what I *did* do—intelligence work is still something of a mystery to me." He directed a self-disparaging smile in Huppenkothen's direction. "But I was never asked to do anything I thought improper. And I'm afraid I've no knowledge of the files you speak of."

An unexceptionable start, he thought. Modest, cooperative, conceding a little to the original charge against him, and yet not compromising his patriotic standards—all in all, a very reasonable statement of position.

Then Sonderegger leaned forward into the light, and Bonhoeffer saw that the rules had changed.

"Let me advise you," he said. "Don't be clever. This isn't a court of law. You're not a military prisoner. You've no rights, and no one can

214

help you. You will tell us everything you know of this affair. I mean to pick you clean—by force if I have to."

"Then I beg you not to overestimate my importance." He looked again toward Huppenkothen. "I'll tell you all I can, but my knowledge of the Abwehr's work is limited, to say the least. I think that came out in the War Court."

"From what I found at Zossen, there were certain things you forgot to tell the War Court. So let me warn you about that, too. If necessary, I'll bring people here to jog your memory. Your parents, for instance. Or your fiancée."

"That won't be necessary." He lowered his gaze. "Ask anything you want to know. I've nothing to hide. Threats merely confuse me."

"Quite right," said Huppenkothen, from the shadows. "Dr. Bonhoeffer is a sensitive, intelligent man. I'm sure he's fully aware of the dangers of his situation. And I've no doubt he's as anxious as we are to get to the bottom of this business."

"Thank you, Herr Section Leader. I've waited eighteen months for an opportunity to clear myself. I look forward eagerly to appearing before the People's Court."

"Ah. Well, there I must disappoint you. The evidence that came to light at Zossen is of such a delicate nature, touching so closely upon the welfare and security of the Reich, that the Führer has ordered us to deal with it in the strictest confidence. I'm sure you understand. Neither you nor any of those implicated will appear in court."

Bonhoeffer did his best to look bewildered. "I'm not to stand trial? Then how shall I prove my innocence? I'm a minister of the church. My reputation . . ."

"Just try to think of *this* as your trial, said Huppenkothen. You've no one but Commissar Sonderegger and myself to convince. The Führer has empowered me to dispose of your case in any way I see fit."

"But my defense?" Bonhoeffer peered anxiously into the darkness. "I'm not prepared."

"So much the better. Your answers will be all the more revealing." He leaned into the light, holding out a gold cigarette case. "Do you smoke?"

"Thank you."

"There are matches on the table. When you're ready, perhaps

you'll tell us about these files your brother-in-law kept."

Bonhoeffer drew powerfully on his cigarette. "As far as I know, Herr Section Leader, the Abwehr's files were kept at the Tirpitz-Ufer center, here in Berlin. After my arrest, I heard that the building had been bombed, so perhaps they were then moved to Zossen for safekeeping."

"The section leader is referring to Dohnanyi's secret files, documenting an army conspiracy to overthrow the Führer and make peace with our enemies," said Sonderegger.

Bonhoeffer looked at him anxiously. "You mean they were *not* Abwehr files? I'm sorry. I don't understand. Hans once told me that an important part of his work was anticipating situations that *might* arise, so as to be ready for them. And also *inventing* stories and situations to gain useful information from the enemy or confuse or mislead them. I had some experience of this myself. The mission I undertook for Admiral Canaris in 1942, when I met Bishop Bell in Sweden, was like that. It was to talk about possible peace terms, so as to get some idea of British government thinking. So when you mentioned making peace with our enemies, Herr Commissar, I wasn't sure if you meant that or something else. Because if you *did* mean that, then it was official Abwehr business, and the file should be with the others." It was disconcerting not to be able to see their faces.

"The files I'm referring to," said Sonderegger after a pause, and Bonhoeffer learned nothing from his voice, "were compiled by Dohnanyi over a period of years. They show that he conspired with Canaris, Oster, Beck, Goerdeler, Hassell, Halder, Witzleben, Josef Müller, Leuschner, Wirmer, Schacht, and many others to murder the Führer and overthrow the government. There are documents, many of them in his own handwriting, containing detailed plans for this *Putsch*— even listing the names of those selected to replace the present ministers of the Reich. There is a considerable quantity of photographic and other material, also collected over a period of years, that was obviously intended for use afterward in an attempt to discredit the Führer and justify this treasonable conspiracy to the German people. Now, you say you were close to Dohnanyi. Are you telling us you had no knowledge of what he was doing?"

Bonhoeffer had listened with what he hoped was a nice blend of

216

incredulity and dismay. "I find it totally inconceivable," he said flatly. "I know my brother-in-law to be a loyal and dedicated servant of Germany."

There was another silence. "Then you'll be surprised to hear he's confessed," said Huppenkothen mildly. "Indeed, he could hardly have done otherwise after being confronted with the evidence."

"Yes. I'd be very surprised." He was getting tired of twisting his head from side to side, and the light hurt his eyes. "I'd like to see this evidence."

"Please. You'll find copies of the key documents in front of you."

Bonhoeffer pulled a few of them toward him with the air of a man neither anxious nor easy to be convinced.

"Among them are reports by your friend Dr. Müller on his dealings with the enemy through the Vatican," Huppenkothen went on. "But of course you know about that. You and Dohnanyi went there together in 1942."

"The Catholic Church was one of the Abwehr's principal sources of information on Allied public opinion."

"Evidently. On the strength of Müller's findings, your brother-in-law wrote a memorandum in March, 1940, urging Generals Thomas, Halder, and others in the High Command to arrest the Führer and make peace on terms already agreed in outline with the British government." He directed his attention to the table. "You'll find a copy there somewhere."

Bonhoeffer fingered the papers blindly. "It must have been prepared for some other purpose," he said. "Perhaps to test the loyalty of the General Staff."

Huppenkothen laughed. "Very ingenious. But I'm afraid not."

"He's fencing again," said Sonderegger.

"Is he? Well, you know him better than I do. That really wouldn't be wise, Dr. Bonhoeffer. Were you aware of the real purpose of these negotiations with the Vatican or not?"

"As far as I know," he said, stirring himself, "the idea was to test Allied thinking, to find out what their war aims really were. And the best way to do that, we found, was to make some sort of unofficial peace overture."

"As you did later—with Bishop Bell in Sweden?"

"Exactly. It's obvious you can't just contact the enemy and say, what are your intentions? You have to approach them in secret, ostensibly to talk about some matter of mutual concern, and then try to get them to show their hand. I'm no expert, but I would have thought this was standard procedure."

"Quite. But was it also standard procedure to prepare *two* reports? One for the official record, and another—quite different in tone, content, and purpose—for those we now know to have been plotting against the state?"

Bonhoeffer stubbed out his cigarette carefully. If they had found a copy of his private report to Beck on the mission to Sweden, then the game was over. "Certainly not."

"Well, your friend Dr. Müller did. On each occasion, he made one report for the files—to cover his tracks—and another for Dohnanyi. Now, didn't you do the same? And please think before you answer."

"I don't have to." That at least was true. Not knowing exactly what they had found at Zossen, he had long since decided to brazen it out. If they had positive proof against him, he was finished in any case. If not, he still had a chance. "After every mission, I'd report verbally to Admiral Canaris or General Oster or my brother-in-law— sometimes to all three—and afterward in writing. The written reports were then, I imagine, filed in the usual way."

"You did this after your visit to Sweden?"

"I did."

"And the point of that mission, you say, was to test Allied opinion in the context of secret peace talks?"

"It was."

"Then can you explain why papers relating to that mission were found with these other treasonable documents in the conspirators' secret files?"

Bonhoeffer shook his head cautiously. "To my knowledge, there *were* no papers relating to the mission—apart from my report."

"Oh, but there were. Letters. Memoranda. All very damaging."

"To whom, Herr Section Leader? Surely not to me? There may have been some routine correspondence about travel arrangements and so on, but I would know nothing of that. And as for what happened to the report after I wrote it, or what use was made of it, I really can't say."

"He's lying," said Sonderegger, and Bonhoeffer sat back, offended.

Huppenkothen crushed out his cigarette. "I can't think he would be so foolish. Are you suggesting that your brother-in-law deceived you? That the object of your mission may not have been what he represented it to be?"

"Not at all. He always stressed that the first principle of intelligence work was to tell no one more than he needed to know—and to tell one's family nothing at all. It was understood that I would simply follow instructions and leave the rest to him and his superiors. There was no question of deception."

"All right. But isn't it then possible, not being in possession of all the facts, that you *unwittingly* served this conspiracy? That these traitors *used* you—for your foreign connections?"

"I don't understand." The bait was tempting, but poisoned. "In what way?"

"Well, what if the *peace* discussions were the real object of your mission, and the testing of opinion merely the pretext for getting you to undertake it? Suppose they took advantage of your inexperience? Isn't it at least possible that in all innocence you were induced to take part in an operation harmful to the national interest?"

"No." He looked at Sonderegger, who had once offered him a similar way out. "I know my brother-in-law too well for that. I think what may have happened is that he set aside his secret files on all these sensitive operations in case the documents they contained should be misunderstood or misinterpreted by those unfamiliar with the Abwehr's methods. And in view of what's happened, I would say his fears were justified."

Sonderegger jutted impatiently into the light, stabbing his finger at the papers on the table. "That's six years of treason. We're not dealing in suspicion. These are *facts.* You're still alive because we mean to sift the whole business through from the beginning, but this isn't a trial. You're guilty. You, Dohnanyi, Oster—all of you. And there's the proof."

Suspiciously, Bonhoeffer again pulled some of the papers toward him, and Huppenkothen laughed.

"You know, I begin to understand poor Roeder's difficulty," he said. "Dr. Bonhoeffer is a very elusive fellow. With all the evidence of his guilt set out there, instead of him pleading with *us*, we're pleading with *him* to acknowledge it."

"How will it help you, Herr Section Leader," said Bonhoeffer, "if I confess to crimes I didn't commit, or pretend to knowledge I don't possess? The Herr Commissar knows we covered this ground again and again in the War Court. I don't think there's much to add—a few details, perhaps—but I'll gladly go over it once more if you think it necessary."

Huppenkothen settled both elbows on the table and rested his chin on his hands. "You disappoint me. I hope it won't be necessary after all for Commissar Sonderegger to try the methods he seems to favor. I'd prefer to deal with a man of your stamp in a more civilized way."

"If you've assumed I'm guilty, Herr Section Leader, then clearly nothing short of a confession will satisfy you. But I can tell you only what I know. If it's not what you expect, or want to hear, I'm sorry. I'm doing my best."

"I don't think so. You must bend a little. Help us. Help your family. It's clear that you've always opposed the Führer and National Socialism. It's obvious from your record. So why not admit it? Show us you mean to cooperate."

Bonhoeffer looked down at the papers. He was ready to make a concession. If they meant to pick over the ground since 1938, as Sonderegger had said, it might take months—provided he could keep them interested, and away from the family.

"I can't simply answer yes or no, Herr Section Leader—not if you want the truth. I'm a pastor. I try to follow the word of God. I must oppose anyone who interferes with the proclamation of His word."

"Very well. You oppose the Reich to the extent that it involves itself in church affairs, is that it? You can surely say yes or no to that."

"Yes." He hesitated. "Although it would be truer to say that I oppose the German Christians. The dispute is theological, not political."

"All public disputes are political. And insofar as the ideals of National Socialism, and of the German Christian movement, are embodied in the person of the Führer, so then are you opposed to him?"

"I have sometimes opposed the policies of his ministers."

"Come now. You *consistently* oppose the policies of his ministers —and in opposing them, you oppose him."

"I am concerned only with matters affecting the Christian faith. In all other respects, I acknowledge the Führer's claim on my obedience."

"Indeed? In connection with the Treachery Law? The Nuremberg laws? The oath of loyalty? The laws relating to military service? Or are these also matters of theology?"

"They must all yield precedence to God's law. I think the Führer is sometimes misled by his advisers."

"The Führer can no more be separated from National Socialism than Christ from Christianity." Huppenkothen seemed pleased with his apothegm. "If you oppose his works, you oppose him."

Bonhoeffer pushed up his glasses and rubbed his eyes. "When forced to choose, I must follow Christ."

"The Jew?"

"The man. The son of God."

"Against the Führer?"

"Wherever He leads me."

"To conspiracy? Treason? Murder?"

"Christ was himself the victim of treason and murder."

"At the hands of the Jews. Like the Führer. Although God seems to look upon the Führer with more favor than you, Pastor Bonhoeffer. He did, after all, save him from your friends." He smiled. "They *were* your friends, were they not?"

Bonhoeffer hesitated, judging he had gone far enough for the moment.

"A very eloquent silence." Huppenkothen leaned forward. "You opposed the war and our solution to the Jewish problem. You defied our attempts to instill a proper sense of duty in the Evangelical Church. You identified yourself with a bourgeois clique that dared obstruct the

221

will of the German people. You justify your presumption by claiming that God has led you against the Führer. You admit that those who treacherously plotted his murder are your friends. Do you *still* deny that you are, and always were, opposed to the Führer? And this time, I really must insist on yes or no for an answer."

Bonhoeffer remained silent. His sight was so blurred he could scarcely make out anything in the shadows. If it was to do any good, they had to believe his admission was forced.

"He needs softening up," said Sonderegger.

"Possibly. Perhaps his family can help us."

Bonhoeffer let his shoulders droop. "There's nothing they can tell you."

"That can hardly be true of your brother Klaus," said Huppenkothen, smiling. "Or your brothers-in-law. But I wasn't really thinking of them. I was thinking more of Fräulein von Wedemeyer. And perhaps your mother."

"They know nothing."

"Nothing of substance, I'm sure. No gentleman would involve his womenfolk in such an unpleasant business. But they will at least know who came to the house. Where you went. Who your friends were. And they could hardly fail to be aware of your general attitude toward the Führer. A word here. An expression there. Do you see what I mean? They can surely tell us—in the most general terms—whether you support National Socialism or oppose it?"

Bonhoeffer looked at him for a long moment. "I oppose it," he said.

"You are opposed to the Führer and National Socialism?"

"Yes."

"And have been from the beginning?"

"Yes."

Huppenkothen nodded. "So you're a realist after all." He held out his cigarette case, but Bonhoeffer ignored it.

"He's told us nothing," said Sonderegger. He sounded bored.

"On the contrary. Dr. Bonhoeffer has told us there'll be no more of these tedious evasions. We can get down to business now. Isn't that so?"

"I'm at your command, Herr Section Leader."

222

"You see?"

Sonderegger sniffed, and retreated into the gloom.

"But if you'll forgive me, I'll leave you now to the commissar. It's been a long day and I'm rather tired." Huppenkothen came around the table and stood opposite Bonhoeffer, forcing him to squint against the light. "I'm glad we understand each other. I shall look forward to our next meeting."

They were both silent after he left, Bonhoeffer soiled and depressed by the tawdry performance, and Sonderegger apparently at a loss to restore some sense of purpose to the proceedings. After several heavy sighs, he pulled the papers toward him and began to ask Bonhoeffer about the Kleists, the Kleist-Retzows, the Wedemeyers, and other landowning families he knew from his days at Finkenwalde. The hostility he had shown in front of Huppenkothen was now gone. He seemed almost to be killing time, and for this Bonhoeffer was grateful, for his friends in Pomerania had suffered badly in the purge. The silences lengthened between questions, and after about an hour, Sonderegger suddenly went to the door, called a guard, and had Bonhoeffer returned to his cell.

Thinking about it afterward, as he lay on the bed, Bonhoeffer remembered how Sonderegger's interventions in the past had always seemed to work to his advantage. Though sharp and formidable on the surface, they were generally directed against the strongest points in his defense rather than the weakest, and whenever they had talked alone, Sonderegger had shown the same lack of zeal. It was not from any positive desire to help—Bonhoeffer was sure of that. It had nothing to do with him personally. He was inclined, rather, to think he was simply the unwitting beneficiary of some secret contempt for his work or associates that Sonderegger had walled up behind his professional reserve. He had sensed it in the commissar's dealings with Roeder, and now with Huppenkothen. There was a cross-grained tension between them, not openly expressed, but leading each to thwart the other in small ways. And as Sonderegger was a calculating man, his threats to extort a confession by force or by involving the family might almost have been intended to steer Huppenkothen in the opposite direction.

In the weeks that followed, suspicion became a certainty. In the presence of Huppenkothen, Sonderegger was invariably terse and hostile, provoking his superior into ever more elaborate debates and courtesies—and so long as Bonhoeffer consented in the end to yield, Huppenkothen seemed content with the most trivial admissions. But alone, Sonderegger would soon lapse into something close to indifference, taking Bonhoeffer through his story in more detail than before, but without threats or pressure or even much evidence of skepticism. After a few hours of this, the questions becoming more and more desultory, he would then call the guard, and the session would be adjourned for another two or three days.

Though sometimes tempted to show he knew that Sonderegger was following a course of his own, Bonhoeffer judged it best to leave well enough alone. He was also careful not to seem to take advantage of the commissar's leniency, and made a point of always answering as fully and as truthfully as he could without compromising anyone he thought might still be alive or whose family might in some way be vulnerable. Time was passing, disagreeably but not intolerably. He was at peace with himself and working well. The guards, for the most part, were friendly, though not to be trusted. He had his friends about him, which helped offset the worst effects of isolation, and although news of the war was hard to come by, it seemed hardly possible that it could drag on much longer. They were now spending as much time in the Himmler bunker as in their cells.

Then the interrogations suddenly took a new turn. For most of November they had been left to Sonderegger, who would send for him two or three times a week to go through the next phase of his story, generally in chronological sequence; but one bitterly cold morning in December, almost two months after his transfer from Tegel, he was taken to the bunker as usual and ushered, not into the examination room, but into Huppenkothen's private office, where he was greeted more as a guest than a prisoner. Even Sonderegger seemed affable for once, and Bonhoeffer sat back in the comfortable chair he was offered, waiting to hear the latest inducement to turn informer. But when they returned him to his cell an hour or so later, he was still at a loss to explain the new cordiality. There had been none of the usual playacting. Huppenkothen had questioned him seriously about his contacts abroad in the ecumenical movement, going back to the early thirties, and as they were all safely out of reach, he had answered fully and politely, even exaggerating their importance a little so as to impress him with their value.

The next day, he was sent for again, this time to discuss his American connections. And when, on the third day, they got around to the substance of his talks in Sweden with Bishop Bell, he realized that the whole thrust of the investigation had changed. The Gestapo were no longer interested, if they ever really had been, in connecting his missions abroad with the conspiracy; Huppenkothen apparently accepted that they had been carried out in good faith. What he now wanted Bonhoeffer to do was to supplement the reports he had written about them for Canaris. They were looking to put his connections abroad to some use, and the only use Bonhoeffer could think of was the one the resistance had recognized—sounding out the Allies on possible terms for peace.

The thought was electrifying, and to lend it substance, the now daily sessions in Huppenkothen's office were accompanied by a noticeable loosening of restrictions. His cell door was sometimes left open to give him more air, his meals improved, and best of all, the next laundry and food parcel was sent through by Sonderegger without delay, and with a scribbled note from Maria to say the parents were well and thinking of him. The guards also seemed to be looking the other way more often while he and Schlabrendorff braved the morning shower, and as he surreptitiously shared out among the other prisoners the bread and tobacco sent in by the family.

In less cautious moments, he even allowed himself the daydream of being sent to make contact with the British through his friends in Geneva, and to encourage the idea, added a little more each day to his account of the talks with Bishop Bell. As Huppenkothen's main worry seemed to be the threat of a new Russian offensive in the east, Bonhoeffer held his respectful attention for almost a week by "remembering" how Bell had told him that a strong body of opinion in England, led by men of such opposite views as Sir Stafford Cripps and Lord Beaverbrook, was greatly perturbed by the prospect of a Bolshevik advance into Europe, and that Beaverbrook for one had already looked into the possibility of making common cause with Germany against it.

But then the Führer intervened. On December 16, taking advantage of the winter storms that had grounded Allied aircraft for several days, he launched twenty-eight divisions against the American First Army in the Ardennes sector, with the object of breaking through to Antwerp and Brussels and encircling the British forces to the north. When Bonhoeffer heard about it from a jubilant Huppenkothen three days later, he was more surprised than alarmed that the Wehrmacht was still capable of such an effort, and put it down to a last-ditch attempt to improve Germany's bargaining position. It certainly did nothing to weaken Huppenkothen's interest in British politics, and at the end of the session Bonhoeffer was rewarded with permission to write a Christmas letter to Maria.

> These will be quiet days in our homes. But I have had the experience over and over again that the quieter it is around me, the clearer do I feel the connection with you. It is as though in solitude the soul develops senses which we hardly know in everyday life. Therefore I have not felt lonely or abandoned for one moment. You, the parents, all of you, the friends and students of mine at the front, all are constantly present to me. . . . It is a great invisible sphere in which one lives and in whose reality there is no doubt. . . . Therefore you must not think that I am unhappy. What is happiness and unhappiness? It depends so little on the circumstances; it depends really only on what happens inside a person. I am grateful every day that I have you, and that makes me happy.

His calm acceptance of whatever might happen had not, however, impaired his curiosity about it. Although the guards were not to be drawn on the progress of the Ardennes offensive, Bonhoeffer could tell from their manner that it was not going well, in which case it could only have brought Germany's final surrender that much closer. As a further test of his standing with Huppenkothen, he asked for permission to send a birthday letter to his mother on December 28, and this was granted at once.

> Dear Mother,
> I want you to know that I am constantly thinking of you and father every day, and that I thank God for all that you are to me and the whole family. . . . It's a very great comfort to me that Maria is with you. Thank you for all the love that has come to me in my cell from you during the past year, and has made every day easier

for me. I think these hard years have brought us closer together than we ever were before. My wish for you and Father and Maria and for us all is that the New Year may bring us at least an occasional glimmer of light, and that we may once more have the joy of being together. May God keep you both well.

Satisfied at last that Bonhoeffer could tell him nothing more about his journeys abroad, Huppenkothen turned the questioning back to Sonderegger. By now, Bonhoeffer was more amused than persuaded by his fantasy of preparing the way for peace talks as Himmler's emissary, but he was also increasingly confident that the war would be over before his case ran its course. By the middle of January, the Wehrmacht had been forced halfway back to its starting line in the Ardennes salient, and in the east, the whole central front was crumbling under the long-awaited Russian offensive. If it had done nothing else, the failure of Hitler's last military gamble had proved even to his most fanatical supporters that the war was lost—and with that, it was reasonable to suppose that every member of the SS and Gestapo would now be considering what his position might be after the surrender. A good many, particularly the senior officers, would go down with the party elite in one final orgy of blood and destruction, having few claims to mercy in Allied hands, but Sonderegger was no fanatic. The habit of obedience was too strong for him, and others like him, to break, but Bonhoeffer had no doubt they would now be looking to improve their chances of survival. And what better way than by saving a prominent political prisoner to testify afterward on their behalf? He was sure this explained Sonderegger's oddly ambiguous attitude toward him ever since his transfer to Prinz-Albrecht-Strasse. Well ahead of the party zealots, he had probably recognized the inevitability of defeat and tried to steer a course between duty and self-preservation, not disobeying his orders but, as far as he dared, neglecting them.

"Have you finished with me, Herr Commissar?" Bonhoeffer asked one day, breaking a long silence.

Sonderegger looked up from the file he had hardly even pretended to study for the past ten minutes, and lit a cigarette without answering.

"For today, I mean."

The commissar considered him for a moment, then slid the pack down the table, and his matches after it. "Don't delude yourself," he said. "You're in this with the rest. When the Führer decides to finish them off, he'll finish you, too."

"Herr Huppenkothen seems satisfied with my explanations."

"He's satisfied he can hang you. You're an enemy of the Reich, and your friends are all traitors."

Bonhoeffer looked at him steadily. "So you'll keep me alive for as long as I'm useful." He stressed the "you" just enough to make the suggestion personal if Sonderegger chose to take it that way.

"Naturally." He was studiedly neutral.

"And no doubt the same applies to my brother-in-law Dohnanyi?"

"His case is different." Sonderegger slapped the file shut.

"That's a pity." Bonhoeffer hesitated. "In some situations, you'd find him *most* useful. I'm thinking particularly of his influence abroad."

"Dohnanyi planned the whole thing—and the Führer trusted him. Nothing can be done. It's his own fault."

"But what if he were given a chance to redeem himself—to take advantage of his credibility with the enemy, perhaps. . . . I don't know much about these things, Herr Commissar, but surely that might be worth considering? Dohnanyi's connections abroad are far more extensive than mine."

"Dohnanyi is useful only to the extent that he can help us clean house." Sonderegger slumped back out of the light. "And Section Leader Huppenkothen is interested in what *you* have to say only because it amounts to a confession. You, Canaris, Oster, and Dohnanyi deliberately broke an agreement restricting political intelligence work to Reich Security Head Office. That's a hanging matter in itself."

Bonhoeffer was quiet for a moment. There was no sense in pushing him too far. "I'm sorry, Herr Commissar. Dohnanyi's a sick man. I'm very worried about him. Can you say how much longer you think this will last?"

"That depends on Dohnanyi." He began to gather in his papers. "We're bringing him here to speed things up."

As Bonhoeffer struggled with his absurd pleasure in the idea of sharing a prison with Hans, they both heard the distant howl of a new alert, the third that day. "And it also depends on the enemy," Sonderegger added.

"Well, there I can't judge," he said, smiling faintly to show how little he really fancied his chances of tricking the other into giving him an answer. "Are the Russians over the Vistula yet?"

"The Vistula?" Sonderegger snapped his case shut. "The Bolsheviks are eighty miles from Berlin."

Bonhoeffer saw his hands shake, and hid them in his lap. The glass inverted over the carafe of water jingled against it, fractionally ahead of a rumbling explosion nearby.

"Then it's got to stop," he said. "Before Germany is destroyed."

Sonderegger inspected his nails. "That's treason. By order of the Führer, anyone who says the war is lost will be hanged as a traitor. Regardless of rank."

Bonhoeffer watched him, almost with pity.

"I'm a policeman," said Sonderegger. "I don't make the laws."

Bonhoeffer nodded, but this only annoyed him.

"You don't understand. I swore to obey. Are we Germans or rabble? If Germany breaks faith with the Führer now, then God *should* destroy us."

"If Germany is destroyed, Herr Commissar, it'll be because *we* broke faith with God."

Sonderegger relapsed into boredom. "Then I'll answer for it in the hereafter. Meanwhile, I have my orders."

"Then may God have mercy on us all."

"Amen," he said, and the bunker trembled again.

Hans von Dohnanyi was brought in by stretcher a few hours later. He was paralyzed in both legs. They left him lying in the middle of his cell with his head toward the open door, and although Bonhoeffer passed by several times, there was no way to attract his attention. He then offered to help carry Hans out of the bunker at the next alert, but the guards said they had orders not to move him, even to the lavatory. Incensed, Bonhoeffer loudly demanded to see Sonderegger to protest about this brutal neglect of a sick man, hoping that Hans would hear his voice, and was told that Commissar Stawitzky was in charge. Stawitzky was notorious for ill-treating his prisoners, and as the guards urged Bonhoeffer back to his cell, one of them warned him in an undertone not to interfere.

The following morning, February 2, Carl Goerdeler, who had

been tried and condemned with Hassell and Leuschner on September 8, was taken from his cell and hanged at Plötzensee, along with another prominent member of the resistance, Johannes von Popitz, a former Prussian Minister of Finance. As the news spread among the prisoners, the building went quiet, and Bonhoeffer ached for his friend Schlabren- dorff, who was due to appear before Freisler in the People's Court next day.

A few hours later, in the early evening, Huppenkothen sent for him, seated him comfortably in his office, gave him a cigarette, and casually announced that his brother Klaus and Rüdiger Schleicher had both been sentenced to death that afternoon. Hit hard, Bonhoeffer looked so straight at Huppenkothen that he seemed glad to end the questioning ten minutes later when an alert sounded.

It was a long and heavy raid, but Bonhoeffer was blindly grieving and hardly noticed. At the all-clear, the guards had to push him into line, and he found himself leading the way back with Josef Müller and Schlabrendorff. As they came to the open door of Dohnanyi's cell, he saw the guard in front had his back turned, and on an impulse he darted inside, braced against a shout that never came.

Hans smiled when he saw who it was, and Bonhoeffer gripped his hand. "Are you all right?"

"Better than I look." He lay, gaunt and gray, in a pool of urine. "Don't worry. Have they hurt you?"

"No. Just threats. Klaus and Rüdiger were condemned today."

Hans grunted softly. Then, "How do *we* stand?"

"As before. I had to say I always opposed them. And they know the trips were not military. But that's all."

"Good. Say it's my fault. You can't harm me. We need time."

Bonhoeffer glanced at the door. The others were shuffling by too fast. "The Russians are on the Oder."

"I heard. I'll try to stay ill till they get here." He squeezed Bon- hoeffer's hand and smiled. "Go now. Don't let them see."

"God keep you, Hans."

"And you, Dietrich."

He pulled himself away and stepped boldly out into line with the last half-dozen prisoners, the guard behind them rounding the corner as he did so, but looking the other way.

230

In the morning, he said goodbye to Schlabrendorff in the washroom; condemned prisoners were not normally returned to Prinz-Albrecht-Strasse. But the sirens sounded soon after, and as they lined up outside their cells in the passage, he saw Schlabrendorff was still there, a few places behind him. The guns were already firing as they hurried into the bunker, and the first muffled bomb bursts silenced the buzz of talk inside even before they reached their usual positions in the corridor.

It was the worst daylight raid of the war. Within a very few minutes, an avalanche of destruction rolled right over them, crushing their heads with noise, then rumbled past like a huge iron drum. Another followed on the echoes of the first, before the ground had even stopped shaking, and trampled by to give way to the next. They looked at one another, startled, and a child began to cry, infecting others, until the troughs between these thundering waves were filled with wailing. Sixteen feet of concrete was now thin as an eggshell. Then there were no troughs. They were gripped in one long tremor. Some slid quietly down the walls, folding their arms about their heads. Others jerked and twitched, faces shining with sweat. The bunker filled with smoke, the sour smoke of burning brick, and the guards turned uncertain, muttering together in groups or pushing roughly through the crowd. When Bonhoeffer went to help an old man pulling feebly at his collar, one of them barred the way, unbuttoning his holster.

Then they were hit. He knew it would happen a second beforehand. Out of the blanketing uproar, he heard one, two, three clumping footfalls, and as the fourth split upon the roof, he looked up to meet it. The concussion stopped his ears. The air went solid for a long instant, and the bunker seemed to burst outward rather than in, bucking free from the ground. Plumes of dust jetted down and the light turned yellow, but the concrete held. Jarred to the bone, Bonhoeffer smiled, faintly puzzled, at Schlabrendorff, and as the screaming started, turned to helping the others to their feet. Then he remembered Hans, left behind in his cell.

The raid lasted two hours, and it was another two before they were allowed out. The Gestapo building was gutted. The roof and upper stories had gone, reduced to a shell by fire, while the lower floors had been flayed open and choked with rubble. The air smelled foul with smoke and dust, but the cellars were still intact. Gangs of men had already cleared a path from the bunker and restored order inside, shoring up the ceilings with balks of timber and hanging oil lamps at intervals along the corridors. When Bonhoeffer reached his brother-in-law's cell, he saw him propped up talking to Stawitzky by candlelight, and leaned against the wall for a moment to catch his breath. In his own cell, the floor was littered with fallen plaster, but his manuscript was safe, and a friendly guard eventually brought him a stub of candle.

By nightfall, he was shaking with cold; the heating system had also been knocked out. And when his turn came to visit the washroom, he discovered there was no running water either, just a choice of scummy bowls in which most of the prisoners had obviously washed already. Unable to follow their example, he was nevertheless forced to use the least offensive of the lavatories, wincing with disgust. But Schlabren-dorff was still there, and that redeemed everything. As they whispered together while waiting to be locked in, he told Bonhoeffer that the People's Court had been hit, and Roland Freisler was dead—he'd heard it from one of the guards.

Next morning, February 4, Bonhoeffer celebrated his thirty-ninth birthday by being the first to use a fresh bowl of cold water in the washroom. But the place stank intolerably from the overflowing lavatories, and he was glad to escape to the yard, where an open latrine had been dug, with a bar nailed across to sit on. Except for two short spells in the bunker, he spent the rest of the day on his bed in the dark. He had been told to use the candle sparingly, and in any case found it too trying to read or work by.

Two days passed. The stench of the lavatories hung in the air like a poisoned fog. There was no hot food, no light, and as the guards kept them locked in their cells, preferring to pass the time above ground, some of the older prisoners were so crippled by the biting cold that they had to be half-dragged, half-carried to the bunker whenever the alert sounded, which was now every four or five hours. They existed in a vacuum; the official machine had stopped running, and no one knew what to do. There were no interrogations, no trials, no purpose in being there, and the strangeness of living like rats in a broken sewer affected the guards as well. Few of them made any attempt to enforce normal discipline; some sat up half the night with Bonhoeffer talking about

232

their families and what would happen when the Russians came.

Wednesday, the seventh, was laundry day. Having heard nothing from his parents on his birthday, he had no great hopes of their getting through now. By midday, he was sure that no one would come, but then the guard appeared with his parcel as usual. Besides clean clothes, there was bread, tobacco, writing paper, books—including the Plutarch *Lives of Great Men* he had asked for, and a note from his father:

Dear Dietrich,

Because of the raid, our birthday letter for the 4th, which we wanted to bring you on Saturday, didn't reach you. We sat in the Anhalter station in the S-Bahn during the attack, and it wasn't very pleasant. Nothing happened, except that afterwards we looked like chimney-sweeps. But later, when we tried to get to you, we were very anxious because we weren't allowed to go in because of the unexploded bombs. The next day we heard that nothing had happened to the prisoners. We hope that is true. . . .

Karl-Friedrich had thought of the Plutarch for you for your birthday. I hope this letter reaches you. We are looking forward to being allowed to visit you soon. At our age, there are many things to be arranged that have to be discussed with one's children. I'm typing this to make it more legible. Our warmest greetings.

Your Father

As he read it through again, there was a commotion in the corridor, and he heard the number of his cell called out, among others. Putting the letter away, he quickly packed his few possessions in his suitcase, protecting the manuscript between his clothes and placing the food and tobacco on top to spare casual thieves the trouble of disarranging everything. If he was to be killed, he intended to ask Sonderegger to return the case to his parents. But when he joined the others outside, he saw that they also had their baggage with them, which presumably meant they were being moved. As they passed Hans's cell, he called out, but there was no answer.

Two prison trucks, ringed by armed SS men, were waiting on the deserted street, and as the file of prisoners came up the steps from the cellar, the guards herded them through the ruins to where Sonderegger stood checking off their names against a list on his clipboard. Bonhoeffer asked politely where they were going, but he seemed not to hear, and a guard pushed him toward the larger of the two waiting groups. He knew most of his companions, although only Josef Müller returned his smile. The rest had retreated again behind the wall of apathy they presented to one another in public. Among them was General von Falkenhausen, once governor of Belgium and northern France, Ludwig Gehre and Franz Liedig, both officers of the former Abwehr, and Hermann Pünder, the Catholic ex-mayor of Münster. But there was no sign of Schlabrendorff. The group waiting by the second truck included Canaris, Oster, Karl Sack, Generals Thomas and Halder, Hjalmar Schacht, and the one-time Austrian Chancellor, Kurt von Schuschnigg.

There were twenty prisoners in all, and when they started to board the trucks, only Müller and Bonhoeffer were held back and handcuffed. Bonhoeffer turned to Sonderegger, holding out his wrists for him to see, but the commissar looked right through him and climbed into the other truck.

That night Bonhoeffer's group arrived in Buchenwald. There was no sign of the other party, and when he asked the guard who took off his handcuffs what had become of them, he was told they had gone farther south to Flossenbürg. He and his companions were then led into one of the SS barracks outside the main perimeter of the camp, where the commandant himself assigned each of them to a cell in the basement. The whitewashed walls were wet to the touch and patterned with mildew, but there was more room in cell No. 1 than Bonhoeffer was used to, and no smell to speak of from the adjoining lavatories and washroom. Another difference was that when an air raid alert sounded a few hours later, the two guards bolted everyone in and made themselves scarce.

He found out why next morning, when the trusties came in from the camp at six to make the beds and clean up. Standing, as ordered, by the open door of his cell, Bonhoeffer got to talking with an amiable young NCO named Sippach, who told him that the cells occupied only half the basement area; the rest was used as an ammunition store. He also learned they would not be allowed outdoors for exercise, but could stretch their legs in the corridors provided there was no talking. Müller, he discovered, was at the opposite end of his row of cells, in No. 8, with Falkenhausen between them in the much larger No. 5. This faced an archway to the main central corridor running parallel with theirs behind a partition wall. Another arch opposite led to a third parallel corridor with four large cells, Nos. 9 to 12, and the guardroom. Seeing Bonhoeffer free to move about, some of the others asked Sippach if they might do the same, and by the time the trusties had finished, the prisoners had all managed to exchange a few words.

Despite the cold, their immediate circumstances had improved enormously. There was light and running water; the guards seemed slightly awed by the importance of the new arrivals, and the food was much better. They were given generous helpings of soup at midday, and about a pound of bread each, with butter and preserves, in the evening. By then, the prisoners' uncertainty about the Gestapo's intentions had ceased to weigh on them very heavily. They had not been moved for humanitarian reasons, but equally they would never have come so far if it were just to meet their deaths; there was no shortage of hangmen in Berlin. If they still had some value, that, for the moment, was enough. They were content to rest after months of incessant bombardment and the constant strain of interrogation. Although there were often four or five alerts every twenty-four hours, nothing fell close to the camp, and after the first few nights, Bonhoeffer found he was sleeping through them as often as not.

With fewer interruptions, he also returned to work with a new energy, adding page after page to his manuscript in smaller and smaller handwriting as his stock of paper ran down. In some respects, conditions were now closer to those he had known at Tegel. Although the young NCO was not to be trusted, he soon gave up trying to enforce the no-talking rule, and the guards, instead of allowing the prisoners out one by one, as ordered, for their half hour's exercise every day, generally preferred to release them in twos and threes so as to get it over with and return that much sooner to the warmth of the guardroom. In this way, Bonhoeffer soon made a friend of his neighbor Dr. Pünder, and often managed a good long talk with Müller.

They even kept in touch with the progress of the war. The guards were so nervous about it that they asked Falkenhausen to listen to the Wehrmacht bulletin on the radio every afternoon so that he could explain the latest position to them on his staff map. Afterward, he passed the news around to his fellow prisoners, and their hopes of liberation would rise a little higher each day. There had been no sign of interest in them on the part of Reich Security Head Office for more than two weeks.

Then, on February 24, a new batch of prisoners arrived from Berlin. The first Bonhoeffer knew of it was when two trusties carried in another bed and the guard told him he would now have to share his cell with a general. After so long on his own, he greeted the prospect with resignation rather than pleasure, but was most agreeably surprised when the camp commandant eventually ushered in General Friedrich von Rabenau. Though they had never met before, they knew each other well by reputation. A friend of Goerdeler's and active in resistance circles from the start, the general had retired in 1942 to study theology at Berlin University. Before the day was out, they had settled on a timetable to suit them both—Rabenau was writing his memoirs and no more anxious than Bonhoeffer to be distracted from his work —and laid the foundations of what promised to be a marathon theological dispute.

The others were less fortunate. The mistrust that had once divided the original party now united them against the newcomers, two of whom were women. This added inconvenience did nothing to lessen their resentment at being overcrowded, particularly as one of them had the earmarks of a Gestapo spy. She called herself Miss Heidl. A short, stocky blonde in her twenties, she had traveled with the others from Sachsenhausen, where she had been living under the protection of an SS officer in the camp brothel. Though she claimed to have worked for Allied intelligence, this seemed hardly enough to warrant her inclusion with such notable prisoners as General von Rabenau; Erich Heberlein, the former ambassador to Madrid, and his wife; two Englishmen, Captain Payne Best and Squadron Leader Hugh Falconer, and Lieutenant Vassili Kokorin, a nephew of Molotov, the Russian Foreign Minister. Suspicions deepened when the commandant installed her in a large cell next to the guardroom and crammed the Heberleins into a small one, but Miss Heidl proved to be so vain and silly a creature that Bonhoeffer for one found the spy theory hard to accept. He was inclined to agree with Payne Best, to whom Rabenau introduced him in the washroom one morning, that the SS officer had probably attached his mistress to the party as a convenient way of saving her from the Russians, who were about to overrun the camp at Sachsenhausen.

Bonhoeffer liked Best on sight. He was one of two British intelligence officers who had figured in the so-called Venlo incident in the early days of the war. They had been kidnapped by the Gestapo on neutral Dutch territory and carried over the frontier while trying to make contact with the German resistance. His imperious manner with the guards, perfected after five years' detention at Sachsenhausen, amused Bonhoeffer as much as it alarmed some of the others, who saw their best chance of survival in meekness and compliance, but it helped break the ice between the original group and the newcomers, and worked so well that they were soon free to do much as they pleased. Best was also very generous with his possessions, freely lending out clothes, books, playing cards, and two pocket chess sets to anyone who asked. He even shared his small stock of tobacco, and when that had gone, organized a black market supply through a Ukrainian trusty.

But he could do nothing about their rations. Soon after his party arrived, the bread allotment was cut back to one slice a day, and the midday soup turned to dishwater. Complaints to the commandant went unanswered, but they learned from the guards that all available food and fuel had been requisitioned for the thousands of refugees flooding into Thuringia ahead of the Russian advance. Nor was there much hope of receiving fresh supplies, for the railways had been bombed and strafed to a standstill, and road traffic could move only by night. The last telephone, telegraph, and postal links with Berlin had been cut, and all communications with the capital were now by radio or courier.

The Third Reich was collapsing into chaos. Almost every day, Falkenhausen had some new disaster to report. On March 5, the Allies occupied Krefeld. On the sixth, they entered Cologne. On the seventh, they crossed the Rhine at Remagen, and by the twelfth, held the west bank from Nijmegen to the junction with the Moselle at Coblenz. Two weeks later, all German resistance west of the Rhine had ceased, and Allied armies were deploying eastward from the Remagen bridgehead and, farther north, from Wesel. On the Eastern front, the situation was no better. Russian forces had cleared Hungary and were driving deep into Austria while they regrouped in the north for their final assault on Berlin, now only fifty miles distant.

On Easter Sunday, April 1, Bonhoeffer woke early, cramped with cold and hunger pains. It was very quiet in the cellar—the others, including Rabenau, were still asleep—and as he lay there, summoning the strength to get up, he heard a faraway rumbling. It was too regular and continuous for thunder, and not close enough to be yet another raid on Weimar. He asked the NCO what it was when he opened the cells at six, and the other hesitated. They were guns, he said. The Americans had reached the Werra. He had orders to ensure that the prisoners were ready to move on twenty minutes' notice.

Bonhoeffer received the news serenely, but it threw the others into high uncertainty. Everyone knew the standing orders for camp commandants. Before they abandoned their posts to the enemy, all political prisoners were to be shot. The American advance therefore meant liberation or summary execution, depending upon the morale of an SS officer they had seen only once, and whose future in Allied hands would hardly be affected one way or the other by what he did to them. All day long they pestered the guards for some clue as to the commandant's intentions. One said they would be leaving on foot, which touched off a scare that they were to be shot in the woods nearby. Another said a truck was waiting, which calmed them again. The NCO had nothing to offer, but confided privately to Best that he meant to desert just before the Americans arrived.

They listened to the guns for forty-eight hours, anxiety forcing each of them back into isolation and silence. Then, midway through the afternoon of Easter Tuesday, the NCO told them they would soon be leaving, and at ten o'clock that night, Bonhoeffer emerged with the others into the open air for the first time in nearly eight weeks. Waiting in the yard was a prison truck half full of wood, which its engine had been adapted to use for fuel. There was so little room inside that by the time they were all aboard with their luggage, the guards had to put their shoulders to the door to get it shut. As they did so, an alert sounded, and the seventeen prisoners were left squashed together in the dark to dispose themselves as best they could in a space hardly big enough for eight.

There was only one small ventilator, and when the guards came back from their slit trenches after the all-clear, the atmosphere was stifling. It then became rapidly worse as the engine was fired up.

Within a few minutes, the truck had filled with such choking fumes that some of the party thought they were being deliberately gassed and started to panic. Only when they moved off did the air clear a little, and by then General von Rabenau and the two women had lost consciousness. At Bonhoeffer's suggestion, the others laid them out flat, joining hands to cradle them across their arms and knees until they recovered, but the three were no sooner sitting up again than the truck stopped to have its generator restoked and the flues cleaned. This, they soon learned, had to be done every hour, and each time it restarted, the same thing happened. The concentration of fumes would rise in the back until they were all coughing and gasping for breath, eyes streaming, pulses thumping, and then slowly drop back to a more tolerable level as the truck trundled on again. Sleep was impossible, although as the woodpile diminished, they were able to stretch out more. By dawn there was room enough for them to stand at the window two at a time to get a little fresh air, but they were all very weak. They had been given nothing to eat or drink—and there was nothing to smoke after Bonhoeffer had shared out the last of his tobacco.

As the light grew stronger, they realized they had been traveling southeast, which was ominous, for Flossenbürg lay in that direction, the most notorious of extermination camps. But most of them had a more immediately pressing problem, and after they had battered on the sides of the truck for several minutes, their three guards grudgingly let them out to relieve themselves along the side of the road, keeping them covered with their machine pistols. Afterward, the three rather unexpectedly produced some bread, sausage, and ersatz coffee, and the prisoners' spirits revived a little. To pass the time, Bonhoeffer persuaded Kokorin to start teaching him Russian.

At midday, the truck pulled up outside the police station at Weiden, the village closest to Flossenbürg, and the guards went in to report. They were gone some time, and came out obviously at a loss. Bonhoeffer watched them for a moment or two as they stood talking in the street below, and tapped on the window. They stared up at him in silence. Then the driver shrugged and opened the door. The camp was full, he said. The commandant wouldn't take them.

Not quite daring to believe him, the prisoners returned to their seats. If they were not to be killed, then the game was over. The Reich lay in ruins. There was no time left to play out the farce of political trials. They were going to survive. As the truck moved off, they looked at one another as though afraid they were dreaming.

About a mile beyond the village, the truck was overtaken and stopped by two men in a police car. After conferring with the guards and inspecting their papers, they opened the door and ordered Müller and Liedig to climb down with their baggage. But there was some sort of discrepancy between the guards' list and the policemen's orders, for instead of closing the door, they stood arguing in the road. Then they turned again toward the truck, and as Bonhoeffer leaned back in the shadows, Ludwig Gehre jumped down to meet them, demanding that they take him, too. He and Müller had become very close while sharing a cell at Buchenwald, and he had evidently decided they should stay together to the end. Presented with a third prisoner, the police seemed satisfied, and a few minutes later, the truck rolled on, still heading south.

The others sat quiet for a time, subdued by the loss of their friends, but as they left Flossenbürg farther and farther behind them, there was no suppressing their sense of release. The mood of the guards had changed, too. With no final destination in view or definite orders to follow, they became almost human, allowing everyone to get out of the truck while they restoked it, and once, when they stopped near a farmhouse, waiting until they had all had a wash at the pump in the yard. Nor did they object when the farmer's wife gave Bonhoeffer two loaves of bread to share out and a jug of milk. By late afternoon, the tension had so eased that they were taking it in turns to lie down and rest. With the window wide open, the air was breathable; the sun shone and the danger had passed.

They reached Regensburg at dusk. Stopping several times to ask the way, their driver eventually found the courthouse and insisted on handing them over, although the jail was already full. After much confusion and argument, the warders locked them in, five to a cell, to sleep on straw mattresses laid side by side on the stone floor, but they were hungry, and so confident of survival now that they refused to settle down, keeping up such a clamor that the prison staff was finally browbeaten into bringing each of them a bowl of soup and a chunk of bread.

Though exhausted by the journey, Bonhoeffer was up and waiting when the cell doors opened next morning, but it was almost an hour before he got to the washroom. The corridor outside was packed with people he knew, men, women, and children. They were the "family prisoners," relatives of Goerdeler, Hassell, Halder, Stauffenberg, and others involved in the plot, and as his companions from Buchenwald came out to join the reunion, the last vestige of prison discipline broke down. No one paid the slightest attention to the warders' attempts to separate them, and they condescended to return to their cells only when told that their breakfast was waiting for them there. But the meal was no sooner over than an air raid alert sounded and they had to be let out again to go down to the basement shelter, where the hubbub broke out once more. With that, the warders gave up, and the cell doors stood open all day.

At five o'clock, their SS guards returned to collect them. After exchanging promises to meet again as soon as the madness was over, Bonhoeffer and the others climbed aboard the truck in a glow of optimism that lasted about four miles. They were bumping eastward, parallel with the railway, along a road littered with burned-out vehicles, when the truck suddenly slewed to one side and stopped. The steering had collapsed. A passing cyclist was told to report their position to the Regensburg police, and they settled down to wait, the guards keeping an uneasy watch on the sky while the light lasted. From the wrecks strewn about and the bomb craters in the fields between them and the railway, it was clear that enemy aircraft were used to treating this stretch of road as a shooting gallery.

By nightfall, it was very cold. No one else came by after the cyclist, and with nothing to eat, drink, or smoke, the prisoners huddled miserably together till dawn, listening to the rain on the roof. As the light grew stronger and the weather cleared, the guards agreed to let them out, and they stamped up and down by the truck, trying to get warm. There was still no sign of movement on the road, and after watching the horizon anxiously for several hours, the guards had just decided that one of them would have to go back for help on foot when they heard a motorcycle far off in the aching stillness. Rather than trust anyone else to deliver a message this time, they flagged the rider down as he approached, requisitioned his machine, and sent their own driver back into Regensburg to report in person.

Two hours later, at about eleven o'clock, a magnificent, shiny bus, commandeered in town by the Security Service, pulled up alongside the crippled truck. The prisoners were disconcerted at first to find that besides changing vehicles they were also exchanging their three Buchenwald guards for an escort of ten security guards armed with submachine guns, but they were soon nodding off in the forgotten luxury of deep upholstered seats. After dozing a little, Bonhoeffer began to enjoy the drive. Once across the Danube, the bus took the back roads through peacefully beautiful country and climbed steadily into the Bavarian forest. The others, too, became entranced with the views on either side, and as the guards were aloof rather than unfriendly, the atmosphere soon more closely resembled that of a tourist bus than a prison transport. When the driver stopped to give a lift to some giggling village girls, he told them his passengers were members of a film company on location, and they believed him.

In midafternoon, the bus reached the village of Schönberg, at the head of a wooded valley high above Passau. After the misery they had left behind them, it was another world, and as though encouraging them to feel they were out of danger, the guards installed them in a bright, sunny dormitory on the second floor of the village schoolhouse. There was a feather bed for each of them, and windows on three sides looked out on the mountains. When the wife of the school janitor produced two bowls of boiled potatoes for supper, they had their gayest meal in months.

Next day, April 7, the villagers sent in two large loaves of bread and some potato salad, little enough for fourteen, but a real sacrifice, for no supplies were getting through. The "family prisoners" had also arrived from Regensburg, as Payne Best discovered when he went into their dormitory by mistake on returning from the washroom. The guards were more careful after that and kept all the doors locked, but this was no great hardship. There was plenty of room to move about, and the more energetic members of the party spent much of the day walking around and around the long center table. For his part, Bonhoeffer was content to sun himself at the open window, with Pünder and Kokorin. The clean chill of the air and the silence of the mountains worked on him like a benediction. He watched the cloud shadows slide down their slopes and cross the green valley all day, and when at last it filled like a bowl with darkness, the sky still in a pale blaze above the rim, he stretched out on his bed in peace and gratitude and slept without stirring until the sun roused him again.

It was Low Sunday. When Pünder suggested he should hold a service, Bonhoeffer at first refused. The group was mostly Catholic, and in any case, he thought it might embarrass Kokorin. But the Russian joined with the others in urging him to change his mind, and so he said some simple prayers and read them the texts for the day: "With his stripes we are healed" and "Blessed be the God and Father of our Lord Jesus Christ! By his great mercy we have been born anew to a living hope through the resurrection of Jesus Christ from the dead!" He then spoke for a few minutes about the spirit that had sustained them, and their hopes of sharing in Germany's deliverance. And as he ended by asking a blessing upon them all, he saw two men in plain clothes standing at the door.

"Prisoner Bonhoeffer?" said one.

He understood their purpose.

"Get ready to come with us."

He packed his things, hesitating for a moment before taking his manuscript, but deciding to leave the Plutarch instead to mark his trail. When he was ready, he said goodbye to each of his companions in turn, coming last to Payne Best.

"If you get home safely," he said, "I would like you to take a message to my friend George Bell, the bishop of Chichester. Tell him that for me this is the end but also the beginning. With him I believe in the principle of our universal Christian brotherhood, which rises above all national interests, and that our victory is certain. Tell him, too, that I have never forgotten his words at our last meeting."

Best shook hands on it, and Bonhoeffer went downstairs between the SS men to their waiting car.

They drove all day and reached Flossenbürg camp in the late evening. He was then taken to a cell in a wooden hut, and told to change into prison clothes. Just before midnight, two uniformed guards brought him before a summary court-martial convened by SS Judge Otto Thorbeck on instructions from Berlin. Section Leader Huppenkothen was there to act as prosecutor, and he immediately confronted Bonhoeffer with Admiral Canaris, General Oster, and Dr. Sack, who had already been tried. He then examined him once more on his associations with the Abwehr, asking long leading questions to which he politely answered yes or no, or remained silent. He neither feared nor resented these proceedings, for they could alter nothing, and when the time came for him to speak in his own defense he declined to do so for the same reason. Back in his cell, he prayed on his knees through the night.

He now willed nothing for himself. He had surrendered everything at last—his past, his pride, his own self. He awaited what was to come with the purest concern, wholly involved and yet wholly at peace.

On the morning of April 9, shortly before six o'clock, he was brought from his cell, and the other prisoners from theirs, to hear the verdict. They had been found guilty of high treason and condemned to death, the sentence to be carried out at once. The guards ordered them to strip. They then walked naked down the stone steps leading through the trees to the place of execution. At the foot of the scaffold, Bonhoeffer looked up at the gray sky. A moist breeze lifted the leaves and he shivered. After kneeling for a few moments to touch the earth, he then mounted the steps, the others following. A guard bound his hands behind him and gently took off his glasses before settling the noose about his neck.

Then he was alone, blindly trusting. As he heard the trap creak, he yielded humbly to the rope, and in the sudden wrench, was no longer separate from his God.

His body was then taken down and burned, along with his suitcase and manuscript.

✝ ✝ ✝

Hans Von Dohnanyi was hanged in Sachsenhausen on April 9, 1945, at about the same time.

On the night of April 22, Klaus Bonhoeffer and Rüdiger Schleicher were taken from the Lehrter Strasse prison with fourteen others and shot dead in the street by SS men. Eberhard Bethge escaped unharmed from the same prison two days later.

On April 30, three weeks after Dietrich Bonhoeffer's execution, Adolf Hitler committed suicide in his Berlin bunker. A week later, Germany surrendered unconditionally, and the war in Europe was over.

Maria von Wedemeyer was then searching for Bonhoeffer in the west. She had learned of his removal from Berlin on February 14, when she called at Prinz-Albrecht-Strasse with his weekly parcel. As the Gestapo refused to tell her where he was, she set out to search for him, carrying a case of warm clothes. Turned away from Dachau, she traveled on to Flossenbürg, covering the last miles on foot, but the SS again denied all knowledge of his whereabouts. When the same thing happened at Buchenwald, she made her way back to Berlin, exhausted by her nightmare journey, but still determined to find him.

It was June before she learned that Bonhoeffer was dead, and July before the news reached his parents.